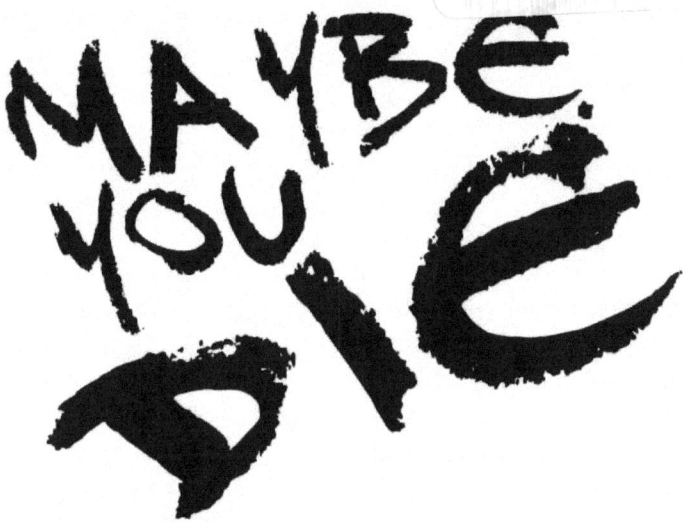

NANCY LEE

Black Rose Writing | Texas

©2020 by Nancy Lee
All rights reserved. No part of this book may be reproduced, stored in a retrieval system or transmitted in any form or by any means without the prior written permission of the publishers, except by a reviewer who may quote brief passages in a review to be printed in a newspaper, magazine or journal.

The author grants the final approval for this literary material.

First printing

This is a true story. In order to maintain anonymity in some instances, the author may have changed the names of individuals and places. The author may have changed some identifying characteristics and details such as physical properties, occupations and places of residence.

ISBN: 978-1-68433-442-1
PUBLISHED BY BLACK ROSE WRITING
www.blackrosewriting.com

Printed in the United States of America
Suggested Retail Price (SRP) $20.95

Maybe You Die is printed in Gentium Book Basic

*As a planet-friendly publisher, Black Rose Writing does its best to eliminate unnecessary waste to reduce paper usage and energy costs, while never compromising the reading experience. As a result, the final word count vs. page count may not meet common expectations.

To my mother, Valerie, who had the ability to see beyond peoples' facades. I didn't believe her premonition when she first told me. But I came to believe it the day I died.

To my second husband, John, who hounded me and typed and retyped this book, hoping it would give me peace. Thank you, babe.

To my best friends and special gifts from God, Bob and Anita, and Dr. John and Anne. They saved my life more than once.

To my brave children, who did their best to work through the chaos of a new life.

To my mother, Valerie, who had the ability to see beyond peoples' facades. I didn't believe her premonition when she first told me. But I came to believe it the day I died.

To my second husband, John, who hounded me and typed and retyped this book, hoping it would give me peace. Thank you, babe.

To my best friends and special gifts from God, Bob and Anita, and Dr. John and Anne. They saved my life more than once.

To my brave children, who did their best to work through the chaos of a new life.

MAYBE YOU DIE

PREFACE

This book is based on my life story. Some names and places have been fictionalized but the events are real. Certain people portrayed in this book might have memories of events that differ from mine.

INTRODUCTION

As she cradles my hand in hers, she smiles and bends close, touching her nose to mine. Her eyes sparkle as I look into her wrinkled face. Then she turns my hand over, palm side up. Mary Kubbiachi is going to tell me my fortune. This is her wedding gift to me. I eagerly await her prediction.

Mary is sixty years old and is a mysterious person. No one at school really knows her, but everyone likes her. I have been told that she has been a student here at the Chicago Academy of the Fine Arts for over twenty years, declaring no particular major, just dabbling in a variety of arts that interest her. She was in one of my fashion illustration classes and did very well.

As I sit waiting to hear my fortune, I notice how beautiful the weather is. The sun is shining and a gentle breeze blows through my long, blonde hair.

"How perfect a day it is," I think to myself.

This is my final day of college classes. I, Nina, am now a fashion designer.

I sit in anticipation as Mary scrutinizes the lines in my hand, all the while, her face beaming. Then, in her singsong Japanese-American accent, she says, "Oh my, you love to spend money!"

I reply with a nod and a sheepish grin.

"No need to worry. I see you have plenty to spend. See? More lines going this way than going that way," she shows me as she traces them on my palm.

"Oh, good!" I exclaim as I wiggle with excitement.

"You have two, maybe three children," she informs me.

"Wow, Mary, this is fun!" I say, eager for more. Her finger traces a long line on my palm, and her smile broadens even more as she announces, "You live a long time!" Then, just as she says this, she gasps and her demeanor changes. Her smile fades and her eyebrows furrow closer. She puts her face next to mine and whispers, "*Maybe*."

"What do you mean, '*maybe*'?" I ask.

"See? See here?" She shows me.

"See the break in the lifeline? A big, big break." Her face becomes drawn and her voice becomes low as she whispers, **"Maybe you die."**

I stare at her. I am speechless.

She quickly changes her tone. "But if you live, you live a long time!"

My jaw drops and I ask, "How old will I be when the break occurs?"

"Maybe thirty or forty," she answers.

Just as those words leave Mary's mouth, Ms. Schmidt, the head of the art department, appears out of nowhere. Having overheard Mary's prediction, she grabs Mary by her arm, yanking her up onto her feet, and drags her away from me. I can hear her being scolded.

"You have been warned before, Mary, not to tell fortunes."

I watch Ms. Schmidt as she pulls Mary up the stairs and out of sight. As my eyes leave them, I notice that my palm is still turned upward. I place my hand back on my lap and notice that the once gorgeous, sunny day has turned gray, and the soft breeze has given way to a cold wind.

A sense of foreboding envelops me.

"Oh, good!" I exclaim as I wiggle with excitement.

"You have two, maybe three children," she informs me.

"Wow, Mary, this is fun!" I say, eager for more. Her finger traces a long line on my palm, and her smile broadens even more as she announces, "You live a long time!" Then, just as she says this, she gasps and her demeanor changes. Her smile fades and her eyebrows furrow closer. She puts her face next to mine and whispers, "*Maybe.*"

"What do you mean, '*maybe*'?" I ask.

"See? See here?" She shows me.

"See the break in the lifeline? A big, big break." Her face becomes drawn and her voice becomes low as she whispers, **"Maybe you die."**

I stare at her. I am speechless.

She quickly changes her tone. "But if you live, you live a long time!"

My jaw drops and I ask, "How old will I be when the break occurs?"

"Maybe thirty or forty," she answers.

Just as those words leave Mary's mouth, Ms. Schmidt, the head of the art department, appears out of nowhere. Having overheard Mary's prediction, she grabs Mary by her arm, yanking her up onto her feet, and drags her away from me. I can hear her being scolded.

"You have been warned before, Mary, not to tell fortunes."

I watch Ms. Schmidt as she pulls Mary up the stairs and out of sight. As my eyes leave them, I notice that my palm is still turned upward. I place my hand back on my lap and notice that the once gorgeous, sunny day has turned gray, and the soft breeze has given way to a cold wind.

A sense of foreboding envelops me.

CHAPTER ONE
DAY ONE
IN THE HOSPITAL

I have never noticed how sweet is the taste of blood.

My tongue slides over my lips and I swallow the fluid that fills my mouth. "Please call a priest for me. I'm going to die," I beg through lips that feel as though they are frozen. "Can anyone hear me?" I ask again in a louder voice.

"You're not going to die. Relax, dear. You are safe now. Are you aware that you are in a hospital? Do you know why you are here?" a soft, feminine voice asks me.

"Yes, I'm aware of why I'm here," I answer.

"Is your name Nina?" she asks.

I nod my head up and down.

"That's the name we found on your driver's license in your purse. Nina, we need to notify your family that you are here. Whom shall we call?"

"My family," I think to myself, pondering, and then answer, "My family lives in Chicago. My father's name is Lester and my in-laws' names are Sara and Steven." I give her the phone numbers. "You must also notify our Peoria family. They are our dearest friends. Their names are Bernie and Andrea Sellers. Oh! Also, Dr. McGinn and his wife, Ann, please." I relay their phone numbers as well. "Then call our babysitter, Lucy, at our home. Tell her I'm here. Tell her we were in an accident, and that we will be okay." As I finish this sentence, I begin to feel nauseated. I am going to be sick.

"Be quick," a voice orders. "Get a pan. She's going to vomit."

I feel someone lift my head and turn it to the side just in time for me to throw up. My head is lowered back onto a pillow. Now I do not taste the blood, only the vomit. I am trying to open my eyes, but I cannot. They do not want to cooperate and with that realization, a fear sweeps over me that I may have lost my vision. My head feels as though it is on fire!

"Nina," a voice calls to me, "I need to remove some of your clothes. I will try not to hurt you."

Someone lifts up my shoulder, and I feel the fur collar of my new coat as it slides across the side of my face. It feels cold, wet and sticky. I realize it is drenched in my blood.

"Nina, I will have to use scissors to cut off your bra. We removed your blouse when we slipped off your coat. I do not want to turn you over to unhook your bra, so I will cut it off from the front. You're going to feel the cold metal." As she does this, she remarks, "Dear, I sure hate to do this. It looks like a brand new bra."

Indeed, it is new. All the clothing I am wearing tonight is new. My husband, Bob, bought all of it for me as a Christmas gift and I have not worn it until today. I saved it for a special occasion. I smile as I remember back to how proud Bob was of choosing these gifts for me all by himself.

I begin to relax. I feel so very tired. I drift off to sleep until I feel a twinge of pain. "Ouch," I moan.

As someone turns my head to the side, I hear people whispering, but I cannot hear what they are saying.

"Please give me something for pain," I beg.

"I'm sorry, Nina. We've given you all that we can," a male voice answers.

"All that you can?" I think to myself, worried. I remember someone told me once that medical personnel cannot give a person anything for pain in a severely traumatic circumstance, especially for patients whose injuries have not yet been diagnosed. Medications can interfere with certain, life-threatening conditions and cause further injury or death.

"Please, I need to see a priest. I'm dying," I plead.

"We won't let you die, Nina," a comforting voice assures me.

I am not convinced. "You've heard all of those dumb Polack jokes, haven't you?" I ask the person who just spoke to me.

"Sure have," the voice answers.

"Well, they're true. I'm a fully pedigreed Polack and if I had any sense at all, I would just pass out so I wouldn't have to feel all this pain." I hear people laugh at my self-deprecating remark. Once again, I feel myself drifting off to sleep and the pain begins to subside.

"Nina!" A loud voice calls to me and shocks me out of my peaceful place. "I'm Father Carroll. I am the chaplain. You asked for me. Would you like me to hear your confession?"

"Confession?" I ask. "No, Father. will you please give me the last rites? I believe I'm going to die."

"The doctors are doing their best to make sure that doesn't happen. Would you like me to hear your confession first?" I am confused, but I agree. "Whenever you're ready," Father Carroll whispers to me.

I try to think of the sins I have committed, but for some reason, I cannot recall any. I know that I have sinned, but my mind is blank. "Father," I say, "I know that I have sins, but I just can't remember any."

With that said, I drift off to sleep again. I no longer feel any pain, just a sense of utter peace and well-being. Everything grows dark and I am in a beautiful, serene place.

OUR FIRST YEAR OF MARRIAGE — AUGUST 1958

"Think, Nina. Try to remember," I think to myself. "Where did it all go wrong?" I ask myself over and over as I strain to recall our early years as husband and wife.

I remember the day in 1957 that Bob gave me a beautiful engagement ring he purchased with his summer earnings. It was a one-and-one-quarter-carat blue-white diamond, almost perfectly cut. I was so excited to show Bob's parents. I will never forget his mother's response. She barely looked at it.

"What do I get? I'm putting you through school and you spend your money on a ring?" she screamed at him.

Bob grabbed me by the arm. "I think we had better leave," he snapped at his mother. He rushed me through the door.

I was stunned. "Didn't you ask or even tell them?" I asked.

He apparently figured that because he had earned the money, spending it on a ring was his choice. According to his parents, it was not a good one. In all the years we were together, his mother never did ask to see my ring. A few months later, after things had quieted down, we told them we were thinking of getting married late the next summer. They thought it was a good plan, as did my parents. His Mom still never asked for a close look at my ring.

Bob's parents' marriage seemed ideal to me. Both of his parents worked full-time jobs. His Mom worked at an optical firm and his father worked at a steel company. He has a brother, James, who is ten years younger. His family lived on the second floor of the duplex they owned and his grandmother lived on the first floor with Bob's aunt. His folks never drank and only occasionally argued. I sure wished my parents lived like that. Every day I came home from school or work, I wondered whether they would be fighting.

Bob and I decided that we would have a very small but elegant wedding instead of the standard "hoop-de-la" wedding chosen by everyone else in our Polish community. We wanted our wedding to be classier, to represent our high hopes for the future and our desire to leave our blue-collar lives behind. We were both professionals. We wanted "the good life" and we were willing to work for it.

Then it happened.

"What the hell is this?" my mother exclaimed. "Sara is inviting the whole damned town! You said to keep the guest list down to family only. She has a list of over two hundred people she wants to invite!"

"Bob's Mom tells us she can't cut back because she's gone to all their families' weddings all her life, so these people owe her," I explained.

"Well, if she's going to invite all these people and we're paying for the wedding, then we should have all of our friends, too."

And so it was. We lost control of our own wedding and it became *their* wedding. Our small, intimate ceremony turned out to be dinner for six hundred and fifty people - the largest Polish wedding our community had ever hosted.

My wedding gown was my final design project for college. It was a simple, elegant design with no beading and no lace. It was made of the heaviest silk Marshall Fields could order from France. I remember the day the fabric buyer at Marshall Fields called me to inform me that the silk I had ordered had arrived.

I rushed to the store to examine it. "Beautiful!" I exclaimed. "How much do I owe you?"

"Two hundred dollars," she says.

"Two hundred dollars?" I repeat in shock.

I start to feel faint. The silk on display in the store was not nearly as heavy as I wanted, but it was only a few dollars a yard. I assumed that if it were heavier, it would just be a bit more expensive.

"But this is so expensive," I thought to myself, "*six times* more expensive!"

"I'll pick it up in a couple of days," I inform the saleslady, attempting to conceal my terror.

I realize I have a serious problem. Since I special-ordered the fabric, I cannot have it sent back to France. Besides, as a part-time employee at this Marshall Fields store, I could have purchased a wedding gown for that price from the Marshall Fields' elite store for couture clothing (The 28 Shop). I don't have a choice - I have to buy it.

I have to tell my Dad how much it will cost and I am paralyzed with fear. All the way home on the train, I rehearse the explanation to my father, scared to death of what his response will be.

I arrive home shortly before my father. As he walks in the door, I say, "Dad, the fabric came in today for my wedding gown. It's a lot more expensive than I thought it would be."

I start to cry. "It's two hundred dollars, Daddy. I am so sorry. I am so sorry, Daddy. It never occurred to me that it could cost that much. I should have asked. I thought it might be a dollar more a yard, but it was much more. I am so sorry, Daddy. I'm so, so sorry."

My Dad walks around the living room, pacing back and forth, repeating the amount of money again and again. He then disappears into the bedroom. I sit on the edge of the sofa with my head hung low, sobbing. After a few minutes, he comes out of the bedroom and hands me the money.

"Thank God you are making this gown. What would it have cost if you had to purchase it?" he asks.

I sit there with my hand extended, still holding the money, in complete disbelief. My father is very naïve and I realize that I am one very lucky daughter.

Sometimes my mother would call my Dad a "dumb Polack," but he was far from dumb. He was offered an executive's position at the printing factory where he worked, but in order to accept that job, he would also have had to join the Masons. As a Catholic, he could not belong to any secret organization. At that time, his father was still living, and my Dad felt it might kill his father if he joined the Masons, so he did not take the job.

Not only did I design and make my wedding gown with that fabulous fabric Dad paid for, but I also designed and made my bridesmaids' dresses. I used orange silk organza and laid it over yellow taffeta, creating the effect of a soft, iridescent melon color. The girls carried bouquets of frosted, melon-colored, artificial grapes with green ivy. I was a fashion designer. I had to be different, after all.

On our wedding day, it was a scorching ninety-eight degrees. The men wore cutaway tuxedos made of wool and they had perspiration running down their faces.

My Dad looked so proud and handsome. He walked me down the aisle and when he turned his face to kiss me, tears were rolling down his face. He put my hand into Bob's hand, kissed me, and slipped into the pew next to Mom. Tears welled up in my eyes and I tried to compose myself. I looked into Bob's eyes and they were sparkling with happiness.

During the ceremony, Bob kept brushing his hair out of his eyes. He and his Mom argued the night before the wedding. She insisted that he wash his hair, but he argued that if he did, it would be falling into his eyes during the ceremony. His blonde locks were very coarse and more easily managed if he washed it the day before, as he had already done. But she won the argument and thus, his hair fell into his eyes during the ceremony.

Father Kelly shortened the ceremony because of the heat, and we left the church through a shower of rice. I have a candid picture of that moment and it was our favorite picture from our wedding. It was even better than the one taken by the professional photographer.

Immediately after the ceremony, the driver of our car, Bob's uncle, took us to a studio to have our formal wedding portraits taken. The photographer commented that he wished all brides were as easy to pose as I was.

"Hell, it should be easy to pose her. She's a model," Bob said.

"No wonder," he replied.

We headed off to our reception. It took four hours to feed our guests, who were served family-style. They feasted on sausage, chicken, sliced beef, gravy and of course, *kapusta*, or Polish-style sauerkraut.

After dinner was served, we cut the cake. It was the most beautiful cake I had ever seen. The baker melted peppermint candy and draped it over the whole cake. When it hardened, it looked like glass. It had doves on top and ribbon draping around it, both of which were also made of the hardened candy.

We celebrated the *Wykup* next. This is the Polish version of a reception line that takes place after dinner rather than after the wedding ceremony. The bride and groom stand at the beginning of the line and the bridal party stands next to them. The guests, headed by the bride's parents and then the groom's parents, form a line passing the bridal party to congratulate the bride and groom.

Before the guests congratulate the couple they pass by a special table. Sitting behind the table are two uncles, one representing each of the two families. One offers each guest a cigar and the other offers each a shot of whiskey. In the center of that table is a large cardboard box decorated with crepe paper made to resemble a house. A slit is cut into the top into which guests drop envelopes that usually contain money.

Polish people almost always give only money at weddings. I received all sorts of gifts at my bridal shower months before the wedding. Everything from kitchen utensils to sterling and crystal. We were so grateful for all of our beautiful gifts, both practical and extravagant.

During the procession of well-wishers, the bridal party rocks back and forth and yells out a Polish phrase, "Jeszcze nasza," which means, "She's still ours!" The guests try to buy the bride by putting money in the box so they can keep her.

My Dad led the line. He kissed me on the cheek and whispered into my ear. "Don't forget! Every little girl gets three spankings in her lifetime, and you'll never be too old or too far away that I can't get to you and give you the other two."

"Daddy!" I exclaimed.

Then I saw tears in his eyes and knew what he was talking about.

It had happened about five years before, when I was sixteen years old. I had gotten into a nose-to-nose argument with my mother.

"God damn it!" I said, frustrated.

She stopped her arguing, stepped back and yelled over to my Dad, "Lester! She swore at me!"

"Dad, I didn't swear at Mom. I swore, but not at her!" I pleaded.

"You swore at your mother!" He slapped me across the face. Afterward, he walked away and closed the bedroom door behind him. From outside the room, I could hear him crying.

My mother and I looked at each other, stunned. My father had never hit me in my life and my mother looked so righteous. I ran into my bedroom and I, too, cried. I wore that handprint on my cheek for the rest of the evening. It turned out to be an event that neither Dad nor I would ever forget. And I will never forget that special moment with my father.

Slowly, the guests made their way to the end of the line. I remember how proud I was to be Bob's wife and how excited I was as people wished us happiness for our future.

They then formed a double circle, one inside the other, with one circle moving in one direction and one circle moving in the other. All the while, they sang the song "*I Love You Truly*." Bob was seated on a chair which was placed in the middle of the circle. I sat on his lap while my maid of honor removed the bobby pins that had been holding my veil in place and she gave them to my bridesmaids to keep as a good luck token. My veil was placed over Bob's arm and I stood up as my bridesmaids tied a satin apron around my waist that had tiny little rubber babies attached to it by pink and blue ribbons. This signified my transition from a bride to a wife.

Bob and I danced until my father and my new father-in-law interrupted us to dance with me. And so it went until it had gone full circle with our immediate families, at which point I was finally free to dance with my new husband again. The waltz ended and he took me back into his arms, scooped me up, and carried me out of the hall with great flare and drama.

I can still hear myself laughing, "Bob what are you doing? Your mother said we had to wait to say goodbye to all of the guests."

"To hell with that! Those people are never going to leave and it's already ten thirty."

The door closed behind us and I saw a car waiting. Evidently, Bob had already made arrangements with one of his uncles to have our car ready for a fast getaway. We left without saying goodbye to anyone. We were exhausted and we knew that these receptions could last hours longer. We also knew that we could not.

I snuggled up to him as we drove away. "This is our new life. It begins today," I said as I closed my eyes and smiled with a feeling of contentment I had never experienced.

We spent the night at a hotel and made love all night long. The next morning, we returned to my parents' home for the after-party, called the *poprawiny* in Polish, a celebration to use up all the leftover food from the night before.

My Mom met us at the door and pointed angrily at Bob.

"Do you know what she did? Last night, after you left the reception, Sara, *your mother*," she added, still pointing her finger at Bob, "tried to steal the extra food from the reception hall. She had her brothers take boxes of chickens and put them into the trunks of their cars. One of the cooks thought it was strange as it was *us*," pointing to herself, "who paid for all that food! The cook found me and told me what was happening. I went outside and found them standing by their cars with the trunks loaded with *our* food! I made them unload the cars and return all the chickens and other leftovers to the kitchen.

"Your mother was furious, telling me that there were plenty of leftover chickens, that she had many out-of-town guests, and that she was planning on fixing a meal for them the next day. I told her that if she had come and asked me, I would have been happy to give her whatever she needed. But instead, she thought I'd had enough beer to drink that I wouldn't notice, so she decided to *steal* them!"

We stood there listening to my mother's tirade as we watched friends and family leaving my parents' house, carrying bags of chickens as they wished us well.

"Mom, how come we had so many extra chickens to begin with?" I asked.

"Your father wouldn't listen to the old Polish cooks. He complained they did not have enough food to feed the two hundred fifty people at your bridal shower. He discounted their suggestions and over-ordered. I suggest that the two of you get straight to your house, Bob! Your mother and father took the money box home with them; you had better check it out. She probably helped herself to some of that, too!"

The expression on Bob's face conveyed it was time to get the hell out of there. We kissed them and thanked them for everything. When we reached the car, we just sat there in silence. Bob started the car and said, "Well, I guess we had better get this over."

As we walked into Bob's home, his mother walked up to us with fire in her eyes, prepared to tell us her side of the story.

"I'm sorry that happened," I said after she finished talking. "My Mom said that if you had just asked her, she would have given you anything you needed."

As soon as the words left my mouth, she turned on her heel, walked to the dining room table, picked up a piece of paper, and slapped it into Bob's hand. It was the bar bill. At a Polish wedding, the drinks are free for the guests. Usually, the groom's family takes care of the tab. She agreed to this when we planned the wedding.

"I don't think we should have to pay for all of this," she told us. "After all, Nina's family did most of the drinking. Most of our family doesn't even drink!"

"But my family paid for the orchestra, all the food, the hall, the flowers and the cake," I quietly noted, thinking that would make her realize that this bill was, indeed, much less than what my parents had paid.

However, it did not seem to matter to his Mom. She just continued to complain about one thing after another while brought his packed suitcase from upstairs, took it outside and placed it into the trunk of our car. We sat down at the dining room table, opened each wedding card and wrote the amount of money given. Then we placed the cards back into a box so that when we returned from our honeymoon, we could take the time to enjoy reading them. Meanwhile, his mother continued to complain about the bar bill.

Finally, Bob reached the limit of his patience and suddenly stood up. He was so angry that he grew pale. He shouted out to his parents, "Forget the damn bill! I will pay for it!"

We left their home and drove to the hall to pay the bar bill. We never told my parents about it because they already hated "the thieves," as they referred to Bob's parents. They probably would have gone to Bob's family house, knocked on the door and called them something worse had we shared this news. My parents had already paid enough for our huge wedding that neither they, nor we, ever wanted. His parents insisted on it and they got it at my family's expense.

When we got back in the car, Bob turned to me and said, "Not exactly the way I expected our lives to begin, Kitten." Bob's terms of endearment for me were "Kitten" and "Kitts." We did not speak to each other for the entire three-hour trip to Bloomington, Illinois, where we had rented our very first apartment. I think we were just in shock from the events at both parents' homes that morning.

Bob was entering his fifth year of college at Illinois State University's teaching college, where he would continue his major in physical education. We planned to leave Bloomington for California the next year. Bob would study physical therapy. I left my dreams of being a fashion designer behind to follow him until he earned his physical therapy degree from Stanford. We then planned to head back to Chicago to pursue my designing career.

I had already been offered the top-paying job in my class as a designer for Maidenform bras. I interviewed, just for the heck of it, as I had already planned to wed and move away. I was offered the job, but of course, I turned it down.

However, it did not seem to matter to his Mom. She just continued to complain about one thing after another while brought his packed suitcase from upstairs, took it outside and placed it into the trunk of our car. We sat down at the dining room table, opened each wedding card and wrote the amount of money given. Then we placed the cards back into a box so that when we returned from our honeymoon, we could take the time to enjoy reading them. Meanwhile, his mother continued to complain about the bar bill.

Finally, Bob reached the limit of his patience and suddenly stood up. He was so angry that he grew pale. He shouted out to his parents, "Forget the damn bill! I will pay for it!"

We left their home and drove to the hall to pay the bar bill. We never told my parents about it because they already hated "the thieves," as they referred to Bob's parents. They probably would have gone to Bob's family house, knocked on the door and called them something worse had we shared this news. My parents had already paid enough for our huge wedding that neither they, nor we, ever wanted. His parents insisted on it and they got it at my family's expense.

When we got back in the car, Bob turned to me and said, "Not exactly the way I expected our lives to begin, Kitten." Bob's terms of endearment for me were "Kitten" and "Kitts." We did not speak to each other for the entire three-hour trip to Bloomington, Illinois, where we had rented our very first apartment. I think we were just in shock from the events at both parents' homes that morning.

Bob was entering his fifth year of college at Illinois State University's teaching college, where he would continue his major in physical education. We planned to leave Bloomington for California the next year. Bob would study physical therapy. I left my dreams of being a fashion designer behind to follow him until he earned his physical therapy degree from Stanford. We then planned to head back to Chicago to pursue my designing career.

I had already been offered the top-paying job in my class as a designer for Maidenform bras. I interviewed, just for the heck of it, as I had already planned to wed and move away. I was offered the job, but of course, I turned it down.

instead, she thought I'd had enough beer to drink that I wouldn't notice, so she decided to *steal* them!"

We stood there listening to my mother's tirade as we watched friends and family leaving my parents' house, carrying bags of chickens as they wished us well.

"Mom, how come we had so many extra chickens to begin with?" I asked.

"Your father wouldn't listen to the old Polish cooks. He complained they did not have enough food to feed the two hundred fifty people at your bridal shower. He discounted their suggestions and over-ordered. I suggest that the two of you get straight to your house, Bob! Your mother and father took the money box home with them; you had better check it out. She probably helped herself to some of that, too!"

The expression on Bob's face conveyed it was time to get the hell out of there. We kissed them and thanked them for everything. When we reached the car, we just sat there in silence. Bob started the car and said, "Well, I guess we had better get this over."

As we walked into Bob's home, his mother walked up to us with fire in her eyes, prepared to tell us her side of the story.

"I'm sorry that happened," I said after she finished talking. "My Mom said that if you had just asked her, she would have given you anything you needed."

As soon as the words left my mouth, she turned on her heel, walked to the dining room table, picked up a piece of paper, and slapped it into Bob's hand. It was the bar bill. At a Polish wedding, the drinks are free for the guests. Usually, the groom's family takes care of the tab. She agreed to this when we planned the wedding.

"I don't think we should have to pay for all of this," she told us. "After all, Nina's family did most of the drinking. Most of our family doesn't even drink!"

"But my family paid for the orchestra, all the food, the hall, the flowers and the cake," I quietly noted, thinking that would make her realize that this bill was, indeed, much less than what my parents had paid.

Marshall Fields also offered me a position as an assistant buyer. Positions in buying at Marshall Fields were very prestigious. Most of the buyers there came from Harvard and Princeton, so I was extremely honored. I turned that one down, as well, thinking, "Oh, well. First things first. We will be back in a couple years. Then it will be time for my career."

When we arrived at our apartment, we only unpacked our overnight suitcases. We left our large suitcases in the car for our honeymoon. Our apartment was full of the boxes of gifts from our wedding shower, as Bob had driven them to our apartment the week before. We planned to unpack them when we returned from our honeymoon.

We fell onto the sofa and looked at each other with love. We were so tired from the drive and the chaos of the day. We bathed, climbed into bed and fell asleep. In the middle of the night, I awoke to go to the bathroom. I turned the light on and screamed. Bob came running to the bathroom.

"Holy shit! Cockroaches! Holy shit!" he repeats over and over, as they scurry off into the nooks and crannies of the bathroom.

"We are *not* staying here!" I yell at him. "Didn't you check out this place before you rented it?"

"I was here during the day, not at night!" he says.

"Get dressed. We are out of here. Let's pack up our things," I say. We load the car.

"Just be sure to check each box before you put them into the car," he yells to me.

We did not have to pack furniture, as we had rented a furnished apartment. We went to breakfast and purchased a newspaper to seek a new place. The very first apartment we saw was perfect.

"This is lovely," I say as we sign the lease.

It was on the second floor of a huge, lovely brick home owned by the Burns family. They occupied the first floor and half of the second floor. We lived on the other half of the second floor. Our section was not connected to theirs and we had a separate entrance. It was a very tiny apartment, but it was all we needed for the year we were going to live there. We did not have a normal bed; it pulled out of the sofa.

We move our treasures in and head to our honeymoon destination, the Cloister at Sea Islands in Georgia. Bob looks at me, beaming, "Well, Kitts, we're on our way to our new life."

As we pull out of the driveway, I close my eyes and think about the previous two days. I imagine my parents were still giving away chickens and chuckle. The drive to Georgia takes two days.

When we arrived at the Cloisters, we pulled into the long driveway and up to a magnificent mansion. A young man dressed in a red attendance outfit opened the door and welcomed us. As he and another attendant unpacked our car, I heard one saying to the other, "I haven't seen an old car like that for a long time."

"Old car," I thought, "you should see our own car!" We were driving Bob's parents' car, which was only two years old. We knowingly looked at each other and laughed.

The young men carried our luggage into the reception area. When we entered the building to check in, our jaws dropped. We had never seen such opulence. The young men in the red suits put our luggage onto a rack and led us to the guest cottage we had rented. It was lovelier than we could have ever dreamed, complete with a balcony that overlooked the ocean. Bob took me in his arms and kissed me. We stood there in silence; and in awe.

We picked up the information book about the resort and noticed that dinner was to be served at seven o'clock. We unpacked our clothes and dressed in our finery for a formal dinner. Bob wore a dark suit, and I wore a dress made of silk organza. Several ladies commented on the elegance of my dress. Bob proudly explained to them that not only did I design it, but I also made it.

We spent a lot of time in bed, as typical honeymooners do. I remembered one of my friends saying, "If you put a penny into a jar for every time you make love the first year of your marriage and then take one out every time you make love after that first year, you may never empty the jar."

"Perhaps time will tell," I thought, unconvinced.

I could hardly wait to experience the ocean for the first time in my life. After breakfast the next morning, we changed into our beachwear and walked out to the water. I was swimming in water up to my neck when something caught my eye.

"Sharks! Sharks!" I screamed.

Everyone scurried up onto the beach. I was shaking as Bob came to meet me and help me to the shore.

"Sharks," I pointed out again to everyone on the beach.

Someone laughed and said, "Sharks? Those are not sharks. They're dolphins!"

The beachgoers erupted in thunderous laughter and for the remainder of our honeymoon, people pointed at me and told the story of the "Shark Lady."

"Oh, well. It'll give us something to talk about someday," I said to Bob.

The next day on our honeymoon I started my period. I always suffered from terrible cramps, so I spent a quiet day moaning and groaning. It really put a damper on our vacation but we made our best efforts to enjoy the time we had there anyway.

The following morning we decided to collect seashells, and Bob got sunburned so badly that we had to make a hospital visit. Both of us were miserable and it wasn't any better back at the hotel.

"You want me to wash your handkerchiefs?" I asked, incredulous. "Take them to the laundry in the main building?"

"No, I want you to wash them!" he said.

"Where do you think I can wash them? Here in the sink?" I asked.

He nodded in agreement.

"You have to be kidding. There is no way that I am going to wash those snotty, hay fever-infested handkerchiefs by hand. No way in hell!" I yelled at him.

He grabbed the handkerchiefs and retorted, "I ask you to do one thing for me, but no, you're too good!"

"You bet I am!" I yelled in response as he left our suite.

"What the hell was that about?" I thought. "I guess it must be some test of my loyalty. I failed!"

We were happy that our trip at the Cloisters had come to an end. We were grouchy as hell. On the way back home, we decided to optimistically dub it a "newlywed challenge." It did not help. We did not talk to each other all the way home.

I remember thinking to myself, "How could this have happened? We dated for three years and never had an argument. All of these past years were happy. This first week of marriage was awful."

When we arrived at our new apartment, Bob dove right into his studies while I scanned the employment section of the newspaper. The small town of Bloomington had no need for my talents. Money was going to be the name of the game. I needed any kind of job that would pay for the rent.

During the following two weeks, I was hired into and quit six different jobs. I remember that I would interview during my lunch hour, be hired, quit the old job, and start the new job the next day. I finally ended my search when I was hired as a darkroom technician in a photography studio. I really liked the job.

Bob had a wonderful personality, and he was so funny. But early into our marriage, I became his straight man. I never knew what to expect, and I did not appreciate my new position.

Our first grocery shopping adventure was quite the challenge. I had never cooked a day in my life. And I had never even shopped for groceries, so I had no idea what to buy. Back home, I went to school and worked part time. My mother did the cooking, and I came home from school and did the dishes. I knew nothing about cooking or shopping.

For my first attempt, my Mom suggested that I prepare a ham. Mom told me it was easy to fix, a no-brainer. All I had to do was heat it in the oven. I figured I could handle that.

I went to the grocery store with Bob and we proceeded to the meat department. I picked up a ham and squeezed it. Bob asked why I was doing that, and I responded while still looking at the ham, "I don't know, but my mother always says that you squeeze it. I want to look like I know what I'm doing, so I'll squeeze the hams."

When I finished speaking, I turned and looked up to discover that Bob was nowhere in sight. I noticed that people had stopped their own searching and were looking at me, as it appeared to them I was talking to a ham. All of a sudden I heard his voice. He walked up behind me and asked dramatically, "Who put eight great tomatoes in this little bitty can? Who did it? Let me see the guy who did it!"

All the while he stood there, holding a can of Contadina tomato paste. Contadina would have been proud of how well he executed their famous television commercial. He looked like Sherlock Holmes, holding his eyeglasses over only one eye like a monocle.

He asked again, "Did you see the guy who did it?"

People had collected around us and were laughing. It *was* really funny. I had to laugh, too.

I picked up a few other items and proceeded to the checkout. Bob disappeared again and he had the money. I grew anxious. The clerk was almost finished ringing up our purchase when suddenly Bob appeared out of nowhere and put a bag of grass seed on the counter to be added to our bill.

"I want this. It's on sale," he dramatically insisted so that everyone in the store could hear.

"It's a wonderful bargain," said the clerk.

I glared at Bob and said under my breath, "Put it back and give me the money. I'll pay this bill."

"But I want it!" he whined.

With pursed lips, I demanded, "Give me the money for the groceries and put the damn grass seed back!"

With that, he grabbed the bag of grass seed and yelled, "You never let me have anything I want!"

He looked at me menacingly, and the clerk looked at me as I if I were the Wicked Witch of the West and said, "It's a great price, madam."

I looked at her, my eyes narrowing, and said, "We don't need grass seed! We live in a second-floor apartment!"

He laughed all the way home. At the time, I was pissed. But it turned out to be such a funny story that I have told the story many times over the years.

We had to make adjustments to coexist. I did not squeeze the toothpaste tube the right way, and he never noticed that he had taken the last pair of underwear until he opened the drawer in the next morning and he discovered he had no clean ones.

That first year, we competed constantly for the "head of household" designation and tried, begrudgingly, to adjust to one another's idiosyncrasies. It was frustrating, but I did have one moment of retribution.

Bob's classes for the day had adjourned early because of a heavy snowstorm, so he picked me up early from my job at the photography studio. We went to the grocery store, figuring that we might be snowed in for a few days. The blowing snow made the journey slow and slippery. As we left the store and headed home, it had become apparent that it was no longer light snow, but a blizzard.

We parked our car at the back of our apartment building on a narrow street. The snow slipped into my high-heeled shoes as I snatched some grocery sacks out of the trunk of the car. As we walked to the house, Bob said casually, "By the way, hon, I need some papers typed tonight. They're due tomorrow."

"Tomorrow? I have worked overtime every night this week. I still have to prepare dinner and now you want me to type? This assignment was not just given today, Bob. You probably already had it for a week!" I growled.

We trudged through the snow on the street and up the sidewalk. We were almost to the house when our landlord's three children came running up to us. They adored Bob. Often, he would stop and play with them after school.

"Come play with us!" they begged.

"No, no. Not tonight. We have work to do," he said.

The children continued to beg.

"Come on, Bob," I said, already annoyed at him because of the hours of typing that were facing me.

Bob always waited until the last minute to turn in an assignment. I hated that because, with my hunt and peck typing system, it would sometimes take me until the wee hours of the morning to finish. All the while, Bob would be sleeping.

"Please, please!" they cried.

"No, not tonight, kids," he replied.

"Come on, please? Or is she going to holler at you again tonight?" they asked innocently, looking a little sideways at me.

Bob and I realized they must have overheard our bickering. I will remember the look on his face forever. His nostrils began to quiver, his eyes filled with fire, and his teeth clenched. He looked like Napoleon Bonaparte as he stood up straight, placed the groceries onto the snow-covered sidewalk, looked at me with defiant eyes, and bellowed, "I will play with you, children!"

He shoved the grocery sacks at me, sneered at me, and left me standing there as he marched off with his little army of supporters.

"Damn!" I exclaimed. I was madder than hell. I had to type a report that could have been done days ago, but it was due the next day. It was all because he was fooling around with his buddies over the weekend watching football and forgot about the assignment.

I struggled up the narrow, winding stairway with the groceries and entered our apartment. As I put the groceries on the table, I looked out the kitchen window and saw Bob holding the child-sized sled. The children stood off to the side watching him.

He pulled the sled up to his chest as his rather short, stocky legs began to run faster and faster. He leapt onto the sled, planning that it would carry him to glide down the road. However, his sled stopped when it hit the pavement and he did not. He went sliding down the street, not on the sled, but on his stomach and the side of his head. He finally stopped and the kids ran over to him. I opened the window and could hear them saying, "Mister, mister! Are you okay?"

He creakily stood up and removed the snow from the inside of his ear. With the support of the children, he got up, onto his feet and crept back to the house. I could hear him promising to play with them again tomorrow.

"Yes! Yes! That was great! Oh, God, it doesn't get any better than this! At last I am vindicated. Justice is mine! I win! I win!" I celebrated aloud to myself as I danced around the kitchen.

I could hear him coming up the stairs. The kids opened the apartment door, helped him in, and left him sitting in a chair at the kitchen table.

"Are you okay?" I asked.

I tried to look interested and concerned, but I could only do it for a minute before I broke out in laughter, holding my stomach. I laughed hysterically while he sat there in the chair, still wearing his coat.

He finally lost his dejected look, smiled, and said, "If you can stop laughing, I'll tell you what happened."

"I saw it all!" I squealed.

"Okay, okay. I'm calm let's hear it." I said to him.

Bob began to give me his explanation of what happened. "I was running faster and faster, and as I fell on the sled, I mistakenly stepped on the rope. So the sled stopped, but I didn't!" he admitted.

"I saw it all," I repeated, smiling.

"Well, you didn't see it all!" he said. "Guess where the handlebars got me?"

I laughed hysterically.

"That's not funny!" he said weakly.

"It's more than funny. It's hysterical!" Eventually, even he had to laugh.

For some reason, after that incident, the jockeying for positions came to an end. There were no losers and there were no winners. We found our places, peace and plenty of laughter.

All of these memories come easily to me and they form a path to the present. But it is a confusing present I do not understand. "I'm so tired of this journey," I think. "I can't continue now. I need peace again." Please Dear God, I'm tired of looking through this "My life" album.

CHAPTER TWO
DAY TWO
IN THE HOSPITAL

"Ooh," I moan softly, with the little strength I have.

My face and head feel as if they are on fire. "Is someone here? Can anyone hear me?" I say in my strongest voice, which is just above a whisper. "I need help," I beg. "I can't breathe. Something is around my neck, and it's choking me."

I jump as I feel someone taking a hold of my hand, and I try to free what feels like a tourniquet around my neck.

"Just relax, dear. You need that. It's called a compression bandage, and it is wrapped around your head and neck. It's kept tight to stop the bleeding," a voice tells me.

"Who are you?" I ask in fear as I weakly push the person's hand away from my arm. I am not consciously aware of why I am afraid but the feeling envelopes me.

"My name is Sister Josephine," the voice answers.

"I'm afraid, Sister. Is anyone else here with us?" I ask.

"It's only me in this room with you. Some of your friends are sitting just outside the door. They are allowing you to rest. No one can hurt you here, Nina. We'll keep you safe," she tells me. "Do you know where you are?"

"No, no I don't," I answer. I feel so drugged and so groggy, as if in a thick, gray fog. I am mentally dull and feel as if I am lost in space and time.

"You're in the hospital. Do you know why you are here?" she asks.

"I'm in the hospital," I repeat her words without thought or the meaning really having taken hold. "No. Why am I here?"

"You don't remember anything?" Sister Josephine asks.

Suddenly, my body stiffens and I try to sit up as the visions begin to fill my head. "Oh, God. Oh, God. Yes, yes, I remember," I say. Again, I try to loosen the bandage and again, Sister Josephine grabs my hands and holds them to keep me from grabbing at the bandages.

"Try to calm down, dear. The bandaging is pulled tight because there are parts of your scalp missing. The doctors couldn't pull the skin together, so the only way to stop the bleeding is to put pressure on the area." I hear Sister Josephine's voice from what seems like a distant place.

"Sister, I can't open my eyes. My eyelids are so heavy, and I can barely speak. My lips feel numb," I tell her as I become aware of my physical senses.

"Your lips are swollen, as are your eyes. They will return to normal soon," she tells me. "Right now, all you need to do is relax. You are safe here. A lot of good people are taking care of you. No more harm will come to you. It is over," she reassures me in a comforting tone of voice. Then instantly, in a brighter tone, "No more talking for you now. You need rest. God will heal you and the rest of us will protect you."

I find my body giving way to her tenderness and I accept what I have heard. I drift in and out of sleep. Occasionally, I feel people tending to my needs but I have no strength to move and no desire to do so. It occurs to me that, completely out of character, I have no will to live or die. I feel that a greater power is handling this for me. I keep falling asleep, but I must not. I need to stay awake. I must try to figure this out. I must try to remember everything that I can.

"How else can I fix this? How am I to understand it if I can't figure out how and why it happened?" I ask myself. I need to continue to remember, to work through my memories of the sixteen years of my marriage.

"Now, where did I leave off? Try, Nina," I encourage myself. I want to remember the happiness and laughter of our early years of marriage so I can try to find out where it all went so wrong.

YEAR TWO
OF OUR MARRIAGE

"A telegram from Stanford University," Bob reads. "They've made an error. In checking over my transcripts, somebody screwed up. I'm missing one hour of chemistry to get into the physical therapy program." He looks at the paper in his hand in disbelief. Moments earlier, the telegram with this terrible news was delivered to our door.

There are boxes all over the apartment. We are packed and readying to leave for California. We have planned this for months and months.

"Well, what are we going to do?" I ask.

"I don't know."

"But we're supposed to be leaving in a week! Why wasn't this discovered earlier? Where else can we go?" I ask Bob.

"I'll be damned if I know," Bob says. "Let me call the admissions office at Stanford and see what I can find out." He walks to the living room, picks up the phone and calls the Stanford University Admissions Office in Palo Alto, California. I perch myself on the edge of the sofa. I am just as shaken as he is and I am eager for an explanation. I have already quit my job, and Bob, who has just graduated from college, is ready to begin a physical therapy program.

He speaks to someone on the school switchboard and they transfer him from person to person until he finally speaks to the one with the answer. The admissions employee asks Bob to hold while he verifies his transfer credits. A short while later, the representative comes back to the phone and explains that the telegram is correct. The representative tells Bob that he should have been notified earlier, but someone messed up and failed to send the notification. He goes on to explain that now, the class is full and Bob cannot even appeal the decision. The representative explains that it is simply too late.

"How can this be? You have made a mistake. I only need one hour of chemistry. I applied an entire year ago and nobody caught this? Now you are telling me I have to wait for another entire year and attend another college to take a chemistry class for one lousy hour of chemistry? This is crazy! This is ludicrous! Can't you make an exception? I had plenty of time to make this up. This is your fault!" Bob says, with voice getting louder with each sentence.

"The class is already full, sir," the representative repeats. He hangs up on Bob before he is given another tongue-lashing. Bob holds the phone, staring at it, too dumbfounded to put it down.

"He hung up," Bob says. "There's nothing we can do. Nothing!"

We spend the next couple of days making phone calls. Bob frantically calls schools all over the country trying to find a physical therapy program with open seats where his credits will apply. There are not many schools offering this fairly new major, so this will be quite a chore.

A few days pass, and Bob receives tentative acceptance to the Mayo Clinic in Rochester, Minnesota and to Hermann Hospital in Houston, Texas. The Mayo Clinic program is nine months longer because students are required to work as assistants to the licensed therapists while they attended school. It is not as expensive as Houston's program, but the Hermann program takes only fifteen months and students are not required to work as they study. This sounds better to Bob. His parents already agreed to pay the tuition to Stanford, so the money is not an issue. He decides that we will move to Houston and I am fine with that decision. None of the three options was better than the others location-wise. We were going to be far from our families, friends and any chance of me starting my career no matter which school Bob chose.

Bob is happy with his decision because Hermann's program is substantively comparable to that of Stanford's. He is sick of school so he is happy the program is shorter, too. He has been in college for five years already because he switched his major from architecture to physical education, and now to physical therapy, so his education has already taken longer than either of us expected. Bob and I prepare to leave for Texas and my bosses at the photography studio in Bloomington help me with ideas for jobs in Houston.

"Why don't you go to Sieldings?" Fred, my boss, suggests. "It's one of the most prestigious photography studios in the world."

I'd like to get into fashion design but Houston isn't exactly a Mecca for fashion. Hell, I don't even know if there are any dress manufacturers there. I am hoping there are but if not, I will apply for another darkroom position. I will work anywhere and do anything. "After all, it's only fifteen months," I tell myself. "I just need to earn enough money to support us for fifteen months. Then we'll go home to Chicago where I can begin my career as a designer."

Two weeks later our car is packed and dragging a U-Haul trailer behind it, leading us to the start of a new dream. The drive takes two very long days.

As we approach Houston, I am surprised. It is not arid and dry, like a desert, as I had expected. It is subtropical: beautiful, lush, green, and terribly humid. We stay in a hotel our first night in town. Early the next morning, we purchase a newspaper and search for an apartment. There are many options but we finally decide on one. For the next three days, we move in, then out of, three apartments, each time finding a different bug population sharing our new home.

The bugs in Texas are gigantic. Cockroaches in the Midwest do not compare to what Texas has to offer. Their version is a massive, reddish-brown creature with wings. They call them "palmetto bugs." I joke that I could put a saddle on one and ride it. The old saying rings true. Everything certainly is bigger in Texas.

We are exhausted from all the moves. For many nights we don't sleep well. We just keep looking for bugs. We wake up often and check all night long, paranoid that we will experience another infestation. After a week, Bob makes the announcement, "We made it! No bugs! I guess we have landed. Today we'll start unpacking and I'll run out and get a newspaper so you can see what's available in the job market."

"Okay," I agree as I pull the coffee pot from its box. "I'll put on the coffee."

After we have coffee, Bob runs some errands and reappears with the Sunday newspaper and a phone book.

"Where did you get the phone book?" I ask, surprised to see it.

"I met the guy next door and told him what we were doing here in Houston. He offered to loan us his phone book until our phone is installed. The phone company will give us one then."

"First, we need some groceries. Then we'll get to business," I say.

We bathe, dress, and drive off in search of a grocery store, which we find a few blocks from our apartment. We shop, return to our apartment, unload our groceries, and find enough pots and pans to make breakfast. Then we open the phone book.

"There's only one dress manufacturer listed. I will call them tomorrow. I look up the number for Sieldings too. Get the Houston map, honey, and let's look to see where these places are located," I say to Bob.

As the hours pass this day, we unpack everything we have. When the last box is empty Bob grabs me and pulls me into his arms. "Welcome to Houston, Kitts! Let's put the sheets on the bed and mess them up." He leads me by my hand to the bedroom and we make love for the first time in our new home, in the city where we are beginning our new life.

On Monday morning I pick up the phone and dial. "My name is Nina," I say. "I'm a recent fashion design graduate and I'd like to apply for a job with your company."

The woman who answered tells me they are not hiring now but that she will take my name and phone number. She seems interested in my qualifications and tells me if she does not contact me in two months, I should call back.

"Oh, well," I think. "I guess I'm not surprised. I think I am even more surprised that there is even *one* dress manufacturer in this city. It is not exactly New York or Chicago. I decide I will call Sieldings and if that does not pan out, I will get the newspaper and look again. I can always work in retail after all my years at Marshall Fields." I call Sieldings and am surprised that they agree to interview me the next day for a position as a darkroom technician.

Tuesday arrives before I know it. Bob leaves the apartment to get the car to drive me to my interview and I take one last look into the mirror. "Way too classy for a darkroom job," I say aloud to myself. I am wearing the Italian raw silk suit I designed and made for our honeymoon. I even wear the matching silk pillbox hat with the long, brown feather on the side. I look as though I should be having lunch at the country club, not interviewing for a blue-collar job.

I hop into the car and, using the trusty map, navigate us to our destination. We notice the sign for Sieldings and pull into a parking spot. The building looks as though it was once someone's mansion. It is landscaped beautifully and looks very impressive. I open the door to the building and walk in. A lady walks up to me and asks if she can help. I inform her I have an interview with Mr. Hildebrandt. She offers me a seat in the reception room but I do not take it. I am too fascinated with what I see to sit.

The room is probably twenty by thirty feet and it is filled with portraits: individual portraits, family portraits and portraits of famous people. I walk around looking at the photographs, amazed. I have never seen such fantastic pictures. Even with my limited knowledge of photography, I recognize that this exhibition is notably exquisite. I remember Fred at the little camera shop where I worked in Bloomington telling me that the photographers here are all master photographers, a title earned through rigorous competitions.

"Nina," a voice calls to me. "Mr. Hildebrandt is ready to see you."

The manager of the studio shows me to his office and ushers me in. A large, handsome man sits behind a desk. He looks up at me and I notice the look on his face immediately. He is pleased with what he sees.

"You are not what I expected," he says to me. "Have a seat. I believe that you are applying for a job in the darkroom. Is that correct?"

I nod in agreement.

"I don't have your resume, so tell me all about you."

I brag about graduating at the top of my class and tell him I had one of the best job offers when I finished fashion design school, adding that Marshall Fields, where I worked part-time all the years I was in college, also offered me a position as an assistant buyer. I explain that I modeled for the Stevens Agency in Chicago but that when we moved to Bloomington, the best paying job I could find in that little college town was as a dark room attendant.

"They trained me," I say. "When I left, I made them aware that Houston might not offer many fashion industry positions, and they suggested I look up this studio. I must say, I've never seen portraits of the same quality as those in your reception gallery."

Mr. Hildebrandt sits back in his chair and studies me. He is silent for a few moments and then says, "Nina, I wonder if you might consider another position we are seeking to fill. We need a receptionist. The receptionist position at Sieldings is an important one to us. The receptionist sits at an antique desk in the lobby and reflects the elegance and quality of this business. She must be able to speak well and denote a touch of class. I think you will be perfect for the job. I, personally, would not want to hide you in the darkroom. What do you think of the offer?"

"Well, does the reception position pay better than the darkroom?" I ask unabashedly.

"Much," he answers.

"Well then, you have yourself a receptionist!"

I fall in love with my job. I love to sit and chat with the clients while they wait to speak to a salesperson or to be photographed. I receive praises from other employees who think I am a wonderful asset to the studio. Our client list includes the President and the Vice President of the United States, debutantes, the Southwest's elite, the brilliant scholars, the movie stars and occasionally, the average Joe who saves and saves to have a portrait made by the world-renowned Sieldings Studio.

Today a man appears at the door holding a picture. He says it is his young daughter who has recently passed away. It is of poor quality but it is all he has left of her. His hands are shaking and I notice his clothes are not of the standard I am used to seeing here. He says he wants to have a larger picture made. He tells me he works in maintenance at the airport and that he has admired the beautiful photographs of Houston's finest hanging there over the years. He says that he had hoped one day to have Sieldings photograph his daughter, but she did not live long enough for him to save enough money to have it done.

"I have saved some money. I do not know if it is enough. Can you make this picture bigger and maybe a little better? I don't know if I even have enough money," he repeats apologetically. I look at the little roll of money in his hands and he places it on my desk. Our portraits start at one hundred dollars and I am sure that he does not have the minimum. I show him a chair in the gallery and tell him I will be right back.

I go to Mrs. Miller, who is in charge of sales, and notice that she is wearing the hat I designed and made for her birthday last month. It is a small, red hat with cherries hanging off of one side. She looks beautiful in my design. I sit in the chair in front of her new desk and explain the sad story. She instructs me to ask Dorothea, the studio's maid, to pour the man a cup of coffee and tell him she will be with him in a few minutes.

Fifteen minutes pass before Mrs. Miller returns to meet with him. She takes the picture and his money and gives him a receipt. He leaves the studio and curiosity gets the best of me. "I saw you take the money. Are you going to do something for him?" I ask.

"I went upstairs and found Mr. Sieldings, Sr. and relayed the story to him. Tears welled up in his eyes and he told me to tell the gentleman that he would be honored to make him a portrait and to just accept whatever money the janitor had to pay. We are going to make a sixteen-by-twenty portrait. We will copy the original and then one of our professional artists will color over it in heavy oils, thus making it look like a fine oil painting. We'll give the original back to him."

Today the janitor is scheduled to pick up the portrait. A good portion of our staff is present. He arrives and is presented with the portrait. He is overwhelmed. He cries and cries and we all cry with him. I know in my heart that I will remember this humble little man forever. I am reminded of a saying my Mom uses often: *"Do what you can for those in need. For one day, when you are in need, someone will be there for you."*

"What would you think of our purchasing a mobile home?" Bob asks as he enters our apartment after school and drops his books on a chair. "One of my classmates is selling the one they live in because it has only one bedroom and they are expecting a baby. It's the kind you can hook up to a car, so we can drag it back home and live in it for a year or so. I will call Mom and Dad and ask if they will loan us the money. We can pay it back when I start my job. It is nice. I have seen it. What do you think? They have it parked in a mobile home park and the rent for the space is much less than our rent here."

"Sounds good to me," I answer. "Run it by your parents."

They agree, so we purchase it and move in two weeks later.

The months are flying by and Bob and I are becoming very thin. We look great, really. Dinner is on a three-day rotation. One night, we have goulash made with hamburger, which I purchase at three pounds for a dollar and use half a pound at a time. The next night, I fix cornmeal mush, and the third night, we have pancakes. Every day for lunch, we each eat a peanut butter and jelly sandwich and one apple. I purchase the peanut butter and jelly in gallon jars. I plan to keep these jars so I will never forget how tough it was once upon a time. I vow to myself that once we get out of here and find good jobs, I will never eat peanut butter again.

I barely earn enough to make ends meet. It is not easy living on one very small income. Bob loves his classes and it is wonderful to see him so happy. He never complains about any of his subjects and he has even become a solid "A" student. I knew he always had the potential but before entering this physical therapy program, he had always been satisfied with A's, B's and C's.

He loves his classmates, too. He casually talks about a girl named Nellie Mayor. She plays in a semi-pro ladies baseball league and she keeps pestering him to catch for her sometime during their lunch break. He ignores her and tells me he cannot imagine catching for a girl. He was once the first string catcher for the University of Illinois baseball team. He informs me he has finally weakened to her pleas and has told her he will catch for her the next day.

Later the following day, he relays to me he arrived with his glove and squatted into catching position with his glove out, awaiting the pitch. Nellie wound up and zoomed the ball into his catcher's mitt, knocking him on his ass. Their classmates applauded and Bob was humbled. He had not even positioned himself properly as he did not expect her to throw as hard as she did. He promised her they will play more often and they continue to do so for the rest of the school year.

Bob's days in class and his evenings at home are spent studying. We are starving, happy, and oh, so in love. Life is good and we tell ourselves one day, it will be even better. We will have to work hard to get there. We are willing to do it.

One of our weekend hobbies and distractions from our hard work is crab fishing. It's a way to have fun and eat well on our tight budget. Our neighbors know just how to help us. Crab fishing is the solution.

The night before crabbing, we purchase a dozen chicken wings and leave them outside overnight. By the next morning, because of the Texas heat, they are rancid but a delectable treat for the crabs. We drive approximate fifty miles to Galveston which is on the Gulf of Mexico. We find a long fishing pier; tie a chicken wing on a long, heavy string; lower it to the bottom of the water; and tie the string to a post on the dock. Every so often we pull the string up slowly. We can tell by the weight of the line whether we have a crab holding onto the chicken wing. Once a crab grabs it, it will not let go. We pick up a net and scoop up the crab. We then put it into a bucket along with the others we catch that day. We take them home. Our neighbors teach us how to make gumbo, too. Mmm, real food. We enjoy our fabulous crab gumbo and the company of our neighbors.

We also spend a lot of time playing pinochle at the Altons. Danny Alton is a classmate of Bob's, and his wife, Nell, is a stay-at-home, expectant mom. We can hardly wait for those nights. Their folks support them financially so they eat like real people. On the nights we play cards, Nell fixes fried bologna sandwiches and homemade potato chips. It is such a welcome break from our three-day menu plan. We cannot wait to live like they do one day, like normal people.

I love my position at Sieldings but financially, it barely suffices. Two months pass and I call the dress manufacturer again to inquire if they have any new openings for a designer.

"Come in for an interview tomorrow morning at ten," the lady requests.

I call in sick to Sieldings and arrive at a restaurant near the dress manufacturer at eight o'clock, two hours early for my appointment. Bob drove me here early in order to get to class on time. I sit and sip coffee until the time comes for my interview.

"Hi, Nina. I am Peter Black. What I really need is a pattern drafter. We start all of our designers off as pattern drafters. Have you ever done drafting?"

"Yes, of course I have, but I'm better at draping." I answer.

"We don't do draping here. Do you think you'd like to try your hand at drafting?" he asks.

"Of course."

"Come with me," he says as he leads me past fifty women working at sewing machines.

I had never been in a dressmaking factory. I am excited to be here. We come to an enormous room. There are literally thousands of patterns on hangers, filling dozens of racks. Huge pattern-cutting tables sit nearby. I take it all in and feel exhilarated. This could be the beginning of my designing career.

"I'd like you to make a paper pattern of this design," he says, as he shows me a picture of a dress.

"Now? You want me to draft a pattern today?" I ask, astonished.

"Sure! You will notice each rack has a variety of basics. One has a selection of raglan sleeves; another, set-in sleeves; and so on and so forth. Take any one of these bodices, sleeves and so forth, and draft a pattern of this dress. I'll be in that office." He points to a glass office. "Come get me when you're finished." He walks away, leaving me all alone.

I watch him as he sits down at his desk and I notice that my palms are sweaty. I didn't plan on this. "I guess it's now or never," I think to myself.

I put down my purse and begin the search for the sleeve, bodice and skirt that most closely resemble the drawing. Alas, I am ready to draft. I work for a few hours and check my final product. When I am satisfied with my newly crafted pattern, I walk over to Mr. Black's office and ask him to come to the cutting room to check my work.

He scrutinizes each piece and then proceeds to show me where I should have made corrections. He does not look as though he is displeased and yet he does not immediately praise me for my work. Finally, he says, "You know, you're pretty good, young lady. Not bad for a kid fresh out of school. You will get faster and more accurate with practice. I would like to offer you a position as an assistant pattern drafter. We manufacture high-end, ready-to-wear dresses. You'll have to earn your way to a designer position."

He tells me what he would pay me and explains that I would be on a three-month period of probation. If I made it and decided that I liked the job, we would then talk more about money. He offers me slightly more than what I am earning at Sieldings. "Think about it over the weekend and give me a call," Mr. Black said.

We shake hands and I leave. I walk out of the building and to the restaurant where I had coffee that morning to call a cab. I slide into the back seat, give the cabbie our address, take off my hat, and sink deep into the seat, numb and still shaking. *"Pretty good for a kid just out of school,"* I replay in my mind.

I think to myself, "Well, Nina, so far you've interviewed for two designing positions since school and you got both of them." I start weighing my options, my mind working quickly through all the thoughts. "I passed up the first one with Maidenform. Should I take this one? It would be a great learning experience and would definitely improve my chances of landing a design position when we return to Chicago. On the other hand, it is a three-month trial. What if I don't make it? What if the people I work with don't like me and feel that I am too slow? What if I do not measure up for any other reason and they have to let me go? I could not go back to Sieldings then. I need to bounce this off of Bob when he comes home from school."

I smile with satisfaction in my skill. I think of my Peppers, as I call Bob, who earned his nickname for always thinking he is hot stuff. I cannot wait to talk to him about my interview. "You'll be proud of me, Peppers," I tell him in my head.

We discuss the offer all evening and come to no decision. "Let's sleep on it, Kitts. Maybe the daylight will find us with clearer heads."

Morning arrives and we go through the pros and cons. The experience would be extremely valuable, but what is making the decision difficult is that I truly love my job at Sieldings. I am fascinated with the beauty of the photography and enthralled by the famous people I welcome into the studio.

"You know, Peppers, as much as I would love the challenge of the drafting position, I don't want to give up the 'Sieldings Experience,'" as I call it. "It's only for a year. I can always become a pattern drafter when we get back to Chicago. I hate pattern drafting anyway. I want to design and drape." I decide to stay at Sieldings and Bob is supportive of my decision. At least we will have a paycheck every week until we leave, even if it is a small one.

As the months pass, I see hundreds of dresses and gowns our patrons wear to be photographed, some made by world-famous designers. I see the names on the labels and dream that one day those labels will have my name on them. Whenever possible, I examine the workmanship and remember the details. Some clients come with unbelievable jewels and furs to match. Sometimes they are even accompanied by armed guards. I have a difficult time processing so much opulence. I have never been wealthy and now I am being exposed to fashion glamour that I never even dreamed existed.

Today, as I enter the studio, Dorothea greets me, excited to tell me about "The Wedding." One of our prestigious brides requested that Dorothea accompany our photographers to her wedding. She wanted Dorothea's expertise in dressing her in her wedding gown.

"Nina, you should have been at that wedding. Mm-hmm," she says in her deep southern drawl, shaking her head. "They covered the trees with live flowers and had live floral arrangements floating in all three of the pools. Mmm. I have never seen such foolishness. Max, the florist said the flowers cost thirty-eight-thousand dollars!"

to talk to him about my interview. "You'll be proud of me, Peppers," I tell him in my head.

We discuss the offer all evening and come to no decision. "Let's sleep on it, Kitts. Maybe the daylight will find us with clearer heads."

Morning arrives and we go through the pros and cons. The experience would be extremely valuable, but what is making the decision difficult is that I truly love my job at Sieldings. I am fascinated with the beauty of the photography and enthralled by the famous people I welcome into the studio.

"You know, Peppers, as much as I would love the challenge of the drafting position, I don't want to give up the 'Sieldings Experience,'" as I call it. "It's only for a year. I can always become a pattern drafter when we get back to Chicago. I hate pattern drafting anyway. I want to design and drape." I decide to stay at Sieldings and Bob is supportive of my decision. At least we will have a paycheck every week until we leave, even if it is a small one.

As the months pass, I see hundreds of dresses and gowns our patrons wear to be photographed, some made by world-famous designers. I see the names on the labels and dream that one day those labels will have my name on them. Whenever possible, I examine the workmanship and remember the details. Some clients come with unbelievable jewels and furs to match. Sometimes they are even accompanied by armed guards. I have a difficult time processing so much opulence. I have never been wealthy and now I am being exposed to fashion glamour that I never even dreamed existed.

Today, as I enter the studio, Dorothea greets me, excited to tell me about "The Wedding." One of our prestigious brides requested that Dorothea accompany our photographers to her wedding. She wanted Dorothea's expertise in dressing her in her wedding gown.

"Nina, you should have been at that wedding. Mm-hmm," she says in her deep southern drawl, shaking her head. "They covered the trees with live flowers and had live floral arrangements floating in all three of the pools. Mmm. I have never seen such foolishness. Max, the florist said the flowers cost thirty-eight-thousand dollars!"

I put down my purse and begin the search for the sleeve, bodice and skirt that most closely resemble the drawing. Alas, I am ready to draft. I work for a few hours and check my final product. When I am satisfied with my newly crafted pattern, I walk over to Mr. Black's office and ask him to come to the cutting room to check my work.

He scrutinizes each piece and then proceeds to show me where I should have made corrections. He does not look as though he is displeased and yet he does not immediately praise me for my work. Finally, he says, "You know, you're pretty good, young lady. Not bad for a kid fresh out of school. You will get faster and more accurate with practice. I would like to offer you a position as an assistant pattern drafter. We manufacture high-end, ready-to-wear dresses. You'll have to earn your way to a designer position."

He tells me what he would pay me and explains that I would be on a three-month period of probation. If I made it and decided that I liked the job, we would then talk more about money. He offers me slightly more than what I am earning at Sieldings. "Think about it over the weekend and give me a call," Mr. Black said.

We shake hands and I leave. I walk out of the building and to the restaurant where I had coffee that morning to call a cab. I slide into the back seat, give the cabbie our address, take off my hat, and sink deep into the seat, numb and still shaking. *"Pretty good for a kid just out of school,"* I replay in my mind.

I think to myself, "Well, Nina, so far you've interviewed for two designing positions since school and you got both of them." I start weighing my options, my mind working quickly through all the thoughts. "I passed up the first one with Maidenform. Should I take this one? It would be a great learning experience and would definitely improve my chances of landing a design position when we return to Chicago. On the other hand, it is a three-month trial. What if I don't make it? What if the people I work with don't like me and feel that I am too slow? What if I do not measure up for any other reason and they have to let me go? I could not go back to Sieldings then. I need to bounce this off of Bob when he comes home from school."

I smile with satisfaction in my skill. I think of my Peppers, as I call Bob, who earned his nickname for always thinking he is hot stuff. I cannot wait

On another occasion, our photographers are picked up and flown in a private plane to photograph a television and radio star's family. Every week, I have another fascinating experience at work. The photographers even use me as a model sometimes to sharpen their skills.

One day, I arrive at work to find the photographers and staff all atwitter. They are wearing terror on their faces. Dorothea whispers to me, "Apparently, Mr. Traina put twenty rolls of color film, taken at '*The Wedding*,' into the solution used to develop black and white film. All of the pictures are muddy and ruined." Mr. Traina is the man in charge of all production and finishing in the darkroom. Because he has been with Sieldings for twenty-five years, he is forgiven.

Thank God, the bride had come into the studio weeks before her wedding to have her formal portraits taken. To make amends, the studio offers her a variety of portraits, some hand-painted miniatures on genuine ivory which retail at four hundred dollars each. They also offer to take the negatives from any of the guests who had used their own cameras and make albums. It costs the studio over thirty-thousand dollars.

Time passes and Bob has only one quarter of his school year left. In order to finish his program, he has to complete three different internships at three different hospitals. He is soon leaving for Dallas for his first one, where he will be working with handicapped children, the field in which he hopes to specialize.

Bob is worried about me staying alone in the trailer for two long months. He decides to buy me a puppy, a Shetland Sheepdog. We name her Prancer, as she was born on Christmas Day.

"She's a puppy. What protection do you think she will be? She's even timid with us," I say. "Well, it's the thought that counts." We are amused to discover that she loves green grapes, cantaloupe and cupcakes. Oh, yes – and beer.

One evening, before Bob leaves for his internship, he gives Prancer a whole can of beer while we are watching television. A commercial comes on for Raid bug spray and Prancer sits up, alert to a buzzing bug. She is mesmerized by what she sees on the television. Suddenly, she jumps at the screen to catch the bug, hits the glass screen really hard and bounces off.

She just lies there, stunned. I run to her and pick her up. Her tongue is hanging out of her mouth.

"I think she's dead!" I scream.

Bob takes her into his arms. "She'll be fine. She's just shocked," Bob says while soothing her.

"Damn you, Bob! I have told you not to give her beer. She could die! That was a stupid thing to do!"

That was the last time Prancer had a beer, although every time Bob opened a can of beer from that point on, Prancer looked at him and barked once. We wonder if she thought of how much she liked it or if she remembered the hangover.

The day arrives for Bob to leave me for his internship, and I am left alone with my "watch puppy." My friends at Sieldings take good care of me and plan many activities so I am not too lonely. Gabby, the bridal consultant at Sieldings, even teaches me how to water ski. In all my twenty-one years, I have never had a tan in the summer. This year, I am golden brown and look damn good in white.

My Texas family helps me understand their love for their country. To them Texas is not a state; it is its own country. When anyone asks any of them where they are from, they stand proud with their heads held high with a superior smirk and say, "I'm from Texas." I love their crazy pride for their "country." No other state boasts residents with the pride of these Texans.

The two months pass and Bob's internship is finally over. My guy is finally coming home, so I fix a special dinner. Bob arrives and storms into our mobile home.

"Hi, Kitts. Oh, God, I've missed you." He kisses me passionately and then he picks me up and carries me into the bedroom.

"Hey, I have a special dinner fixed for you," I say playfully.

"Later," he says, smiling as he places me on the bed. Prancer is not far behind us. Bob tries to wave her off, but she stands her ground and growls at him. I laugh.

"Well, you did get her to protect me, didn't you? You're the biggest danger she's seen so far!" We both laugh and he finally shoos Prancer off the bed. She scampers away with her tail between her legs and Bob wraps me in his arms. Dinner can wait.

The next two internships are in Houston so Bob is able to come home every evening. As the school year comes to a close, Bob sends out resumes to a variety of hospitals, applying for physical therapist positions. He receives three offers and the one he seems most interested in is in Peoria, Illinois. The head of the physical therapy department at that hospital is a highly respected doctor who has written many of the books on therapy that Bob has read in college.

The phone rings and Bob answers it. I overhear some of the conversation. "Next week, I will fly to Peoria for an interview. They are sending me the air tickets," he tells me as he hangs up the phone.

"But Peppers, Peoria is a hundred and sixty miles from Chicago. I need to be in Chicago to be a fashion designer," I reply matter-of-factly.

"I know, Kitts. I need to talk to you about that. I have been doing a lot of research on job opportunities. The doctor that I would be working for is the most renowned physical therapy expert in the country. My idea is to study under him for two years and then I promise we will go back home to Chicago. It'll be a great start to my career," he begs.

"I don't want to stand in your way, but I can't say that I'm happy about it. I do not like my career being pushed onto the back burner once again. It's my turn," I say, attempting to control my temper. "It's been two-and-a-half years. Damn it, it's my turn!"

"I just want to go for the interview. I can always turn it down," Bob insists.

Bob flies to Peoria for the interview. When he returns, he pleads with me to let him take the job. I cannot deny him. He is so excited for this opportunity. My career as a designer will just have to wait – again.

We will be leaving soon and Dorothea has been crying about it on and off for weeks. "I'm going to miss you. I 'sho' will miss your laughter. Who am I going to bring food to? You 'gonna' starve to death without my snacks," she said, shaking her finger at me.

I know I will miss her beautiful, cocoa face and the fondness we have for each other. Dorothea is something special. Her position at Sieldings is patron assistant. She helps the customers dress in their finery and pours coffee for them and those of us in the reception and sales areas. She is as smart as anyone I know and when she enters the building wearing her Pendleton suits, you would think she is a client. She goes into her dressing room and comes out wearing a maid's uniform, a stark contrast. Some maid she is, though. Even in that outfit, she is one class act.

At five o'clock each evening, Wilson, her husband, picks her up in their new Cadillac. Wilson is the *maître de* at Houston's most exclusive restaurant and he makes very good money, especially for a black man in the South. In fact, he does better financially than most white men.

I will miss Dr. Shultz and his wife, Mamie, too. They are our guardian angels here in Texas and the very best friends of my mother-in-law's best friend, Betsy. She asked them to watch over us while we are in Houston and that they have certainly done.

Doc was a very successful surgeon in Chicago. At fifty, he pursued his dream of retiring in Houston. He rents the top floor of a luxury high-rise. He and Mamie live in two-thirds of it, and his brother and sister-in-law live in the other section, compliments of Doc's generosity. Two of the four bedrooms have been converted into closets for Doc, a serious clothes horse. He has racks and racks of dress suits and sport jackets. One of the rooms has two entire walls dedicated to showcasing his cowboy boots and cowboy hats. He calls himself "The Jewish Cowboy of Texas," and the title fits him well.

As his wife's story goes, it did not take long after they arrived in Texas for Doc to become bored with his retirement. He purchased a bleach company that his brother-in-law managed, and then he became a volunteer at the veterans' hospital in Houston. He volunteered for a year but found it too depressing. His next adventure in trying to "give something back to our world," as he words it, was to open a small family clinic where he treats the city's poorest people, many without the funds to pay him. He takes whatever they feel they can give; sometimes nothing. He absolutely loves it.

About a year after opening his practice, he began receiving phone calls from people seeking a cab. He discovered that a new cab company's phone number was one digit different from his. The phone company refused to change the number. Thereafter, when the calls came in the middle of the night requesting a cab, Doc would tell them he would be right there and hang up before asking where they were and where they wanted to go. It took about six months of this before the phone company finally changed the cab company's phone number. Doc is stubborn and he always wins.

Doc and Mamie are our family away from home. Every couple of weeks, they take us to their favorite restaurant for dinner, which happens to be where Wilson works. Wilson treats us as though we are royalty. After dinner, Doc always takes us back to their apartment and loads us up with groceries.

It is Christmas Eve and Doc has asked us to meet them at their apartment before they take us to dinner. We knock on the door and Doc opens it with a flourish. "Voila!" he says. We look around, absolutely amazed at the cages of live chickens and ducks, stacks of cakes, goodies and crates of eggs.

"Holy shit!" Bob exclaims. We carefully walk into the living room. There is no room for a misstep. "What in the hell?" Bob asks.

"Every Christmas Eve, this happens. The patients who are too poor to pay for my services bestow these gifts unto me. In a few minutes, some people from The Boys Club will arrive with vans and take it away. It does my soul good and helps me enjoy my retirement. Here, let me fill a couple baskets for you to take home."

After dinner, we exchange holiday greetings and head home.

"I hope I can do something for someone in need someday. We'll probably never be able to do *that* much, though!" Bob says to me as he drives.

In the wee hours of the morning, the phone rings. "Merry Christmas," I say in a sleepy voice.

"Get over here right now!" Doc demands.

"We were just over last night, Doc. What's up?" I reply, confused.

"Don't ask questions," he orders, "just get here now!"

"Okay, okay," I agree and hang up.

"Bob, get up. Doc says to come over immediately. No questions asked, just get there." We dress quickly and drive back to their place.

We walk through the massive doors to their building and into a lobby full of people. At the far end, I can see Doc waving us over to him. Standing next to him is a huge Black Angus steer with the largest red bow I have ever seen resting on its back. Doc holds something resembling a leash in his hand. Flash bulbs light the room. News media ask Doc questions and Mamie rushes over when she notices us.

"One of Doc's previous patients from Chicago has become a huge success. He credits it all to Doc's generosity and confidence in him, so he rewarded him with the most publicized gift in this year's Neiman Marcus Christmas Book." She beams with pride.

"What's Doc going to do with it?" I ask.

"He's giving it to The Boys Club as a pet. He is a show animal so he is used to people. Taking care of him will be good therapy for the boys." She continues to beam with pride and love for her husband.

On the way home I say to Bob, "I'll never forget this day. I am going to miss them and their goodness. I can't believe our time in Texas is almost over."

On my last day at Sieldings, Dorothea cries all morning. That afternoon, the entire studio throws me a farewell party. A huge cake sits in the middle of the table. "*We'll Miss Our Yankee Baby*," it reads. I burst into tears when I read the message.

"You make sure to come back and see us. We'll be looking for your name on clothing labels," my coworkers say. They each give me a final hug. I begin to clean off my desk when Mr. Sieldings, Sr. pages me upstairs to his office. He beckons me to have a seat. He is a handsome man, about sixty years of age, and one of the most gifted photographers in the world.

"Nina, you are one of the finest employees I've ever had and definitely, the most overqualified for the position. I would like to offer you a recommendation I have prepared for you to use whenever and for whatever you would like. You may never have a need to for it, but I have offered this to very few people in my twenty-five years in this business. You are a great asset and will be one wherever life takes you." He shakes my hand, holds it for a moment, then adds, "May God bless you."

Bob pulls up in our car, but before I climb in, I take one last look at the building in which I learned so much about life. Dorothea stands in front of the door, waving and crying. As I sit down in the passenger seat, my face slides across the collar of my coat. It is wet with Dorothea's tears. I wave back to her until I cannot see her anymore as we drive off to begin the next chapter of our lives.

CHAPTER THREE
DAY THREE
IN THE HOSPITAL

Someone takes hold of my arm and I scream, as I am startled.

"Who are you?" I ask. I still cannot see.

"I'm sorry. I didn't mean to frighten you," a kind voice says.

"What are you doing?" I ask.

"I'm a nurse. My name is Susan. I'm taking your blood pressure; it has a way of bottoming out," Susan says to me as she lays my arm back down alongside of me.

I realize my other hand is fingering a rosary. I wonder why I have it here with me, but more importantly, who put it in my hand? I am in great pain.

"Am I going to be alright?" I ask.

"Two days ago, we didn't think so. Today we're feeling much more positive," she replies.

Strangely, I do not feel comforted. I feel no emotion at all. The only thing I feel is excruciating pain all over my body but especially in my head and neck. I hear other people groaning and moaning. They are in pain, too.

"Nurse! Nurse!" I call.

"Yes, Nina?" she replies.

CHAPTER THREE
DAY THREE
IN THE HOSPITAL

Someone takes hold of my arm and I scream, as I am startled.

"Who are you?" I ask. I still cannot see.

"I'm sorry. I didn't mean to frighten you," a kind voice says.

"What are you doing?" I ask.

"I'm a nurse. My name is Susan. I'm taking your blood pressure; it has a way of bottoming out," Susan says to me as she lays my arm back down alongside of me.

I realize my other hand is fingering a rosary. I wonder why I have it here with me, but more importantly, who put it in my hand? I am in great pain.

"Am I going to be alright?" I ask.

"Two days ago, we didn't think so. Today we're feeling much more positive," she replies.

Strangely, I do not feel comforted. I feel no emotion at all. The only thing I feel is excruciating pain all over my body but especially in my head and neck. I hear other people groaning and moaning. They are in pain, too.

"Nurse! Nurse!" I call.

"Yes, Nina?" she replies.

asset and will be one wherever life takes you." He shakes my hand, holds it for a moment, then adds, "May God bless you."

Bob pulls up in our car, but before I climb in, I take one last look at the building in which I learned so much about life. Dorothea stands in front of the door, waving and crying. As I sit down in the passenger seat, my face slides across the collar of my coat. It is wet with Dorothea's tears. I wave back to her until I cannot see her anymore as we drive off to begin the next chapter of our lives.

"Someone is in pain. Don't you hear them?" I ask.

"You are in intensive care, Nina. You're hearing other patients," Susan answers.

"I want to sleep, I am so tired," I say to her. "But it's so noisy. I might not feel all of this pain if I could just fall asleep."

She chuckles softly. "The first sign that a patient is recovering is that they start complaining. Maybe it is time we move you into a regular room. In the meantime, though, I will give you some pain medication and that will help you sleep."

Shortly after I receive the pain medication, I begin to relax. Then, from what seems to be far off in the distance, I hear my mother singing. I can even see her in our kitchen, her hair shining in the sunlight that is streaming through the window. She is so beautiful. We start to sing "My Happiness" together.

Suddenly, I am awakened from my dream. My hospital bed jerks and feels like it is moving. I hear voices and I groan as the bumps from passing over the floor seams cause waves of pain to overtake my body. "What's happening?" I ask angrily.

"We're moving you to a room of your own, a nice quiet room," a voice tells me.

The motion stops and endless fussing that causes more pain continues for what seems like forever.

"So how do you rate this room? Come on, Nina, open your eyes," someone commands cheerfully. I realize that it has not occurred to me to open my eyes.

Then a feeling of terror strikes and I exclaim, "No, no. I cannot open my eyes. If I do, I will see the blood. I will see the blood squirting all over. No, no. I will not open my eyes. I'm afraid to open them."

I feel someone take hold of my hand. "Don't be afraid. I am here. No one will hurt you. You are safe. Come on, Nina. It's time to come back into our world," the voice says.

Although I am fearful, I attempt to force my eyes to open, but they will not cooperate. I am concentrating, trying harder. Finally, they open and I see large, bright flashes of light. I quickly close them again. "The light hurts," I complain.

"Let me close the shades. The light may be too bright," the nurse offers.

I try again, but I only see blurred images. Everything is a blur and that frightens me as well.

"Take your time, Nina. Give your eyes some time to adjust," she says.

Minutes pass. I try several times to open my eyes and to see what surrounds me. "Everything is blurred. I can't see!" I say in a panic.

"Are both eyes blurred? Cover one of your eyes," she orders, "and look with the other."

I do as she says. "Everything is still blurred," I say.

"Now try the other eye," she instructs.

"I can see! I can see just fine out of this eye," I say, relieved, as objects come into focus, almost like magic.

"Look at me with the eye that's blurred. Believe me, I look better a little blurred. If you could see me with clear vision, my face might scare you," she jokes. "My name is Mary. I'm one of your nurses."

I look at her face and notice that she is very pretty. "You're beautiful," I say to her.

"Compliments won't get you anywhere. I still need to get a blood sample," she replies, smiling.

I glance over to see what she is doing. It has always been so easy to take blood from my arm. As I watch her, I see the blood filling the tube and suddenly become nauseous. I then hear a voice from what seems like a tunnel in the distance. "Come on, Nina. Come on. Are you with us? Are you with us?"

I can hear her, but I cannot seem to respond. I am trying to respond, but cannot. I feel her patting my hand, and she says, "Come on, Nina. Open your eyes again."

I oblige. "What do you want?" I ask.

"We were taking a blood sample and you fainted on us. Does it bother you to have your blood drawn?" she asks.

I have to think about her question for a minute. "No. It has never bothered me before. I have never fainted while having blood taken," I reply.

I look at the vial of blood sitting on the tray and close my eyes. I am becoming nauseated again. I see blood. Blood is everywhere. Oh, God, I am getting sick to my stomach. I remember the blood. And I feel myself slipping away again.

"What are you doing?" I scream as someone pats my hand. I open my eyes and see Mary again.

"You fainted away on me again, lady. The sight of blood is making you pass out. I can understand that. Turn your head away. I will give you an injection for pain."

"Thank you," I tell her as she leaves.

I am alone and I feel a deep loneliness. My hospital room is gray. While my vision is still fuzzy, I see that the room is large and round. It seems so cold. Windows wrap all the way around. I realize I am in the old wing of the hospital. My room is at the top of what looks like a castle tower from the outside. It has two dressers, a desk, an overstuffed chair and two hard chairs. I see a mirror hanging on the wall facing me. It is too high to see myself and I am grateful for that. There is a bathroom in the corner of the room, but I have no need to use it. I usually pee quite often, but I do not seem to have the urge to go. My eyes glance over to the window. The shade is partly open and it looks so cold outside. I hear a noise coming from the doorway and I see the shadowed images of two people.

"That can't be her," a familiar voice says.

I recognize the voice. "Dad, is that you?"

"Oh my God! I didn't even recognize you," my brother whispers to me.

"Do I look that bad?" I ask him.

"No, you look wonderful," my Dad, answers. "It's just that you have so much bandaging covering your head that we can't see much of your face. What I see looks wonderful."

"Dad, you're putting me on," I say in a weak voice. "I'm in a lot of pain. Have you seen the kids?"

"No, and we probably won't. They are in school and when we leave here, we are going back home. The kid," as he calls my little brother, "has a terrible cold. That is why we were not here sooner. We didn't want you to get sicker than you already are."

The nurse comes in and gives my brother a mask so he will not spread any of his lingering germs. They stay and visit as I drift in and out of sleep for the next couple of hours.

"I feel helpless," my Dad says as they prepare to leave. "But it looks like you're in great hands," my Dad says as they leave the room. I know he is in shock and is just as confused as I am. He loves Bob, as everyone who has ever met him loves him. My brother has to get back to his job as a pharmacist, so they must go back home to Chicago. I understand, but I wish they would have stayed longer.

I am about to close my eyes when my in-laws walk in. Mom tells me that my friend, Andrea, came over for a bit to watch the kids so they could come and visit. All my father-in-law can say is, "How could this have happened?" I am certain that they, too, are in shock.

They stay and visit, but I lose track of how long they have been here. I keep falling asleep and waking up. My in-laws tell me that have each taken a week off of work to stay with the children. They hope I might be home by then. They gently kiss me on the cheek and leave to return to the children.

My brain is so fuzzy. But I shock myself as I realize that I have not even thought of my children. Nor have I considered who is taking care of them. I begin to wonder if I will be able to care for them again. I am starting to question many things. I realize my mind is sharpening and I am ambivalent to that fact as I fall asleep again.

Awakening, I notice a shadow moving toward me, and I automatically stiffen my body and my mind, suddenly terrified of who or what it might be.

"It's only me, Nina. I am your night nurse, Karen. I'm here to give you some pain medication," she tells me.

"Yes, please," I say. "I need to be free of this pain." Although I would like more medication, but it makes me sleep. I want to stay awake to see if I can remember. I have to remember back to earlier years because I desperately need to figure out why this all happened.

"Think, Nina, Think. Could you have seen the signs sooner?" I wonder. "When did it all go wrong?"

I remember back to our third year of marriage to resume my search for an answer.

YEAR THREE OF OUR MARRIAGE

Bob has no eyebrows, no eyelashes and no hair on his arms; just a blank look on his face. I look down at my legs. My nylon stockings have melted down to my ankles. I lift my skirt and notice that the garters on my girdle are holding the heavy top of my nylons and nothing else. We look at each other in silence.

After a minute, Bob asks, "Are you okay?"

"I think so," I reply.

"Shit! We could have been killed!" Bob screams at me as soon as I confirm that I am not hurt.

"Well, we're okay. We'll just have to go out for dinner," I say to him.

"Why go out?" Bob asks and then adds, "Now that it's lit, just fix the dinner you planned."

I cover my mouth and my eyes open wide. Bob takes one look at me and snaps, "You didn't! Tell me you didn't shut it off!" He looks into the oven and sees that the pilot light is off. "Christ's sake, Nina! Why the hell did you turn off the pilot light?"

"I thought it might explode again. This damn thing has always been such a pain in the ass to light," I reply. I look at Bob, and he stares back, bewildered. He does not speak, but his expression asks how I could be so stupid. He shakes his head and walks away.

I freeze in that moment, remembering the past few minutes. There was a loud *boom* and the gas range I had been trying to light flew several inches off the floor, tearing loose the bolts that secured it, before falling back into place. We could have been killed. As we calm down, we realize how lucky we are.

"Come on, Kitts. I will get your coat. Take off what is left of your nylons. We're eating out," Bob says to me as he escorts me to the car. "Let's make this a short night because Dad will be here tomorrow. We will just give the roast to the neighbors. You won't be able to cook it when we disconnect all the utilities tomorrow in preparation for the move to Peoria."

The next day, Steven, my father-in-law, arrives on his flight from Chicago to Houston to help us drive back to Illinois. We plan to pull the mobile home with our little, used car. The people we had purchased our mobile home from said that they had hauled it from Iowa with their small car, so they could not see why our car could not pull it to Illinois.

We pick up Dad at the airport, rush home, and connect our car to the mobile home. As we pull out of the trailer park, I ask Bob "Are you as excited as I am?" He just smiles.

Truthfully, though, I think, "Excited is the word he would use. As for me, I cannot help but wonder if my own dream is fading and if I will ever be able to save it."

We drive until dark. We have a terrible time parking our home in a lot at a mobile home park. Bob has never parked anything like this and no matter how he tries to get it on a level spot, he cannot. He ends up parking on an uneven space. The left side is lower than the right side but we do not want to take the time to try to level it again.

Dad is to sleep on the bed, I on the sofa, and Bob on the floor. Bob and I hear his Dad laughing. "Who the hell ever heard of satin sheets? I keep sliding off!" he says.

"We'll pin your pajamas to the sheets tomorrow night," Bob tells him. We all laugh. The trip is not running as smoothly as we had hoped.

bewildered. He does not speak, but his expression asks how I could be so stupid. He shakes his head and walks away.

I freeze in that moment, remembering the past few minutes. There was a loud *boom* and the gas range I had been trying to light flew several inches off the floor, tearing loose the bolts that secured it, before falling back into place. We could have been killed. As we calm down, we realize how lucky we are.

"Come on, Kitts. I will get your coat. Take off what is left of your nylons. We're eating out," Bob says to me as he escorts me to the car. "Let's make this a short night because Dad will be here tomorrow. We will just give the roast to the neighbors. You won't be able to cook it when we disconnect all the utilities tomorrow in preparation for the move to Peoria."

The next day, Steven, my father-in-law, arrives on his flight from Chicago to Houston to help us drive back to Illinois. We plan to pull the mobile home with our little, used car. The people we had purchased our mobile home from said that they had hauled it from Iowa with their small car, so they could not see why our car could not pull it to Illinois.

We pick up Dad at the airport, rush home, and connect our car to the mobile home. As we pull out of the trailer park, I ask Bob "Are you as excited as I am?" He just smiles.

Truthfully, though, I think, "Excited is the word he would use. As for me, I cannot help but wonder if my own dream is fading and if I will ever be able to save it."

We drive until dark. We have a terrible time parking our home in a lot at a mobile home park. Bob has never parked anything like this and no matter how he tries to get it on a level spot, he cannot. He ends up parking on an uneven space. The left side is lower than the right side but we do not want to take the time to try to level it again.

Dad is to sleep on the bed, I on the sofa, and Bob on the floor. Bob and I hear his Dad laughing. "Who the hell ever heard of satin sheets? I keep sliding off!" he says.

"We'll pin your pajamas to the sheets tomorrow night," Bob tells him. We all laugh. The trip is not running as smoothly as we had hoped.

YEAR THREE
OF OUR MARRIAGE

Bob has no eyebrows, no eyelashes and no hair on his arms; just a blank look on his face. I look down at my legs. My nylon stockings have melted down to my ankles. I lift my skirt and notice that the garters on my girdle are holding the heavy top of my nylons and nothing else. We look at each other in silence.

After a minute, Bob asks, "Are you okay?"

"I think so," I reply.

"Shit! We could have been killed!" Bob screams at me as soon as I confirm that I am not hurt.

"Well, we're okay. We'll just have to go out for dinner," I say to him.

"Why go out?" Bob asks and then adds, "Now that it's lit, just fix the dinner you planned."

I cover my mouth and my eyes open wide. Bob takes one look at me and snaps, "You didn't! Tell me you didn't shut it off!" He looks into the oven and sees that the pilot light is off. "Christ's sake, Nina! Why the hell did you turn off the pilot light?"

"I thought it might explode again. This damn thing has always been such a pain in the ass to light," I reply. I look at Bob, and he stares back,

The next day, on the way to our new home, our car suddenly decides to die. Apparently, the trailer is just too heavy for our old car. The transmission has gone out, leaving us stuck in Missouri for the day while the car is being repaired. Bob calls and hires a mobile home mover to deliver our home to Peoria, which we now realize is what we should have done to start. Another life-lesson learned.

Two days later we finally arrive in Peoria. We check out a few mobile home parks and choose one. We stay in a motel while the mobile home is in transit. Meanwhile, we check out the area and the hospital where Bob will work.

On our second day in Peoria, the three of us pick up Sarah, my mother-in-law, from the train station. She took the train from Chicago to Peoria to come see us and explore Bob's new workplace. Over dinner that evening, we share the details of the journey and laugh again about the satin sheets.

"Sounds like you had quite an experience," Mom, as I call her, laughs. "What kind of truck is pulling your home here?"

"*Ah* don't know the name of the company. All *ah* know is that the company uses *raid* trucks," I reply.

I look up and notice the three of them laughing at me.

"What? *Ah* am sorry that *ah* do not remember the name of the company. *Whah* is that so funny?" I ask.

"You've acquired a Texas drawl, dearie," my mother-in-law snickers.

"*Ah* guess those Texas accents rubbed off on me," I laugh with them.

A couple of days later, our mobile home is delivered. Bob's parents help us unpack and put everything in its place. Peoria is about three hours from Chicago, so it's close enough that we can go back and forth to visit in one day if necessary.

Bob takes us to the hospital the day after his orientation and shows us around his new workplace. His parents are so proud of him. I am too, but I am jealous at the same time. I worked so hard to earn good grades and pay for all of my expenses aside from tuition through school. Bob's parents paid for everything and *he* is the one whose career comes first. "Why do men's careers always come first?" I ask myself. And then I think, "I agreed to this, so why am I secretly crying about it?" I try to reason myself out of feeling sorry for myself.

We are, once again, not living in a city where I can use my education. So I decide to go back to photography. I locate the most prestigious studio I can find and decide to convince them to hire me as a bridal secretary. I learned so much from Gabby at Sieldings and I am determined to create a new position for this studio, whether they realize they need one or not.

"How are you?" I ask the owner, Mr. Wilkins. "I'm glad you agreed to see me. I would like to make a proposal. You should hire me as a bridal secretary. Everyone I have spoken with says you are the best photographer in the area, and after having worked at Sieldings in Texas, I cannot imagine working for any other studio that is not of the same quality. I will go after the bridal business. I will increase your sales. I also do not mind doing reception work and general sales. I know that I can increase your profits," I tell Mr. Wilkins confidently.

As soon as I finish my sentence, he says, "You're hired. You start Monday. Be here at nine o'clock. See you then." He got up and left before I could present my entire proposal.

I look at his receptionist, tell her I will see her soon, and leave, realizing that I never had a chance to ask about salary. "Oh well, whatever it is, it is," I say.

I am still surprised that I landed the job so easily. I must have said exactly what he wanted to hear. That night, Bob and I celebrate. And we continue celebrating with real food, the kind of stuff normal people eat. Bob and I eat steak every night for weeks. It is wonderful to have enough money to eat.

Bob loves his job and he is really good at it. Every couple of months, he is praised for his work and he receives a raise in salary.

Within a very short time, we make new friends and enjoy our social life, too. There are the Buckleys, who own the trailer park we lived in. The Helms are both nurses and own the trailer across the street from us. We become friends with the Smyths after I met Vanessa, a beautiful stay-at-home mother.

On this day, Venessa comes walking into the photography studio where I work in a Playboy Bunny outfit. I gasp. "You're not even wearing a coat. It's freezing outside!"

"I got a side job holding trays full of treats at a convention across the street," she says. She explains that she parked her car in the parking lot next door, and when she turned off the engine and pulled the key out of the ignition, the doors would not open. She was able to force the window down some, but she could not squeeze out of it while wearing her fur coat. So she took the coat off and squeezed out of the window, but when she tried to grab her coat, she couldn't reach it. She knew I worked next door to the parking lot, so she came over to borrow my coat.

"Why wouldn't the doors open?" I ask.

"Oh it's another one of Ryan's inventions," she says of her engineer husband. "The doors are electric. When the car died, there was no electric to open them."

"Some invention," I say.

I let her borrow my coat, and she scurries over to the Hotel Pere Marquette to earn her extra money. She is something else. I love her and her spirit and have a feeling that we will be lifelong friends. I'm sure I will never forget her standing at the door in that outfit.

Bob and I enjoy a comfortable year financially, for once not having to watch every penny we spend. We laugh a lot, and we love each other and our friends. It is so nice to be able to afford to go out to dinner and to the theater.

These are some of the best days of our lives, I am sure. The pastures are green and the path ahead is golden. With one year of Bob's promised two-year experience at the hospital here in Peoria down, I am counting the days until our return to Chicago and the beginning of my career as a fashion designer.

CHAPTER FOUR
DAY FOUR
IN THE HOSPITAL

"A gourmet breakfast has been prepared just for you!" a voice announces. I wake up and recognize Mary. "Come on, sleepyhead, wake up!" she says to me.

Food. "How strange for me," I think to myself, "I haven't even thought of food, and I don't remember eating since I've been here." I love to eat and love to cook, so it's hard to believe that I haven't thought of eating. "Yes, yes, Mary. I'd love to have breakfast," I say to her as I open my eyes.

Mary helps me sit up straight and pushes the tray closer to me. I look at the food, but it is not appealing. I look up at Mary and say, "I thought I was hungry, but I don't seem have an appetite."

Mary sits down next to me and picks up the spoon. "Here, try some scrambled eggs. You need some energy," she tells me. She places a spoonful of eggs in my mouth. It tastes like cotton and I almost gag. "Have a drink of coffee," she instructs me, and I take a sip.

"That was good, wasn't it? Come on now. Try to sample a bit of everything. I have to go to another room now. But when I get back, I expect to see that plate clean. Think of my reputation. It would look bad on my record if you starve to death," Mary laughs as she leaves my room.

I sample all of the food and surprisingly, after the awful first bite, it tastes better. As I finish my breakfast, I look up from my tray and notice that taunting mirror. I cannot see my reflection, as my vision is still blurred. And I am still grateful that I cannot. I am not ready for what I imagine I will see.

Just then, Mary enters the room and looks at my tray. "Holy cow! You did great. I told you they fixed a special meal just for you."

"will you please do me a favor?" I ask.

"Sure," she answers, looking over her glasses at me.

"Please, can you take that mirror and turn it around? I'm afraid to see what I look like."

Instead she puts a towel over it.

"Nina, you are beautiful. Do not be afraid. You have some areas that have stitches showing, but you have an excellent plastic surgeon who will remove any scars that don't fade away naturally," she reassures me.

"Mary, I know it's worse than that. My Dad and brother didn't even recognize me," I tell her, adding abruptly, "I wonder why my vision still hasn't come into focus."

"Well, ask the first doctor that comes in and maybe he'll have some answers for you," she replies, walks over to the windows, pulls the drapes open, one window at a time, allowing the sun to filter into my room gently. As she pulls the cord on the last drape, the sun rests upon my bed and illuminates my hand.

"What is this on my hand?" I ask her. "Look, Mary. My ring is taped to my hand." Before she can reply, "Wait a minute! I remember."

I remember the night I first came into the hospital. At one point, someone had been holding my hand, and a woman's voice said, "Your ring is fabulous! It's quite a large pop bottle." Then she whispered into my ear, "I'll tape this ring to your hand so it doesn't *accidentally* get removed."

Mary removes my tray, and I lie back to try to remember as much as I can from that night when a voice interrupts my thoughts.

"Hello, dear." I look up and see my mother-in-law and father-in-law. "How are you doing?" Mom asks me.

"I'm better," I answer. "I've started to eat real food." I smile.

Dad, as I call my father-in-law, sits down on the chair to the side of my bed and says to me, shaking his head, "I don't understand what got into him. He must be sick."

"I don't know, Dad, I just don't know. How are the children doing?"

Mom says, "They don't say much. I know they are confused. They know you're in the hospital. They think you were in a car accident but that you will be okay."

"Has Bob called and talked to the kids?" I ask.

"Yes." Mom answers. "He tells them you were both in an accident because, well, how else can he explain what happened? He tells us he isn't even sure of what happened and that he must have been sick or crazy."

I decide to guide the conversation towards the children and their homework and push the "why" and "how could he" talk aside for now. At this time, we can only guess. I'm still trying to figure out how everything went so wrong with us.

They spend about an hour visiting with me. They are confused, shocked, and I can tell, absolutely ashamed about the actions of their son.

"Well, we better get back to the house. The receptionist at the boarding and grooming kennel, Nora, has opened this morning as she's been doing since this all happened. Colleen is grooming today and she has already started. Everything is going smoothly, dear. You just spend your time getting better and come home soon," Mom says. They kiss me and leave. They look awful, those poor, dear people. I cannot make them feel any better than they can make me feel. We are all dumbfounded and emotionally broken.

As I lay my head back down, I realize how much pain I am in again. At that moment, an unfamiliar voice asks, "Are you Nina?" I look up and see a green hospital uniform in the doorway. Someone is there, but I cannot make out who it is with my blurry vision.

"Yes, I'm Nina," I answer.

"Hello, dear." I look up and see my mother-in-law and father-in-law. "How are you doing?" Mom asks me.

"I'm better," I answer. "I've started to eat real food." I smile.

Dad, as I call my father-in-law, sits down on the chair to the side of my bed and says to me, shaking his head, "I don't understand what got into him. He must be sick."

"I don't know, Dad, I just don't know. How are the children doing?"

Mom says, "They don't say much. I know they are confused. They know you're in the hospital. They think you were in a car accident but that you will be okay."

"Has Bob called and talked to the kids?" I ask.

"Yes." Mom answers. "He tells them you were both in an accident because, well, how else can he explain what happened? He tells us he isn't even sure of what happened and that he must have been sick or crazy."

I decide to guide the conversation towards the children and their homework and push the "why" and "how could he" talk aside for now. At this time, we can only guess. I'm still trying to figure out how everything went so wrong with us.

They spend about an hour visiting with me. They are confused, shocked, and I can tell, absolutely ashamed about the actions of their son.

"Well, we better get back to the house. The receptionist at the boarding and grooming kennel, Nora, has opened this morning as she's been doing since this all happened. Colleen is grooming today and she has already started. Everything is going smoothly, dear. You just spend your time getting better and come home soon," Mom says. They kiss me and leave. They look awful, those poor, dear people. I cannot make them feel any better than they can make me feel. We are all dumbfounded and emotionally broken.

As I lay my head back down, I realize how much pain I am in again. At that moment, an unfamiliar voice asks, "Are you Nina?" I look up and see a green hospital uniform in the doorway. Someone is there, but I cannot make out who it is with my blurry vision.

"Yes, I'm Nina," I answer.

to see that plate clean. Think of my reputation. It would look bad on my record if you starve to death," Mary laughs as she leaves my room.

I sample all of the food and surprisingly, after the awful first bite, it tastes better. As I finish my breakfast, I look up from my tray and notice that taunting mirror. I cannot see my reflection, as my vision is still blurred. And I am still grateful that I cannot. I am not ready for what I imagine I will see.

Just then, Mary enters the room and looks at my tray. "Holy cow! You did great. I told you they fixed a special meal just for you."

"will you please do me a favor?" I ask.

"Sure," she answers, looking over her glasses at me.

"Please, can you take that mirror and turn it around? I'm afraid to see what I look like."

Instead she puts a towel over it.

"Nina, you are beautiful. Do not be afraid. You have some areas that have stitches showing, but you have an excellent plastic surgeon who will remove any scars that don't fade away naturally," she reassures me.

"Mary, I know it's worse than that. My Dad and brother didn't even recognize me," I tell her, adding abruptly, "I wonder why my vision still hasn't come into focus."

"Well, ask the first doctor that comes in and maybe he'll have some answers for you," she replies, walks over to the windows, pulls the drapes open, one window at a time, allowing the sun to filter into my room gently. As she pulls the cord on the last drape, the sun rests upon my bed and illuminates my hand.

"What is this on my hand?" I ask her. "Look, Mary. My ring is taped to my hand." Before she can reply, "Wait a minute! I remember."

I remember the night I first came into the hospital. At one point, someone had been holding my hand, and a woman's voice said, "Your ring is fabulous! It's quite a large pop bottle." Then she whispered into my ear, "I'll tape this ring to your hand so it doesn't *accidentally* get removed."

Mary removes my tray, and I lie back to try to remember as much as I can from that night when a voice interrupts my thoughts.

As the green blur approaches, I can tell that it is a particularly tall man. He walks over to a window and demands, "Come over here. I want to see your face in this light."

Surprised at his audacity, I ask, "You want me to walk over there? I don't know if I can walk. I haven't left this bed since I got here."

"I don't see any IVs," he says indignantly. He walks over to me bed, scoops me up in his arms, carries me about twelve feet to the window, and places me on the window ledge.

"My, my, my," he says over and over as he scrutinizes my face, ears and head. After a couple of minutes, and with no further conversation, he picks me up again and carries me back to my bed. Then he puts my blanket back over me and leaves without saying another word.

I buzz for my nurse. "Who was that?" I ask her.

"I'm not sure what you're asking me," she responds.

"Who is that man that just came in here? He picked me up, placed me on the window ledge, and examined my head. Then he carried me back to my bed and left without saying a single word. What the hell was that about?"

"I have no idea," she says, concerned.

Then it hits her. "You know, I think I saw Dr. Blum down the hall. Maybe he came in to see you. I'll check and be right back."

My nurse soon returns and says, "That explains it. It was indeed your plastic surgeon, Dr. Blum. He has a terrible bedside manner, but he is the best plastic surgeon in the area."

I am appalled. I cannot comprehend how someone could be so callous and rude to someone as pathetic as I am right now. He treated me like an object. He showed no emotion and no empathy. He didn't share what the plans for surgery or recovery are. And I think, "How is he allowed to do that to a patient?"

After the shock passes, I close my eyes and feel like I am about to fall asleep when I am awakened by another bothersome blood pressure check. These are becoming far too frequent. Now I am annoyed both by Dr. Blum and these blood pressure checks.

"How long are you going to keep doing this? At first, it was every twenty minutes. Now it is every single hour. I cannot get any rest. I believe that my blood pressure has been stable for a quite a while now. Can you ask my doctor if this routine can be cut back?" I beg, exhausted.

"I'll check, dear, with the next doctor that comes in," the nurse tells me.

As she leaves, lunch is delivered. I surprise myself again by eating most of it. As soon as I finish, my dear friends, Dr. Jack McGinn and his wife, Ann, come to visit. With them are Andrea and Bernie Sellers, my other best friends. They are laughing about what a coincidence it is that they have stopped in to see me at the very same time.

Dr. Jack McGinn, we call him "Doc," is a pathologist at this hospital. Ann, his wife, was a school teacher but opted to have six children and be a stay at home Mom. She also brags that she has the highest vocabulary test scores ever registered at Holy Trinity College on the east coast. We met them years ago when they purchased a Doberman puppy from us.

Bernie Sellers and his wife, Andrea, met in college at the University of Texas. Bernie is a microbiologist here in Peoria at the laboratory where the method of mass-producing penicillin was invented. Andrea majored in civil engineering and math in college. She wears many hats now. Not only is she the mother of four children, but in her spare time she volunteers for a project called *Suicide Watch* and also one called FISH, an organization that helps people in financial need. We met them at our local kennel club.

"You look great, my dear!" Andrea tells me.

"I do, huh?"

"You look much better than you did a few nights ago. Do you know I was here the night you came in?" Andrea asks.

"No! You were here?" I ask, surprised. "Why were you here?"

Andrea responds, "When you were admitted, you told the staff that your family lived in Chicago but that we were like your family, so you had them call us. You gave them our phone numbers, and they called us at two in the morning. When I got the call, I rushed over here. I was told that you were extremely critical. A priest came to give you the last rites, and he asked me to come with him and pray for you. I held the candle."

"Really? I was that critical? Oh, Andrea, thank you for being here."

"And look at you now!" Doc says cheerfully. "I check your charts every few hours and give Andrea and Bernie the updates. You are definitely on the upswing," he tells me.

They stay and visit for about a half hour, and we chat about the blizzard we had the night everything happened. They tell me it will take a week to clear all the side and rural roads. It was one of the worst blizzards Peoria has ever seen.

In a hurry to talk about something unrelated to my trauma, they begin discussing our dogs and the upcoming Westminster Dog Show. "Oh, my God!" I exclaim. "Ann, you and I are supposed to show Boris at that show in New York." Boris is the beautiful, Champion Borzoi we own together.

"Don't worry your head, my dear. We'll do it next year."

"But we'll never have a better shot at it, Ann. This judge loves Boris," I say in desperation. "He has never lost a show under her. And we already have air tickets to New York."

"Let's see what the next week brings," Ann says, in a motherly tone of voice.

Doc walks to the door and asks very seriously, "Nina, are you aware that there is a police guard outside your room?"

"No," I answer. "Why do I have a guard?"

"You should know, Nina. After Bob was arrested, he bailed himself out. Because he was not in custody, your attorney was afraid that you might still be in danger. He also had the hospital set your phone so you cannot receive any incoming calls. Haven't you noticed that the phone never rings?" Doc replies.

"No, I never noticed that. But I haven't been aware of very much except the pain."

"I think the 24-7 security and the phone block can be stopped for now. Bob's attorney said he would only represent him if Bob committed himself to the mental health clinic for an evaluation, which could take a week. He is there now. Do you want me to call your attorney and have these protections lifted? That way, phone calls can come in and we and the kids can call you whenever we want," Doc suggests.

I shake my head in agreement and I say aloud, "I've been in such a daze that I've only been mildly concerned about the children. I didn't even notice that they aren't calling me. I am such a fierce, protective mother. What has happened to me? What has happened to my priorities?" Bernie responds, "You're doing what you need to be doing, Nina. You're trying to live."

After a few seconds pass, he adds, "Another thing we need to talk about is something that your attorney has asked us to push with you, which is that you definitely file for a divorce. We all know how much you have wanted this marriage to work, but you have paid the ultimate price. We're afraid that you might go back and try to make your marriage work again." That is all he says, letting it sink in while I struggle to process my current circumstances, let alone the rest of my life. No one else says a word and the silence is unnerving. But I have no response for them or for myself.

"It's time for me to get back to the lab," Doc says.

"I've got to get going, too. I have to run a test in about an hour," Bernie says.

"Hurry and get well, lady. We need martini time," Ann whispers in my ear. "Let's hold off on any decision about the dog show until we see how you're feeling."

Everyone hugs me and waves goodbye as they disappear and leave me alone again. I do feel so utterly alone.

I gaze out the window and remember back to the day that Ann and I drove to Ohio to pick up Boris. We purchased him for eighteen hundred dollars, quite a chunk of change in this year of 1973. But we believed he was a prize find. He was already an American Kennel Club Champion at the young age of ten months. It's extremely rare for a puppy, especially a large-sized breed, they mature slower than toy breeds, and to win a Championship at that age, almost unheard of and to top it off, he did it in only three shows, all five-point major wins.

Our agreement was that Ann would pay for him and Bob and I would feed, house, and show him. He blossomed far more beautifully than the breeder expected; otherwise, she would not have sold him, she tells everyone. He has won Best of Breed in every show we entered him, and now he is entered in the Westminster Dog Show, the biggest and most prestigious of them all in this country.

Realizing again that I am in tremendous pain, my mind drifts away from the dog show. So much has happened today that I haven't even asked for pain medication. I push the call button. Mary comes into my room a few minutes later, and she is carrying the blessed needle. "Is this what you're calling for?" she asks me.

I welcome the pinch into my arm because it means my mind will be gone soon, and for a short time, the pain in my heart will be eased as well. "Will I ever be able to heal, both physically *and* emotionally?" I wonder. Today is my fourth day in the hospital, and ever so slowly, I am becoming more aware of the enormity of the situation I face. I force myself to remember our fourth year of marriage.

YEAR FOUR
OF OUR MARRIAGE

"Hey, guys. I need to get in there and clean. Are you decent?" I yell to them.

"Sure, we're decent," someone yells back.

I open the door and there they are, naked as jaybirds. I stop dead in my tracks, and the room full of college baseball players breaks in hysterical laughter. Red-faced, I slam the door shut but I still hear the muffled laughter. I feel a smile creep onto my face as someone in the room yells out to me, "You asked if we were decent. You didn't ask if we were wearing clothes!"

Eight months ago, Bob's folks loaned us the money to purchase our first property. Our friends, the Smyths, owned their home in which they lived on the first floor and rented out the four bedrooms upstairs to Bradley College students.

"What a fantastic idea," we think. A few months later, we "one up" them by purchasing a property to house seventeen students.

The place we purchased had been a fraternity house. We live on the main floor and the students occupy the second and third floors. The basement has been converted into a complete commercial kitchen, recreation room, and dining room. It also features a huge, walk-in shower with five showerheads.

We take possession of the house in May after the semester ends, and we have to have it ready in August. Every night, when Bob and I get home after working our full-time jobs, we get to work on the house. Bob's folks come out every weekend and even donate their vacation time to help us clean, tear down walls, and paint to get ready for our first students to enter this fall. Before we moved in and when our home was still a fraternity house, hired cooks prepared meals for the students in the downstairs kitchen. It is absolutely filthy and should be condemned. We even have to use gasoline around the perimeter of the Coke machine to scrub the sticky grime off the floor. The only dirtier place I have ever seen is a city dump.

Now it's mid-August and the students have moved in. Bob and I each now have a second job. Bob takes out the garbage, sweeps and vacuums the steps and hallways. I clean the bathrooms, which consist of six sinks, five toilets, and two urinals, and then I clean the massive shower room. On the weekends, I vacuum all the rooms and clean the kitchen.

Sometimes the college boys approach us for advice. For some of them, it is their first time away from home and they do not have friends to talk to about their new life experiences. We sit, listen and try to give each one our best advice. I am not sure how good it is, though. We are only twenty-four, and they are about eighteen, but we try.

On a typical night, Bob and I are so busy after work, we do not eat dinner until eight o'clock, at the earliest. Then the next morning we wake up and start all over again. Everything is wonderful, just as we have planned. We are working especially hard and we are building the life we dreamed of, and hoping for, a family.

We learn all too soon that no matter how much *we* plan, God lets us know of *His* plan. This morning, I woke up and noticed that I am spotting and I have terrible cramping. I am about two and a half months pregnant, so I call Dr. Bloom's office and am told to come right in. Next I call the studio to let them know that I will be late. By the time I make it to the doctor, the bleeding is heavier.

After Dr. Bloom examines me, he says, "Either your period is just late, or you're having a miscarriage."

"What do you mean either? Two weeks ago you said I was pregnant!" I reply.

"I said you were *probably* pregnant, but until you missed your third period I couldn't be positive," he says.

"Of course I'm pregnant! I have never missed a single period. I have to be pregnant," I insist.

"Nina, if you are pregnant, the bleeding will stop. Go home and prop up your feet. I will give you some medications to slow or stop the cramping if possible. If the bleeding continues, you are having a late period or an early miscarriage. In either event, it should not be a case that you will be hospitalized; it is still pretty early. If the bleeding stops, you may still be pregnant. That is if, indeed, you are."

Three days pass and the bleeding continues. It seems to be like a regular period, but heavier and much more painful. I know in my heart I am miscarrying. I always assumed that someday I would have a family, but I was not sure when I wanted to start one. We did not plan on this pregnancy, but when it happened, we were delighted. Now that it is ending, we are grief-stricken.

A month passes and I am still experiencing intense pain in my lower abdomen. I feel like I am having menstrual cramps all month long. I see my doctor again and he tells me nothing is wrong. He gives me some pain medication and sends me on my way.

A month later, my cycle resumes but the pain persists. I become terribly depressed. I have barely eaten for the past couple of weeks so I make another appointment with Dr. Bloom.

"Nina, I don't know what to tell you. I find nothing wrong with you. I have someone for you to call. Maybe he can help you. Here is his name and phone number," he says as he hands me the card. I look at the card and read: *Paul Dirk, Psychiatrist.*

"A psychiatrist? I am in physical pain and you are sending me to a psychiatrist? That sounds crazy to me!" I yell at him.

"I don't know what else to do for you. I can't find anything wrong with you physically."

I leave feeling more depressed than I had been an hour earlier. That night, as I sit on the edge of the bed, I ask Bob what I should do. He sits beside me and we both just cry. We are both scared. I consider myself a strong person, but I have apparently become a nervous wreck, with imaginary pain.

"I'll call the psychiatrist tomorrow, honey."

I did call and the psychiatrist asked me to come in that same day. I walked into Dr. Dirk's office and explained why Dr. Bloom sent me to see him. I told him Dr. Bloom thinks I have an emotional problem that is causing the pain.

Dr. Dirk responds, "Nina, I suggest that we hospitalize you for a few days so you and I can have some quality time to work on this problem."

I nearly faint. "You think I need to be hospitalized?" I ask, incredulous that this is actually happening. He nods affirmatively.

I leave the office and call Bob to tell him what Dr. Dirk recommends. "I plan on admitting myself tonight, honey. The sooner, the better, right?"

Bob says he is not sure it is the answer, but he replies, "Whatever you think, Kitts."

That evening, he drives me to the hospital. "Now, Kitts, this is only for a couple days. I am not sure that putting you in the mental ward is the right decision, but just remember, you are here because *you* put yourself here. You can check yourself out any time. Call me, and I'll come immediately."

On the eighth floor, the elevator doors open, we step off the elevator. There is nothing to see but a door and a buzzer. We ring the buzzer and a nurse welcomes us inside. The door loudly locks behind us. And suddenly, I am terrified.

"Bob, why is the door locked?" I look at him with fear on my face.

"See, Kitts, that's why I didn't want you up here," Bob says. As a medical professional, he knows the workings of the psychiatric ward. "I thought maybe they would put you in a different area, not this one." He looks frightened, too. "Now remember, it'll just take a phone call and I'll be here," he reminds me.

A nurse asks for my purse, examines my possessions, takes nearly everything away and gives it to Bob. I am led to a room with a single bed.

"You can leave now," the nurse says to Bob. As he leaves, I notice the tears in his eyes.

I put my pajamas on and turn on the TV. Shortly thereafter, I hear someone screaming. Then I hear someone else yell that he wants to go home. I look toward the door and see that a man in his pajamas has come into my room. He slurs the word, "Hello," as he is brushing his teeth. He leaves, comes back, and just stares at me, still brushing his teeth.

I call for the nurse and she tells me I will eventually get used to the sounds. I decide I have had enough already, after only two hours. I pick up the phone and call Bob. "Come get me, honey. I realize that I'm depressed, but I am not crazy and I shouldn't be here."

Over the next week, I force myself to eat. Sometimes I vomit, but little by little, my appetite returns. But the pain continues and I can't go back to my doctor, who thinks it is all in my head.

"Vanessa, I don't know what to do or where to go," I say to my friend. "I'm in so much pain that at times, I think I'm going to faint! I've tried to 'think it away' and to put up with it, but I just can't anymore."

"Nina, my Dad is a doctor. He says this at least once a day: *Get a second opinion.*"

"But you go to the same doctor, Dr. Bloom, and you say that he's the best. He's the head of obstetrics! That's why you recommended him!" I protest.

"He can still be wrong, Nina. My Dad admits that sometimes even he is wrong. He says that sometimes you do not see the forest for the trees. Why don't you call Dr. Ralph Gilbertson? My friends really like him," Vanessa suggests.

I immediately make the appointment.

When I arrive at Dr. Gilbertson's office, I take a seat in the waiting room. My name is called and a nurse escorts me to the doctor's private office. He comes in and I explain what I have been experiencing these past four hellish months. He directs me to an examining room. His exam is so painful that I wish I could faint. "Please get dressed, Nina, and come back into my office," Dr. Gilbertson instructs me.

I dress and return to his desk. "Did you bring the prescription pills that you have been on for this condition?" he asks. I hand him the bottles. He looks at them and then abruptly throws them into the garbage.

"What are you doing?" I ask him.

"Nina, you are going to need surgery. I could do a simple D&C to scrape some of your uterine tissue, but I already know what I will find. My advice is that we plan on surgery so I can go in and take a good look."

"Surgery? Another doctor told me I have nothing wrong with me and that it is all in my head. Then you come along and want to operate? I really have to think this over, doctor."

"I know this is a lot to absorb. I have another suggestion, however. Take birth control pills for six months. That will give your ovaries a chance to rest and then we can decide," he replies.

"Okay. I can live with that," I agree.

During the six months I am on birth control, I feel absolutely great. I assume the problem has resolved itself. I stop taking the pills as instructed by my doctor. A couple of weeks have passed and I am in greater pain than I was before I began them.

I call Dr. Gilbertson and schedule an appointment for later that afternoon. "I want to go back on those pills. I'm in so much pain!" I beg him.

"Not this time, Nina. Now we need to consider surgery. I am positive you have tumors on your ovaries. I'm sorry to say, you will be lucky if I can save either one of them. This must be done, Nina. I'll schedule the surgery for next week," he tells me.

As soon as I am home, I call Bob and then my Mom. "Mommy, I'm so scared. After the surgery, I may not be able to have children."

"Darling, you cannot live in this pain. You don't really have a choice." We cry together. I suggest that she does not come out until after my surgery. As I will need her help with the students' cleaning chores while I recover.

The day of the surgery is here and Bob holds my hand as I wait to go into the operating room. Bob and I both cry as they wheel me away to surgery.

The next thing I know, Dr. Gilbertson is holding my hand and Bob is standing next to him. "Nina, can you hear me?" Dr. Gilbertson asks. I nod.

"Good. I'll tell both you and your husband what I found. Both ovaries were covered with tumors. I am sure they are benign but the biopsy reports will be back in three days. Your left ovary was totally encompassed, so I was not able to save it. Your right ovary had a tumor the size of a baseball, but I was able to save a quarter of that ovary. You may or may not ever have periods again. You also have severe endometriosis and a dwarfed and tilted uterus."

He pauses and then speaks slower and more deliberately. "The chances of you having normal periods are slim, and the chances of you ever getting pregnant are even slimmer. If that is the case, you can always adopt. I am sure there is a very special baby waiting for you. I wish I had better news. Again, I believe that the tumors are benign. Be grateful for that. You should be healthy after this and able to lead a normal life."

"No babies?" I cry to Bob, looking to him with the hope I don't want to understand what the doctor just said.

"But you are going to be healthy again and we can adopt," Bob reiterates, as though it is any consolation. Within a few seconds, we both break down and we sob as we hold one another's hands.

Five days later, I am finally home and much weaker than I expected so I decide that I really do need my Mom's help. So I call her and ask, "Mom, I was wondering when you'd like to come and spend a few days here."

"Well, dear, I'm sorry that I won't be able to come and help after all. You see, the other day when I was out to lunch with my friend, Flo, something got caught in my throat. The next day, I went to see Dr. Zell. He ordered X-rays at the hospital and well, they discovered a growth on my esophagus. It appears to be cancerous," Mom tells me.

I sit down on the side of my bed, my mind trying to comprehend what my ears just heard. "What are you saying, Mom? Are you going to have surgery?" I ask.

"Yes. Tomorrow," she replies.

"Tomorrow? No. I cannot be there tomorrow. I am confined to this house for the next two weeks. I can't be there, Mom!" I cry, and I can hear her crying with me. "Mom, why didn't you tell me days ago?" I ask.

"What good would it have done? I wanted you to get well, and I did not want to do anything to impede your progress. Dad is taking me to the hospital this afternoon. The doctor is rushing the surgery because he wants to get to it as soon as possible. He feels confident that he will be able to cut out the bad spot and put together the good parts. I will be fine," my Mom says confidently. "Dad will call you tomorrow after the surgery. It will probably be about noon," she says.

My little brother is thirteen years old. Mom tells me he will stay with the neighbors while she is in the hospital.

"I love you, my darling, Nina," Mom says with heartfelt emotion.

"I love you too, Mommy," with the same emotion. I fall into the bed and bawl, holding my stomach to prevent the long run of stitches from bursting.

The following day, I wait for the phone to ring all morning. By two o'clock, I am starting to feel nervous. Finally, the phone rings. "Dad?" I ask before I even say hello.

"Mom is out of surgery. She's fine," he says.

"Did they get it all?" I ask him.

"The surgery was tough. They had to remove ribs, and they told me it's going to be a very rough recovery."

"Dad, did they get all the cancer?"

"Everything is going to be fine," he reassures me.

"Dad, something is wrong. I can feel it, and I hear it in your voice. I am not a child anymore. I have to know the truth. I have to help Mama deal with whatever it is that is going on," I say to him.

Dad starts to cry and comes forward with the truth. "They opened her up and removed some ribs. When they got in there, they discovered that the cancer was everywhere. Her entire esophagus was full of tumors. There was no place to cut and piece parts together. It was all eaten up."

I start crying again and feel as if my heart will breaking.

"The doctor says that we should tell her, Nina, but I don't think we should. We can tell her later, when we do not have a choice. The doctor also said that she has two months to two years to live. They have to place a feeding tube in her stomach and she will need to learn how to feed herself that way because she will not be able to swallow anymore. Oh, God, she will never be able to eat anything through her mouth again. No more of her favorite fried chicken....," he says as his voice begins to tremble.

I stop crying long enough to mumble, "Oh, Dad, you're all by yourself. I need to be up there with you. You're all alone."

"I'm not alone, honey. I am with your Mom. I am going to go see her now. I'll call you tonight," he says.

Mom cannot talk on the phone for several days. When I am finally able to talk to her, I ask her if she is in a lot of pain. She answers in a whisper, "I hope you will never know this kind of pain."

I can feel it anyway, through the tone in her voice. "I'll be there as soon as I can, Mommy. I'll bring food for Dad and Les. I'll do the laundry, too," I tell her.

"I'm supposed to be at your place helping you," she reminds me. "I'm not sure I'll be able to eat your food. The nurses put nourishment into a funnel that leads to a tube in my stomach. I guess I will have to eat like that until my chest and throat heal. The doctor tells me we will not know how long I will have to do that. I guess I can tolerate anything if it helps me get well."

I feel it coming, and I have to get off the phone. "I'll call you later, Mom," I tell her and hang up. I throw up, nauseated by the thought of lying to her, but I know I cannot tell her the truth. I cry until there are no more tears.

The next week, Mom comes home from the hospital. The neighbors bring food for my Dad and my brother. As soon as I am able, we travel to Chicago. I find her in the kitchen. I kneel at her feet and put my arms around her. "I love you, Mommy," I cry.

I get up from the floor and look down at her. She is sitting at her favorite spot at the kitchen table. She looks so frail.

"Sit down, my darling daughter," she calls me as she always has, smiling. "This is rougher than I expected. I'll show you how I have to eat." She shows me the formula she has to put into her stomach.

"Does it hurt when you do that?" I question.

"No, not much. My chest hurts worse. I've discovered that removing a rib is hell to recover from," she answers as I wipe up the formula that spills out of her weak, shaking hand. I look into her beautiful green eyes. She looks back deeply into mine and I feel that she knows she is dying. I wonder who was fooling the other. I get on my knees again, and I put my head in her lap. "Don't worry," she says as she strokes my hair.

Bob and I stay Friday and Saturday night with his folks, who live only three blocks away. We always stay there because they have more room, but we spend the weekend cleaning and visiting with my Mom, Dad and brother. We make the trip to Chicago every week for two months.

Each week I cook enough meals to feed them until I return. We bring their laundry back with us to our home, where I wash it, iron it, and return it the next weekend. Les is only twelve years old, so he is not much of any help. He is very scared at what is happening to Mom. He's never ever seen her sick, let alone this sick. He tries to do little things to help make Mom comfortable. But he has no idea that she is dying. My Dad is not much help, either. After all, he's never had to do any of the housework. After eight weeks of working my full-time job, coming home to work again there, and taking care of the Chicago family on the weekends, I am starting to wear out. Mom notices and begs me to come only every other week. I agree I will consider it.

On the ninth weekend, we enter my parents' home to discover that Mom is struggling to breathe. Dad and I rush her to the hospital and after some X-rays, it is decided that she immediately needs a tracheotomy.

Mom goes home after a few days, but she can no longer speak. She communicates by writing. Mom, Dad and I cry all the time. We are so scared, but Dad and I still have not told her she is not going to get well. We figure optimistically that, after all, the doctors said she may live a couple more years, so we will have plenty of time to talk about it.

Before we leave for our Peoria home and the weekend is over, my Mom writes me a note, *"You're looking very thin!"* She proceeds to give me her regular lecture, but this time it is in writing. Her lecture includes the usual: "You're too thin. You're not eating properly. And you need to take vitamins or you'll never get pregnant!" She wants so badly to be a grandma, and she knows how to lay it on thick.

She continues her note, *"I want you to not come here next weekend. You need to rest. It may be quite a while yet before I am well. I do not want you to get sick, too. Promise me now that next weekend, you'll stay in Peoria."*

After I read it, I look up at Dad. "We can manage. I have become familiar with a lot of restaurants. We'll be just fine," he says.

"Mom, I love you. I'll call you as soon as we get back home," I tell her. I give my Dad a hug and tell him I love him, and then I look at my little brother. "Love you, brat. Behave!"

When I arrive home, I call my Mom every day, several times a day. I hear her pick up the receiver, and then she makes a sound to let me know that she can hear me. Then I tell her about my day and share what is going on in our lives.

A few days after we return to Peoria, Dad calls. "Nina, your Mom is in the hospital again. She couldn't breathe, so they had to make an adjustment in her breathing device."

"I'll be right there, Daddy," I reply.

"No, no. Do not come. Your Mom is feeling much better. As a matter of fact, we took a walk around the hospital. I reminded her of when we were young and how she was as thin as she is now. Then she patted my round stomach, and we laughed together. I said to her, 'I guess I'm not as thin as I once was!' She thought it was really funny. So anyway, I just got back home. Why don't you call her a little later?" he suggests to me reassuringly. He gives me her phone number at the hospital.

"Dad, we're going to the Smyths' for supper. Vanessa says that she needs to fatten me up. I will call Mom from their house after dinner. I love you, Daddy."

That evening, after we finish dinner I say, "I'm going to call my Mom before she falls asleep for the night." I pick up the phone, dial it, and wait while it rings. It keeps ringing but and no one answers. Bob walks over to me when he notices I am not talking to anyone.

"What's up?" he asks. "Mom isn't answering. She must be walking down the hall with Dad again. But he didn't say anything about going back to the hospital," I say to Bob.

I look at Vanessa Smyth's beautiful grandfather clock and notice the time. It is twelve minutes after eight. I put the receiver down and assume Dad decided to stay later.

The phone rings at ten o'clock, just as we enter our home. "Mama died," Dad cries. He sobs, uncontrollably. And soon, I do, too. "She can't be dead.

She just walked with me this afternoon. I can still feel her hand," he lets out through the tears.

The next morning, Bob and I drive back to Chicago to help Dad with the funeral arrangements. We have to purchase a new dress for Mom because all of her clothes are too large. I choose a pink chiffon dress and pink roses to go on top of her casket. Pink was her favorite color.

The funeral is huge because Mom was so young that all of her family and friends are still alive. She was only forty-nine.

As I stand at her grave in the cemetery, I struggle with so many emotions. I am angry at God for taking my Mom and for leaving my brother with no mother. I still have so much of my life ahead of me, and now I have no one to talk to or ask for advice. If I ever become pregnant, I will never be able to ask how it was when she was pregnant with me so we can compare notes. But most of all, I feel a desperate loneliness. I cannot stop crying, and I do not know how I ever will.

We go back to Mom and Dad's house after the funeral. As Bob and I prepare to leave for Peoria, Dad walks out of their bedroom with a piece of paper in his hand. It is my Mom's death certificate, and as Dad hands it to me, my eye catches: *Time of Death: 8:12 p.m.*

I gasp. That was the very minute I had called her from the Smyth's. "Mama," I cried. "Oh, Mom, you were calling to me as I was calling you." I know in this very moment that we are one and that her spirit will be with me throughout the remainder of my life. She will be my guardian, watching over me always.

Bob and I drive back to Peoria without saying a word. We are empty and still in shock. As we enter our home, I pick up the mail. On top of the pile is a letter from Mom. I open it carefully, with tears in my eyes and appreciating her beautiful handwriting. Inside the envelope are some of her favorite recipes along with a note: *"My darling cook, I think I had better get these to you. See you soon, Mom."*

CHAPTER FIVE
DAY FIVE
IN THE HOSPITAL

"Hi, young lady! Is your name Nina?" a man asks as he approaches my bed. "I'm Dr. Bender. I am an ophthalmologist. I've come to check out your eye problem."

A nurse comes in with a wheelchair and tells me we are going to an examining room. They help me into the chair. The nurse pushes me, and we follow Dr. Bender down the hall. After a long walk, we finally enter a room. Dr. Bender retrieves his equipment from his briefcase and scrutinizes my corneas.

"So, your left eye is giving you trouble, Nina?" he asks. I nod. He uses several pieces of equipment, puts a few drops of liquid into my eyes, and tells me, "It's badly scratched but I think within another week, the scratches will heal and it'll clear itself up. This may or may not be the cause of the blurriness, however. There is another possibility, a more serious one. I am concerned about your broken facial bones. I looked at your x-rays before I came to see you. The break on the right side of your face is merely a crack. The left side of your face, however, is cracked completely in half vertically, from your forehead down through your jaw. I will order a new x-ray of your face to see if it is healing properly. You may need surgery to realign the crack. I'll check on you in a couple of days..." he trails off and then quickly reconsiders. "No, maybe we should do the x-rays now."

I return to my wheelchair. We travel down the hall to another room for more x-rays. All the while, I repeat in my head, "My face is cracked in half." With that, I slump to the side and feel as if I am falling asleep.

"Nina. Nina, come on, girl," I hear someone say and look up to see Dr. Bender. He says, "You took a little nap on us." And then he says, "The break is clean. Your face is vertically cracked in half right through the eye socket, but it seems to be healing perfectly. Usually, this kind of fracture requires surgery, but yours does not appear to be separating. This could be the cause of your blurred vision. I will be back in a week and we will x-ray you again. Hopefully by then, your eyesight will be back to normal."

Dr. Bender looks at my x-ray again and examines my head wound. "God bless you, Nina. The amount of damage is so extensive. I would have to say that indeed, God has blessed you. You are a miracle. See you soon," he says as he leaves the room.

The nurse wheels me back to my room. Just as I climb back into my bed, lunch arrives. It looks and smells good. I lift the cover of the main dish, and suddenly, I feel nauseated and vomit all over the tray. I start crying as my nurse comes in and helps me. I don't know why I am crying exactly, I just feel so sad. This news is just overwhelming. The nurse removes the tray and arrives with warm towels and a new gown. She leaves to retrieve a new food tray for me and as my eyes follow her out of the room, I see three men approaching. Two of them are dressed in hospital greens and one is in a suit.

"Hello, Nina," the man in the suit says. "You probably don't recognize us. But at least one of us has been here at least once a day, sometimes twice a day. However, you are usually asleep. I'm Dr. Melborne, this is Dr. Ansel," he points to a bald man, "and that skinny one is Dr. Smith." Dr. Melbourne is a tall, handsome man, even if he is a little blurry. They are all a little blurry. "We're the guys who operated on you several days ago," he adds.

"Three of you? It took three of you to fix me up?" I say in utter amazement.

"You just lucked out," Dr. Smith chuckles. "Our surgical group was on call that night and we were all here because of a big car accident. It involved multiple cars with serious injuries. We had just finished up when you came in, so you got stuck with us. A nurse told us you requested another doctor, Dr. Grey. We called him, but he lives in the country and he couldn't get out of his driveway with all the snow. Besides, there was no time to wait for him. You needed immediate medical assistance, so we took care of you. Ideally, you should have had a plastic surgeon attend to some of your injuries, but time was of the essence. I must say from the looks of you, that we did a fantastic job!" Dr. Smith boasts. "Do you mind if we take a closer look?"

"Why not? Others have, and for all I know they weren't even doctors." Everyone laughs, and they take their turns examining me.

"Gentlemen, look at these ears! Super job, if I say so myself. Who would have thought they would have made it?" Dr. Melbourne says, obviously amazed at their handiwork.

"What do you mean? Are you saying that I might not have had ears?" I ask, flabbergasted.

"Frankly, Nina, we wouldn't have called it a very good bet. There was nothing holding your ears on to your head but a thin layer of facial skin. Honestly, we did not think the blood supply was sufficient to do the job. We see miracles every day, but we consider you to be a week's worth of miracles. The morning after you came in, I had breakfast with your friend, Dr. Grey," Dr. Melbourne tells me. "We told him what we did for you. He was grateful that all of us were here that night because you were a job that required more than just one doctor."

"Six hands were better than two," Dr. Ansel chimes in. "Dr. Grey has checked on you every day. He tells us you and his family are friends and that he cannot believe what happened. We could tell that he was in total disbelief."

I notice that, as they discuss their roles in my care, they are all wearing faces of smug satisfaction. They are certainly proud of their work.

"Well, you keep healing. We will see you tomorrow, or at least one of us will see you. It'll cost extra for all three of us," Dr. Melbourne jokes as they all turn to leave my room.

No wonder my ears hurt so badly. I feel the back of them and can barely touch them. They are so sensitive. I think to myself, "My God! I might have lost my ears! I wonder what I would have looked like. I've never seen anyone without ears."

I start to feel queasy, so I press the call button for a nurse. "Nurse, please get a pan. I need to vomit."

She brings me a pan, and I proceed to be sick. "What happened, Nina," she asks me, "to upset you like this?"

"Do you know that I almost had no ears?" I ask. I can feel tears streaming from my eyes and watch them fall into the vomit. I look down at the pan and notice spots of dark blood. I glance up at my nurse, and she senses my question.

"Don't worry, Nina. You'll have traces of dried blood in your mouth for a while yet." She sits with me for about ten minutes as I try to pull myself together and stop crying.

"Do you feel better?" she asks. I nod my head in the affirmative and then place my head on my pillow, remembering the horrors of the night that put me here. "Do you need something for pain?" My nurse asks as she adjusts my blanket.

"My mouth is hurting."

"Well, your dentist will be in soon to check your teeth," she tells me.

"My teeth?" I frantically run my tongue around my mouth touching each tooth. "Please look into my mouth. Do you see anything obviously wrong?" I beg her.

She looks inside my mouth. "I don't see anything. All your teeth are here, and nothing looks chipped. The doctors are just being thorough.

My head spins with the chaos of the past couple of days. I have learned I have a plastic surgeon, an eye doctor, three surgeons, and now a dentist on the way. I also have my attorney, Rodger Rooker. I do not want to call him, but I know I no longer have a choice. I need some advice about my situation. "I will do that soon," I tell myself.

I am about to ask the nurse for pain medication when the Vanguards arrive. Years ago, Bob and I met them at a dog show. They own a beautiful Doberman named Fab, short for Fabulous, and that he undoubtedly was.

Will Vanguard is a foreman at Caterpillar Tractor Co. He has a great wit. He is also Eric's godfather. Joyce is a home economics teacher. She is brilliant and has an IQ in the genius range. All her siblings do too. For example, her brother's IQ is 171. I liken myself to one of our great presidents. One of his famous quotes goes something like this: "I myself am not a genius but I surround myself with people who are," like the Vanguards, the Sellers and the McGinns.

The Vanguards did not have any children of their own but after they saw the happiness that Brook brought into our lives, they decided to adopt. They were also blessed with a baby girl.

"Hi, Babe," Will calls to me. "Hi, Nina," Joyce says. They both grab a chair and sit, one on each side of my bed. "How is it going?" Will asked.

"I'm still here," I reply, weakened by the last few minutes of realizations and physical sickness.

"That son of a bitch!" he adds. "I heard what happened to you on the morning news on the way to work. I turned the car around to tell Joyce. She was about to leave for school. We decided to call off work and drove straight to your house. Your babysitter had been up all night, so we told her to go home. She informed us that Bob's folks were coming in from Chicago late that evening. We decided to keep the kids home from school because the story was broadcast in all the news media. We did not want them to find out that way. We explained to them, as Lucy already had, that you were in an automobile accident and you were both going to be alright. We kept them all day until Bob's parents arrived that night."

"Oh my goodness, I didn't know you did that. My head is still so foggy. Thank you so much and I love you so much," I replied. How could I still be so unaware of everything that transpired while I have been here?

They stayed for a little while and we reminisced about happier times. They kissed me and promised to return soon.

I call for pain medication. Thankfully, it only takes a few minutes for the medication to start to work. I feel my muscles relax and I realize that I am free of the pain.

This is the fifth day in the hospital. I have to remember back to the fifth year of marriage. I surely must have seen some warning signs somewhere along the way. "What happened that year?" I ask myself. Ah, yes. It is all coming back to me now.

YEAR FIVE
OF OUR MARRIAGE

"No, no, no!" Bob yells at me. "I am *not* going to get a sperm count. If we don't get pregnant and have kids, then I don't want to know that it's my fault!"

"Oh, it's okay for me to think it's all my fault, and it probably is. But you aren't willing to take a simple test and assume any of the responsibility?" I heatedly reply.

"Nina, we're not going to talk about it again. We've had this discussion several times already, and this is the last time!" He proceeds directly outside before I have a chance to respond again.

I know that my chances of getting pregnant are slim to none, but after all I have gone through lately, it is the least he can do for me. It definitely does not appear as if he is willing to do his part.

The subject is not broached again for months. Then, one day Bob comes home from work and announces, "Our baby problem is solved! Dr. Fieldings tells me he has three babies coming up for adoption this Spring."

"Adopt? No way. I am not ready to adopt. Discussion closed!" I say in a huff.

"Come on, Kitts, think about it. I have been giving physical therapy to Dr. Fieldings, an obstetrician. While I was treating him, I mentioned our problem. He came in today and announced that he has our problem solved. Why don't you want to take advantage of this opportunity?"

"I can't yet," I say. "I'm not ready. I believe I can still have a baby of my own. I am just not ready to accept the fact that I cannot get pregnant. I keep praying to Saint Anthony, asking him to intercede for me and to ask God to grant me a miracle. I believe He will." Bob wisely lets the subject go. Months pass, and I continue to pray novenas to Saint Anthony, my patron saint, asking him to ask God to grant me my wish to have a baby.

Early this morning, I wake up and sit on the edge of the bed. A strange feeling comes over me and it is as if I cannot stop myself, nor do I want to stop myself. I walk out of the bedroom and into the pantry. I pick up a yardstick. I return to the bedroom and begin to measure.

The shuffling wakes up Bob. "What's going on?" he asks.

"I'm measuring to find out where we can put the crib," I answer, matter-of-factly.

Bob plops his head back down on the pillow and he begins to cry. I have come to the realization that Saint Anthony *has* answered my prayers.

I call Dr. Fieldings and tell him we would be honored to be the parents of one of the babies he knows is up for adoption. I tell him my preference is a baby boy because I had always wished that I had an older brother.

"Nina, I hope that you can trust my recommendation and that is that you take a particular baby I have in mind, regardless of its sex," he says.

I do not hesitate even for a minute with my answer. "I won't debate that one. I know God is holding my hand. He brought you to us, and I know that you and He are going to fulfill our dreams. When is the baby due?" I ask.

"I'm not looking at the chart, but I believe it's due in March or April," he answers.

Oh, boy, am I excited! It is almost Christmas. I decide to wait until after the holidays to give my boss at least a three-month notice.

On January 10, 1964, I tell my boss that early in the spring I will be leaving to adopt a baby. That very night, Bob and I go to dinner and bump into my boss. He is drunker than a skunk, telling others in his dinner group that I am the best employee he ever hired, and now he is losing me. It makes me feel proud to be so valued, and I am happy to leave on a high note.

Three weeks later, I receive a call from Dr. Fieldings. "Nina? When did I tell you your baby was due?" he asks.

"You said you thought it would be early spring, late March or April," I reply.

"Well, we'd better change that date. It looks more like early March or late February," he informs me.

I have only about a month to be ready, I realize. "I'll be as ready as I can," I tell him.

Two days later, on the afternoon of February second, Groundhog Day, Dr. Fieldings calls again. "Nina, tell your husband he needs to learn to write! All morning I have been calling and getting no answer. So I called information and found out I was reading one digit in your telephone number incorrectly. I thought it was a four, but it was a seven."

"Excuse me, sir. Who are you?" I snap.

"This is Dr. Fieldings. Miss America was born this morning!" he said.

"What did you say?" I asked, stunned.

"You people really do have problems. He can't write and you can't hear," he replies, laughing. Having heard part of my strange phone conversation, Bob walks over and stands next to me. "Are you saying that we have a baby girl?" I ask Dr. Fieldings. Then immediately I turn, "Bob, we have a baby girl!"

Bob takes the phone from me and Dr. Fieldings teases him once again about his handwriting. Were it not for his sloppiness, we would have heard the news hours before now. As soon as Bob hangs up the phone, we call our families and every friend we know to share the good news.

Later that evening, we go out to see a play at the local theater, but we do not hear a single word of the play. We spend every minute in the theater looking around to see if we can spot anyone we know so we could share the news. We want to tell the whole world that we are new parents.

We call our attorney, Ted Huber, the next day to give him the news and to ask what the next legal requirement will be. Ted was the attorney we used to purchase our home and now for the adoption. As this is a private adoption, there will be no agency involved to walk us through the steps, so it is up to our attorney to handle it for us. He is a young attorney and he confides in us he has never participated in a private adoption. Because the situation is new to all of us, plans change several times over the next thirty-six hours. Eventually, we come up with a final plan. On February 5th, our attorney will go to the hospital, take care of the legalities, pick up our baby, and then deliver her to us. The only thing Bob and I have to do is meet him at Trinity Catholic Church at one o'clock, where we will meet our baby.

On the 5th, we pull into the church parking lot by half past noon. Bob and I are nervous wrecks as we wait inside the church. One o'clock comes and passes; then one-thirty, and then two o'clock, and our attorney and baby still have not arrived. We are now getting a bit frantic.

At two thirty-five, the church doors finally open. Our attorney, accompanied by his secretary, walks into the church and I see his secretary carrying our baby. She is all wrapped up in the pink velvet blanket that we sent with them. We run to meet them. I am crying tears of joy as I reach my arms out to hold our daughter. Ted's secretary places her in my arms and Bob moves the blanket, opening up the little cocoon to expose a beautiful face. Her skin is the color of peaches and cream. She has rosy cheeks and her little lips are perfectly shaped.

As I am holding her, Bob looks into my eyes and says, "Nina, she looks just like her mother." He nods at me, and I know he means me. "What a beautiful thing to say," I whisper to him.

"What happened?" I ask, suddenly remembering the attorney's tardiness. "You're late, and we were so worried!"

"When we got to the hospital, the nuns met me as planned. I gave them the clothes for the baby, and I want you to know that the nuns *ooohed* and *ahhhed*. They said that the blanket was the most beautiful one they had ever seen, and they proceeded to dress her. I called the judge and was informed that the birth mother and I would have to take the baby to the courthouse to sign the papers there," our attorney tells us. "I had no idea the birth mother would have to go to the courthouse to sign the papers on what would already be such a traumatic day." He apologizes for frightening us. He reminds us that this is his first private adoption and says that it will probably always be both the saddest and the happiest day in his career. He looks visibly shaken.

We sign the legal papers, hug, and cry some more before parting ways for our own homes. We rush from the church to our car to escape the cold, February wind and Bob starts the engine of our new Mercedes Benz. Before we drive off Bob looks at me holding our baby and says, "I've never seen you look more beautiful!" I feel a sense of peace come over me, a feeling I realize I have never experienced.

We are halfway home when Bob glances over at me and asks, "What are you doing?"

"I'm undressing her just a little. I want to see her toes," I reply as I count them. "They're all here, honey, all ten of them! I've never seen a baby so beautiful." I must admit, I have not seen very many babies. But she does not even look like a newborn. I am told most newborns are wrinkled and red but her skin looks like porcelain.

"Oh, I hope my Mom can see her. Here she is, Mommy. This is Brook!" I say aloud to my Mom's spirit. I noticed tears in Bob's wet, sparkling eyes.

I put my face close to Brook's, and I can feel her breath. She starts suckling as though she is nursing and I notice a wet spot on her cheek. I realize that it is my tear. At this moment in time, I know what my purpose on this earth is. I am to be Brook's mother.

When we arrive home, we place her into her fancy new bed; a large dresser drawer lined with a blanket. We still have a lot that needs to accomplish in preparation for her arrival, but her birth was earlier than we expected so we have to make do with what we have in the meantime. Fortunately, Bob's parents are bringing a bassinet from Chicago.

We begin to change her first diaper. We nervously undress her as if she is made of glass, clueless as to how to change a diaper. "Careful, careful," I insist as Bob removes her diaper. "Don't unfold it. We need to see the pattern of the diaper, or we won't be able to fold the fresh one." We both laugh. We do not even know how to fold a diaper. I never babysat a day in my life.

"Some parents we are going to be!" Bob says. He laughs so hard he cries. As we fumble through our project, she just lies there, watching us.

"Since she was put into my arms, she hasn't cried. I wonder what her cries sound like," I comment.

"I'm sure we'll find out!" Bob replies.

We finish with the diaper changing and re-dress her. I prepare her bottle of formula. The hospital where Brook was born provided us with a list of items we need to have on hand. Bob picked up the list the day after she was born and we purchased the supplies the next day.

I sit down on the couch and cradle Brook in my arms, offering her the bottle of formula. She immediately begins to eat. I look up at Bob as he sits on the arm of the sofa and pats my shoulder. We nod in awe of this brand new experience. It feels so natural.

"My darling Brook, until you came into our lives, I thought we were complete. Now that you are here, I realize it's you who completes our love for each other," I whisper to her. As she finishes the last of the formula, her huge blue eyes close and she drifts off to sleep.

The next day, our neighbor, Aileen Holden, comes over to help me give Brook her first bath. "Holy Cow, Aileen, she's so slippery! I don't think I'll ever be able to do this alone," I tell her, and she laughs at me.

After the bath, I say, "I had to wake her up during the night and give her a bottle. Then I had to wake her this morning for another one, otherwise, she might have slept right through her mealtime. The nuns gave me a feeding schedule and told me to keep her on it. I've had to awaken her every time to feed her because she hasn't woken up and she hasn't cried." With that, Brook begins her first cry.

"Oh, listen, Aileen! She is finally crying! Watch her," I order Aileen and hurry over to the phone to call Bob.

"Honey, listen to this! This is the first time Brook has cried." I hold the receiver to her little mouth. "Did you hear her?" I ask Bob. I can hear him chuckling on the other end of the line.

"You'll be hearing plenty of crying, I'm sure. She probably decided to break us in slowly so we would not take her back. Thanks for the call, Kitts. Everything okay?" he asks. I assure him that all is well and we hang up. I give Brook her next bottle, and when it is all gone, she dozes off to sleep again.

On the second day with our new baby, we take her to an appointment with Dr. Holloway, a pediatrician. As I sit in the office awaiting my appointment, I notice the other mothers looking at my baby and me. They all whisper about how beautiful she is. One of the mothers asks, "How old is your child?"

"Five days old," I reply, smiling.

"Your baby is only five days old? You look terrific!" one of the women comments.

"Thank you," I say, never letting on that I look so good because I had not had a baby. And no, I will not tell them, either. Brook is my baby and I am her Mommy, period. "Nope, I won't tell them," I decide confidently in my head.

I look at the other mothers and I notice they all look tired and disheveled, and for good reason. Their bodies have just gone through a great deal. I imagine that they wondered how I have the energy to fix myself up as well as I do.

Over time, Brook falls into her feeding routine naturally. Some days I still have to wake her to feed her, but most of the time she now alerts me on her own. Our Brook is healthy and well.

Throughout the next month, Bob and I adjust to our new life and enjoy our time with our baby as new parents. Brook is a happy baby. She almost never cries. All she does is smile, eat, and sleep. And, of course, dirty her diapers.

Brook is two months old when her canopy crib arrives. It is the most beautiful crib I have ever seen. It is white with hand-painted flowers on the headboard, footboard and sides. The canopy is made of organdy and lace. It is a bed fit for a princess; our Princess Brook.

My Dad orders an English pram from Marshall Fields and has it delivered to us. The difference between an American stroller and an English pram is that the pram has a very elegant solid body instead of a soft one. Our pram is white and light blue and it has huge wheels with shiny, silver spokes. It is definitely a carriage fit for royalty.

I take every chance I have to load Brook into the pram and walk the neighborhood. I want the world to see our "Miss America." Quite often, people will stop us and inquire about our carriage. Most people in this town have never seen an English pram. I saw them in Chicago years ago and decided that if ever I had a baby, he or she would ride in a pram.

May arrives, and with it, my first Mother's Day. I feel more special than I have ever felt in my life. I make matching dresses for Brook and me to wear on my special day. They are made of white cotton and have red strawberries with green leaves embroidered throughout the fabric, and my outfit is topped off with a red rose corsage Bob bought me to match. Many of the parishioners comment on how cute Brook and I look together.

My Dad, brother and in-laws join us at church this day. It is such a bittersweet day, my first Mother's Day as a Mom and also the first without my own Mom. I wear my mother's diamond and white onyx bracelet, and as I sit in church with my family, I touch the bracelet and feel my Mom's presence. "I'll never let go, Mommy," I whisper to her.

As we leave the church after Mass, Father Miller touches the precious bundle in my arms and says, "I've missed you at daily Masses but I can see that Saint Anthony has answered your prayers."

"Yes he has, Father," I say with a smile. My novenas have paid off, and I am the luckiest Mommy in the world.

About six months later, we stand before the judge and promise to love and care for our special gift, Brook. We are finalizing the adoption of our beautiful child. "You make a very handsome family. She is all yours! May God bless all of you," the judge announces.

Bob and I hug with Brook between us and our attorney congratulates us. We are relieved that someone did not come running in from the corner saying, "You can't have her! I want her back!" I'm sure all adoptive parents have that fear. With the adoption finalized, we drive home from the courthouse, relieved and at peace that Brook is finally ours.

A month later, we dress Brook in the baptismal gown that Bob's father, aunts and uncles all wore when they were baptized. Bob and his brother also wore it at their baptisms and now it is being passed on to the third generation. We cannot button the back of it because Brook is older than most babies are when she is baptized, but it is still beautiful. The gown is made of white voile and it is trimmed with lace. It hangs to the floor, and ribbon runs in and out of the lace and ties at each tier. We throw a party after the ceremony and all of our friends and family, even my former boss, help us celebrate our miracle, whom God has now blessed.

One morning at breakfast, Bob declares, "It's time to give our Brook a buddy. Let's get a dog!" Earlier that month, one of the students who lives at our house left the door open and Prancer, our Shetland Sheepdog, ran into the street and was killed. We have been mourning her death since the incident, so Bob waited to bring up a new puppy until right after we recovered. The timing is perfect.

"Oh, yes!" I agree.

"It has to be a large dog so it can protect her. I've narrowed it down to a Great Dane, a Doberman Pinscher or a Saint Bernard," he announces.

"A Saint," I tell him, making the final decision.

He nods his head in agreement. "Okay, I'll get some dog magazines and we'll look into it," he says.

A few weeks after our first discussion, Bambi joins the family. She is a beautiful two-month-old, soft and fuzzy Saint Bernard puppy. We fence in the small yard and start to work on her doghouse. Bambi lives with us in our house but when we leave for the day, we want her to have a house of her own. The father of one of our college students is a carpenter and he taught his son well. So the student and Bob design and build a huge dog house. It has a triple-track aluminum window, a peaked roof, a front porch and a balcony with real flowers. The doghouse is a reflection of how we believe things should be done; the best way possible. She is too small for it as a puppy, but eventually, Bambi will grow into her canine palace.

Our beautiful baby and sweet puppy add so much quality, love and happiness to our lives. Our Bradley student boarders feel the same. They, but especially Brook, add to the quality of their lives too; their dating lives. They take turns walking with her and while they are out, I clean their rooms. It is a win-win situation. They love to take her for walks, mostly to the girls' dorms. They call her "date bait," and she always accomplishes her job. They come home with a date for the evening every time.

CHAPTER SIX
DAY SIX
IN THE HOSPITAL

My pain awakens me. It is two o'clock in the morning. I press the call button for my nurse. They no longer give me injections for pain because I have graduated to pills, but they do not work as well and wear off much sooner. A nurse enters my room a few minutes later and I ask for a pain pill. "You are all out of pain pills," she answers.

"I'm in a hospital! How can I be out of medication?"

"Evidently, your doctor forgot to order it. It's the middle of the night, so you'll have to wait until morning when he makes his rounds," she snaps haughtily.

"Are you telling me I may have to wait eight hours?" I ask in disbelief.

"You got it!" she sings casually.

"In that case, will you please get me a cup of coffee or tea? I can't sleep, anyway," I say to her.

"I'll get to it when I can. We're busy," she says as she turns on her heel and leaves the room.

Forty minutes pass and I still have no coffee, tea or medication. The pain is becoming unbearable. I cannot deal with this intense pain, so I pick up the phone and dial Dr. McGinn. He answers the phone and his groggy voice tells me he was, of course, asleep. "Jack, this is Nina. I'm in terrible pain and the nurse tells me that my doctor forgot to put an order in for pain medication."

"That's crazy," he mumbles, "surely someone is on duty that can do the job." He sounds annoyed.

"Well, it's been forty minutes since I asked the nurse. She told me she is busy and she will not even bring me tea or coffee. Jack, I feel like my head is on fire."

"Who is your doctor?" he asks.

"I don't know which one is in charge of my pain."

"List them off," he directs.

I name them, and when I get to the name of Dr. Blum, he stops me. "I'll give you his home number. But do not tell him who gave it to you. I'm warning you, he will be pissed that you called him at home, but I assure you, you will get your meds real quick. He is a bastard and all the nurses are afraid of him. When he calls them, action will be taken quickly. Good luck. Call me later; much later, please. And let me know how you came out. Goodnight."

I dial Dr. Blum, and a sleepy man answers. "Are you Dr. Blum?"

"Yes," he answers.

"I'm a patient of yours at the hospital and I'm in a great deal of pain. The nurse tells me I can't have any medication until later in the morning because my doctors forgot to extend the order."

"Who are you?" he asks.

"My name is Nina. You came to see me yesterday," I answer.

"I've only seen you one time, and you call me at home?" he shouts.

"I've only seen all of my doctors once or twice, and I don't know who is responsible for my pain medication. Dr. Blum, I'm hurting very badly."

"How the hell did you get my phone number?" he yells again.

"I have a card with your name and phone number on it here at my bedside. I don't know where it came from," I lie.

"I'll take care of it."

Not more than five minutes later, I look to the door and see my nurse. She places a tray on my table. Her eyes are full of fire and she asks me between clenched teeth, "What did you do?"

"I called my doctor to give me some relief since you wouldn't," I tell her nonchalantly. She hands me a pill and a glass of water. I swallow the pill. As she leaves my room, I notice the tray she brought to me. On it is a pot of coffee, a pot of tea, and a few crackers. "Looks like Dr. McGinn was right," I think to myself.

As I sip my coffee, I think about what I need to do later today. My thoughts drift to Bob and I wonder if he is awake, too, pondering all the decisions that lie ahead of us. I lie awake most of the night, thinking of what is to come.

I sit up to go to the bathroom and swing my legs to the side of the bed. I sit for a few seconds, as the room spins around me. The spinning finally stops and I decide to walk by myself. I have done this with help before, but now I am going to fly solo. I do not want to upset that nasty nurse again. I put on my slippers and as I pass by the windows in my room I stop and notice that it is snowing quite heavily, just like it was the night of the incident. I look to the other side of the room and notice that the mirror on the wall is still turned around so I cannot see into it. I have no idea what I look like, and for now, I am still okay with that.

As I sit on the toilet, I run my fingers over my cheeks and can feel what are probably stitches all over my face and head. I lean back on the seat and rest my back against the back of the toilet. It feels good to stretch out. My back is sore from lying in bed for so long.

Before the incident I considered myself attractive. My blue eyes and nice legs were the reason I was able to model, and the money I made as a model was great. Between modeling and other part-time jobs while I attended school, I was almost never home except to eat and to sleep. I was driven to be a success. I sit a little longer, lost in those memories and old ambitions.

"I'm thirty-seven now," I think to myself, "and I weigh only a few pounds more than I did when I married Bob. My stomach sags after giving birth to three children, but it's nothing a girdle doesn't solve." I make no effort to return to my bed. It feels wonderful to not have a bedpan or catheter anymore. I never imagined that going to the bathroom would be exciting one day. I close my eyes and relax.

"Nina, why on earth are you sleeping on the toilet?" The nurse, Mary, chides me. "Let me help you back to bed."

I stand up, reach behind me, and feel the impression of the seat on my butt. "What time is it, Mary?" I ask as I look out the window and notice it is daybreak.

"It's seven twenty in the morning," she replies.

"Oh, my God!" I say. "I must have been sleeping for hours."

"How about we take a look at your beautiful head," she says as she returns me to my bed and scrutinizes my wounds. "I haven't checked it since we removed the compression bandage two days ago."

"You removed the compression bandage?" I question. "I don't remember that."

"Well, you're pretty groggy from all the pain meds you were on then," she says as she continues to examine me. "That's what I like to see! The blue bruising is turning yellow and brown."

"Oh, no," I shout. "I look better in blue!" We both laugh.

"Look what they did to you," she states. "They shaved your entire head, but they left a little ponytail at the nape of your neck. They may be wonderful surgeons, but they are terrible hairstylists. I will be back in a minute with scissors and I will trim those pieces of hair. You will look much more fashionable. Those silly doctors, to think they were more interested in saving your life than in making you beautiful!"

She returns in a few minutes, snips my hair a couple of times, and steps back to admire her work. I laugh at her as she stands there beaming as though she just finished a piece of artwork instead of nipping a few pieces of hair from a trauma patient's otherwise bald head.

"Nina, you are so much better. You are smiling, and I sometimes even hear you laughing when I am down the hall. You are coming back to us, girl. You are on your way."

The phone rings as Mary leaves my room. I still jump when someone calls. I am not used to the sound of it since I requested the call block be removed. "Hi, Mom," I answer. "How is everything going at the house? Are you having any difficulties with the kids? Are they asking questions? Are they frightened?" I fire off a million questions, and Mom explains that their father calls often and assures them we will both be home soon, so they do not worry.

"Have their classmates said anything to them about all of this?" I ask.

"We never talk about it," she says as she changes the subject. "Dad is at the kennel now doing a few repairs." She fills me in on how everything is going at the kennel. "I'll have the children call you when they get home from school. By then, Jim, my brother-in-law, should be here from Chicago. He will help Dad clean up your van. I love you, dear," she says before hanging up the phone. I hear what she said, but I don't understand why someone would be coming from Chicago to clean the van.

I call my attorney, Rodger, and he tells me that Bob had to admit himself to a mental hospital in order for his attorney to represent him. I must not be the only one who thinks he is mentally ill. I just cannot think of how else this can be explained. There can be no other explanation. Just thinking of Bob makes me panic. I am afraid of him, terrified of him. Rodger tells me he will call me when he has further information regarding Bob's situation.

My mind begins asking a series of questions, simultaneously considering countless other questions as they form a nebulous swirl of uncertainty and fear in my mind. "What will happen if they let him out? Am I safe? I feel safe for now, but what about the days to come? I wonder if he thinks of me. How could he ever explain what he did? I still have not spoken to him. What will I say? How could he ever look at me after what he's done?" I close my eyes to stop the questions and drift off to sleep.

I wake up at four o'clock. "My God," I say to myself. "I've slept all day. No one even woke me for lunch. I guess they decided I needed sleep more than food."

I call home and Sommer picks up the phone. I can hear the other kids arguing about who will be the next one to talk to me. Each one takes a turn and goes into detail about what has been happening in their lives. They never ask me *why* I am in the hospital, they just tell me they miss me and want me home. Eric, who is five, cries. He wants me home *"now."* After almost an hour on the phone with them, we all say our I love you-s and goodbyes. My heart is torn into a million pieces. I want to be home. I want everything to be back to normal. This situation is terrifying, and I am not sure how to deal with it.

A nun brings my dinner in, but I do not eat it and I tell her I am not hungry.

"I'll sit here all night if I have to, but you are *going* to eat!" The nun threatens me.

After I pick at my dinner to appease her, she leaves. All I can do is cry. For the first time since this happened, I am aware of the enormity of it. I try to figure out why this happened but I have no answers. I have only more and more questions. The hours pass, and it becomes dark outside. I am about to drift off when I hear a voice I recognize.

"Hi, babe!" I look up to see Dr. McNamara or Mac for short. Mac is a psychiatrist, and Bob and I share a great bond with and respect for him. When Bob opened a physical therapy office at a hospital in Bloomington, he convinced the hospital to hire Mac as a consultant. It worked out perfectly for Bob, Mac and the hospital.

"Mac, is it you?" I question. "My vision isn't too good these days."

"Sure thing," he answers as he walks toward me. He pulls up a chair to my bed, bends over and kisses me.

I focus my eyes on him and notice that he is wearing a tuxedo. His tie is askew and his usually perfectly placed hair looks windblown. "Hi, babe," he repeats, his speech a bit slurred.

"Mac, you've been partying! You didn't have to get that dressed up just to visit me," I tease.

"I could lie and tell you I dressed just for you, but the truth is, I had to attend a formal hospital dinner. It took a few – well, several – glasses of wine for me to muster the courage to come visit you. I have checked your chart every day but I just could not bring myself to come in to see you. I love Bob, and I have been hoping he has some mental problem that made him do this. I love him like my own son. All of your doctors tell me you're a medical miracle."

He bends down and puts his head in his hands. His suffering is evident. "I talked to Bob's psychiatrist, Dr. Warren, today, and he told me he was present when the police attempted to administer a lie detector test earlier today. They could not complete it because Bob hyperventilated, and they had to give him drugs to calm him down. Dr. Warren said that they weren't going to try to do another test." I ask why and he tells me that since Bob is in the medical field, he may be aware of the ways to make lie detector tests inaccurate, hyperventilation being one of them.

"Dr. Warren did say that blood tests reveal that Bob has hypoglycemia. He said that, in rare cases it can cause bizarre behavior," Mac says. "It's very unlikely that his hypoglycemia caused the incident, though. Dr. Warren says that he feels that you are safe, and that whether Bob knows or remembers what he did, he wouldn't try it again. If he planned it, it didn't work. And even if his illness made him do it, the medication he'll be on and his diet will prevent his hypoglycemia from getting out of hand in the future. He said Bob's condition is completely treatable and you and the children aren't in any danger, Nina." He looks at me and takes me by the hand. He gently kisses my hand and I feel his tears drop onto it.

"I'm afraid of him, but I love him, too. I just don't know if I can ever feel safe again. Mac, I am sorry for you, too. I know he loves you as much as you love him. Have you seen him?" I ask. "I just can't!" Mac takes out his handkerchief and wipes his eyes as someone steps into the doorway.

"Nina, is that you?"

"Yes, it is," I answer. I can tell from the green scrubs he works at the hospital. He holds out his hand, and I shake it.

"Recognize me?" he asks.

"No, I'm sorry, but I don't," I reply.

"I'm Dr. Scalia. I was your anesthesiologist during your surgery." He looks at the man sitting next to my bed and recognizes him.

"Hey, Mac. I didn't realize I had to get all dressed up to visit this lady," he jokes. He looks back at me and winks. He has also noticed that Mac is drunk. "So what do you think of Nina, Mac?"

"I think she's probably lucky to have had you as one of her doctors and doubly lucky to be alive," he answers.

"Lucky? More than lucky! Much more. In all the years I've been an anesthesiologist, only two times did I get so unnerved that, after I finished my job on that particular patient, I had to throw down my gloves and call it quits for the day."

"What happened?" Mac asks.

"I was on duty, and the Ansel team and I had just finished cleaning up multiple auto accident victims when Nina was brought into the operating room. The nurses had already removed her clothes and cleaned up her wounds. She had multiple deep lacerations on her face and head, and part of her scalp was missing. Her vital signs were good, but she kept going in and out of consciousness. At times, she would wake and ask for pain medication. I explained that I could not give her more than I already had. At one time, she answered, 'I know. I'm too close to death,' and then begged me to find her a priest because she said she was sure she was dying. I assured her she was going to be fine."

Dr. Scalia then looks at me and says, "We couldn't believe how calm you were."

He turns back to Mac and explains, "We couldn't give her anything more for pain than we had because it might have killed her. Funny, at one point she said, 'You know what?' I asked her 'What?'"

He looked at me and said, "Do you remember what you asked me, or us?" I shake my head, "No."

"You asked us if we were familiar with all the Polish jokes that had been going around lately. We laughed, and you said, 'Well, I'm sad to admit this, but they're all true. I am a Polack, so I can attest to it. When my Mom would get angry with my Dad because he did something she thought was stupid, she would tell him he was the reason they wrote the jokes. And I am just like him and all the rest of the Polacks - too stupid to pass out and just avoid all this pain! I am the dumbest of them all.'"

Turning back to Mac, "With that, her blood pressure fell and she flat-lined. We were stupefied. Just a second before, she was coherently talking to us, and then she was gone. One second she was telling us jokes about being a Polack, and the next, she was lifeless. Everyone started screaming orders. We acted upon them and were able to bring her back. It was amazing. Just as abruptly as she died, she came back to us. It shook the shit out of me, Mac. It happened so quickly and unexpectedly. When we started the surgery on Nina, the nurses had her all cleaned up, so we did not realize the amount of blood that she had lost. Her blood pressure was normal. It went from normal to nothing, just like that. We had been counting the stitches that the surgeon had put in, and when we reached five hundred, she coded.

"After Nina was stabilized again, I just couldn't calm down. When you are working on a patient whose life is touch and go, you expect a possible death. But when someone seems to be so alert and then dies, you cannot ever prepare yourself for that. I had to go home early that day."

"You mean I actually died?" I ask, completely astonished. Now I am unnerved.

Dr. Scalia suddenly realizes that, caught in the moment, he had said too much. "Only for a minute. But look at you now!" he stutters, smiling, in an attempt to assuage the situation. Dr. Scalia shakes my hand again as he prepares to leave.

"I'm leaving on vacation tomorrow, and I won't be back before you are released. I wanted to tell you how very lucky you are, young lady. I have never seen a patient with a head injury as bad as yours completely recover all mental faculties. I guess it only happens to *lucky* Polacks. Enjoy this new life God has given you," he calls out as he leaves the room. He waves goodbye to Mac.

The discussion seems to have sobered Mac up a bit. He takes my hand and says softly, "He shouldn't have told you all that stuff. You did not need to hear it. But now you know the reason everyone here at the hospital identifies you as their miracle child. Please let me know if there is anything I can do to help you. I'll be in again soon." He leaves me in a complete state of shock.

I died. I really died. I was literally dead, and no one told me until now. "Holy cow!" I think. "I can't believe a doctor would even give a patient all that information." Maybe he just blocked me out once he started conversing with a colleague and kind of forgot I was there. I am sure that I will not sleep tonight - or maybe ever again. I am more frightened than I have ever been.

I reach for my rosary beads and touch them but I am unable to pray. All I can do is remember what happened that night. My wonderful husband, whom I love so much, is the reason I am here. I just do not understand how this could happen. I have a job ahead of me tonight to continue my efforts to remember.

I stare into space, numb. I cannot seem to remember our sixth year together as husband and wife. I keep thinking. "If I look hard enough, maybe I can find the answers. Think back, Nina," I say aloud to myself. "This didn't just happen. There had to be red flags."

With that, 1965 comes back to me.

YEAR SIX
OF OUR MARRIAGE

I can feel someone touching the top of my head, and I know I have just won. I have been crowned Queen of Beta Sigma Phi, a national businesswomen's sorority. I see Bob jump up out of his seat, applauding and whistling amongst the clapping audience. I put my hand over my mouth and dance in a circle as all of the other contestants and judges congratulate me. I have to pose for a million pictures before Bob is finally able to reach me. We jump up and down, laugh, and soak in the moment.

I enjoy my time with Beta Sigma Phi. We take on all sorts of various projects that contribute to the good of the community. Being a part of this sorority gives me an opportunity to get out of the house, meet people, and accomplish civic goals. I love it. I love doing charity work and I especially love meeting new friends and socializing.

Our particular chapter of women voted and chose me to represent our members and compete at our annual dinner dance. A representative from each of the other chapters is also selected. Judges from the TV, radio and newspapers choose a winner. I designed and make a very classy black and white evening dress for the occasion.

Before the crowning, the candidates are individually interviewed by each judge. Then, the judges held a meeting and decided who they thought is the best representative of a woman in business.

Each judge asks the same question: "And what do you do?" "I clean toilets," I said.

"What did you say?" they laughed. I repeated myself.

"How many toilets do you clean?" They are both amused and curious.

"I clean five toilets. I also clean two urinals and a shower room with five showerheads."

"Where is this facility?"

With a big smile on my face, I answer, "At our home." I wait for them to try to figure out what I said, and then I laugh and explain that my husband and I own a boarding house for Bradley University students. I tell them we purchased a huge home that was once a fraternity house and converted into both our home and a home for students and that, in addition to the bathrooms, I vacuum and dust the rooms of seventeen students and I clean their kitchen.

I aimed to impress with my humor, and it worked.

On the way home, Bob teases me, "I guess I'll have to bow down every time I see you from now on!"

"That sounds great to me!" I giggle. It is such a magical night, and I do not want it to end. I feel so special.

When we arrive home, I say, "You take your shower first, hon. I just want to sit in my beautiful gown and be a queen for a little longer." He agrees and I sit on the bed for a few minutes. I begin to undress and unzip my dress. It feels great to get it off because it fit a little snugly. I assume that I must have gained a few pounds since I quit working at the photography studio. I snap off my bra and notice that my breasts are terribly sore. I touch them, and they feel hard.

"Golly, maybe my period is due," I think. "Let me think back. When was my last period? I cannot remember. Good Lord, I've been so happy with our baby and our new life that I haven't even thought about my period. Dr. Gilbertson told me that there was a slim chance I would never have a period again, let alone a regular one, so I really did not think much of it.

"Could I be pregnant?" I ask myself, considering the possibility for the first time. When the bathroom door opens, I ask Bob, "Hey, hon, do you remember when I had my last period?"

"You think I would remember a thing like that? What's up?" he asks, looking worried.

"My breasts are sore and I can't remember when I had my last period. Could I be pregnant?" I wonder aloud to him.

"I don't think that's even a possibility," he says firmly. "Call Dr. Gilbertson tomorrow and see what his thoughts are."

After I shower, I crawl into bed and cuddle up to Bob. "How about tonight honey? With the belle of the ball!" We continue to have a lovely evening.

Morning arrives and Bob leaves for work as usual. I tend to morning chores and then put Brook down for her nap. I think about how wonderful our lives have been since she joined us. I cannot believe the solace she brings to my life. I guess you cannot miss what you have never had, but once she joined our family, I could never live without her.

I look at the clock and call Dr. Gilbertson's office. I ask his nurse if I could speak to him and tell her it is important. After I explain my reason for calling, he suggests I make an appointment. He says he may give me a prescription to start my period so I will be more comfortable, never giving me a shred of hope that I might be pregnant.

That afternoon, I drop Brook off at Aileen's and head to Dr. Gilbertson's office. After the examination, he leans his tall, lanky body against the wall and says nothing. I fear the worst.

"If you were anyone else, I'd say that you were pregnant. I have to add that we both know that would be slightly less than a miracle. Let us run some lab tests. Call me in three days."

Instead, Dr. Gilbertson calls me later and he shouts into the phone, "Well, Nina, you *are* pregnant!"

"Oh my God! I am pregnant! I am pregnant? How can this be?" I ask. "I have to tell Bob!"

"Now, now, Nina," he says in a soothing voice, "you are pregnant, it's true, but the possibility of continuing the pregnancy to term is just as unlikely as it was for you to be pregnant in the first place."

I immediately begin to cry. One second I am ecstatic, and the next, I feel impending doom and feel I have been emotionally sucker-punched.

"The endometriosis that probably caused your other miscarriage could do the same damage this time. I wish I could reassure you that everything will be fine, but I did the surgery. I know the probability of you carrying to term. I have to be honest with you, Nina. Now, having said that, we are going to think positively. I am putting you on a hormone pill and vitamins and we will both pray a lot. Make an appointment for next month. Call me for *any* reason," he sternly tells me.

I pick Brook up from Aileen's and wait for to Bob to arrive home from work. It is strange that he has not even called me, especially knowing that I am to see Dr. Gilbertson. I guess he assumes I heard bad news and does not want me to cry over the phone. He is in for a huge surprise.

I am fixing a special dinner to mark the occasion and I start planning on how I will tell him when he walks through the door. His car pulls into the driveway. I look at the clock, and it is only four. He is home early.

As soon as I see him, all of my potential plans on how to tell him burst into flames, and I shout, "We're pregnant!"

"No shit! Are you sure?" he asks, smiling.

"Yes! I'm positive!" I tell him, beaming.

"I came home early because when I didn't hear from you right after your appointment, I figured you'd received bad news. I thought you would need comfort. Really, Kitts? You're pregnant?" he asks again in disbelief. "When are we due?"

"I don't know yet," I answer.

I know in my heart if I lose this baby, I would be okay because of my Brook. She gives me a reason to live. I decide that if God chooses for me to have this new baby, I will be overjoyed, but I will not fall to pieces as I did before if it is not meant to be.

A few months pass with only minor health concerns, but overall the baby and I are healthy and well.

My brother is graduating from grade school, so we are making our first trip to Chicago since I became pregnant. We are a bit apprehensive because I am due in only three months.

My brother looks so handsome. He looks just like Mom. As I hug him, we both cry about Mom's absence. Being together again reminds us she is gone and my emotions are conflicted. I am so happy to see my Dad and brother and am proud of Joe on his big day, but I miss my Mom so very much.

Joe has enrolled in a Catholic high school and he asks for my approval. There were four schools for him to choose from; two are Catholic, and two are public. It has been ten years since I had been in school and Dad has no opinion, so my brother chose the closest. He decides to spend a couple of weeks with us that summer before he starts high school and I expect him to be bored to death.

And boy, I was right. He is bored to death. We are eleven years apart and more like mother and son than siblings, but he is excited to be the new baby's godfather when he or she is born. At the end of his visit, Dad picks him up and takes him back home to his friends. I miss him when he leaves because, in a way, having him around is like having Mom back, in a sense.

I wonder if I will ever stop crying to Mom, missing her, and feeling cheated that she is gone. She wanted grandchildren so badly and never had the chance to see them, but I know somehow that she does. Sometimes, I put my hand on my stomach and I feel her hand on mine, appreciating the life that is growing inside me. And when I look into Brook's big eyes, I feel my Mom's looking back at me.

The last months of my pregnancy linger on for what seems like forever. I am due in August or September 1965, and the heat really causes me problems. Even with the air conditioning on, I am constantly sweating. I love being pregnant, though. I feel great, and I am so happy. I love my Brook so much that I hope I can love the new baby as much as I love her. Everyone assures me that I will.

I am swollen like a balloon, and I am so clumsy. When I walk through a doorway, I sometimes forget that I am forty pounds heavier than I used to be and I accidently slam half of my body against the doorframe. One of these days, I swear I'll knock myself out. Although Bob seems to think I am a bit grouchy, I feel that I am in good spirits. Pregnancy has been, for the most part, a joyous experience thus far.

On a warm, July evening I am sleeping with no covers on, trying to stay cool, when I suddenly feel as though I am wetting the bed. I feel the bed alongside me and it is dripping wet. I stand up, realize my water has broken, and feel it run down my legs.

"Bob, wake up! My water broke! The bed is all wet. I'm not having any labor pains, but we'd better call the doctor."

I feel my heart racing as I pick up the phone. "Get to the hospital immediately," my doctor orders.

I call Aileen, our neighbor, and she tells me she will come over and wait for Brook to wake up, and then she will take her back to her house. She had already agreed to care for Brook when the time came, so she expects our call.

We dress, grab the hospital bag I packed weeks ago, and head to the hospital. Bob touches my stomach and says, "It's your big day, little one!"

I smile, but I still wonder and worry why I am not feeling any labor pain. As we enter the hospital I begin to feel some pain in my back, but it is nothing like I had expected. We register and are taken to the maternity floor where a resident doctor examines me and tells me I am, indeed, in the early stages of labor. Despite the fact that hard labor has yet to begin, I need to stay at the hospital because my water has already broken, so there is a chance the baby will come faster than usual.

I am taken to a private room. I put on a hospital gown and the nurse prepares me for delivery. The doctor comes in again, and I inform him that the contractions have increased but are not occurring on a regular basis. "I'm a few weeks early," I tell him, "or at least a few, according to my doctor. My periods were irregular, so we're not sure of my actual due date."

"This baby is full term," he replies. "It's a good size and on its way. Do not worry, Nina. Early or not, this baby is ready."

Hours pass and nothing happens. My contractions begin and stop time and again. Finally, late in the morning, Dr. Gilbertson comes in. "Hey, what the heck are you doing here?" he jokes.

days, I swear I'll knock myself out. Although Bob seems to think I am a bit grouchy, I feel that I am in good spirits. Pregnancy has been, for the most part, a joyous experience thus far.

On a warm, July evening I am sleeping with no covers on, trying to stay cool, when I suddenly feel as though I am wetting the bed. I feel the bed alongside me and it is dripping wet. I stand up, realize my water has broken, and feel it run down my legs.

"Bob, wake up! My water broke! The bed is all wet. I'm not having any labor pains, but we'd better call the doctor."

I feel my heart racing as I pick up the phone. "Get to the hospital immediately," my doctor orders.

I call Aileen, our neighbor, and she tells me she will come over and wait for Brook to wake up, and then she will take her back to her house. She had already agreed to care for Brook when the time came, so she expects our call.

We dress, grab the hospital bag I packed weeks ago, and head to the hospital. Bob touches my stomach and says, "It's your big day, little one!"

I smile, but I still wonder and worry why I am not feeling any labor pain. As we enter the hospital I begin to feel some pain in my back, but it is nothing like I had expected. We register and are taken to the maternity floor where a resident doctor examines me and tells me I am, indeed, in the early stages of labor. Despite the fact that hard labor has yet to begin, I need to stay at the hospital because my water has already broken, so there is a chance the baby will come faster than usual.

I am taken to a private room. I put on a hospital gown and the nurse prepares me for delivery. The doctor comes in again, and I inform him that the contractions have increased but are not occurring on a regular basis. "I'm a few weeks early," I tell him, "or at least a few, according to my doctor. My periods were irregular, so we're not sure of my actual due date."

"This baby is full term," he replies. "It's a good size and on its way. Do not worry, Nina. Early or not, this baby is ready."

Hours pass and nothing happens. My contractions begin and stop time and again. Finally, late in the morning, Dr. Gilbertson comes in. "Hey, what the heck are you doing here?" he jokes.

My brother is graduating from grade school, so we are making our first trip to Chicago since I became pregnant. We are a bit apprehensive because I am due in only three months.

My brother looks so handsome. He looks just like Mom. As I hug him, we both cry about Mom's absence. Being together again reminds us she is gone and my emotions are conflicted. I am so happy to see my Dad and brother and am proud of Joe on his big day, but I miss my Mom so very much.

Joe has enrolled in a Catholic high school and he asks for my approval. There were four schools for him to choose from; two are Catholic, and two are public. It has been ten years since I had been in school and Dad has no opinion, so my brother chose the closest. He decides to spend a couple of weeks with us that summer before he starts high school and I expect him to be bored to death.

And boy, I was right. He is bored to death. We are eleven years apart and more like mother and son than siblings, but he is excited to be the new baby's godfather when he or she is born. At the end of his visit, Dad picks him up and takes him back home to his friends. I miss him when he leaves because, in a way, having him around is like having Mom back, in a sense.

I wonder if I will ever stop crying to Mom, missing her, and feeling cheated that she is gone. She wanted grandchildren so badly and never had the chance to see them, but I know somehow that she does. Sometimes, I put my hand on my stomach and I feel her hand on mine, appreciating the life that is growing inside me. And when I look into Brook's big eyes, I feel my Mom's looking back at me.

The last months of my pregnancy linger on for what seems like forever. I am due in August or September 1965, and the heat really causes me problems. Even with the air conditioning on, I am constantly sweating. I love being pregnant, though. I feel great, and I am so happy. I love my Brook so much that I hope I can love the new baby as much as I love her. Everyone assures me that I will.

I am swollen like a balloon, and I am so clumsy. When I walk through a doorway, I sometimes forget that I am forty pounds heavier than I used to be and I accidently slam half of my body against the doorframe. One of these

He looks at my chart. "Can't you make up your mind, little one?" he asks as he taps on my stomach. He instructs a nurse to hand him his instruments, and he examines me.

"You are only dilated to about a three. I still think you are not due yet. The labor may stop completely. We'll just have to wait and see."

"A three?" I think, keeping in mind that I have to be ten centimeters to deliver. I have such a long way to go, and I have already been in the hospital for hours.

As the afternoon passes and evening follows, the pain grows stronger, but the contractions are still irregular and ultimately start and then completely stop several times. A nurse suggests to Bob that he go home, have dinner, and go to sleep. She tells him she will call him if the labor begins again.

Bob looks almost as exhausted as I am. He calls Aileen and tells her he will pick Brook up and call her again when my labor decides to restart. He kisses me and says, "Now, don't you do anything without me, do you hear? We are going to do this together. Natural childbirth, just as we planned."

"I wouldn't think of having this baby without you. You were here from the beginning!" I laugh.

He leaves and calls me when he has picked Brook up and put her down for the night. We say our good nights and eventually, I drift off to sleep.

At three in the morning, I shoot up in bed with a contraction. I call for the nurse, and she calls in the resident doctor. "Well, it looks like this is the real thing," he says.

I call Bob and he readies Brook to go back to Aileen's. He arrives around four o'clock in the morning.

My pain increases, but I am only slightly more dilated than I was yesterday. The contractions are still irregular, and as time goes, the doctors and nurses become concerned. By mid-afternoon, the pain and contractions stop entirely yet again. Dr. Gilbertson examines me and determines that I am experiencing false labor. He says that if the pain continues to subside, I will probably go home. He is leaving on vacation in a few hours and he lets me know that Dr. Reddings, his partner, will be looking after me. He suggests that Bob go back home and assures him I will be following closely behind him if nothing changes soon. Bob takes the doctor's suggestion and goes home from the hospital for a second time.

I receive a light meal and ravenously clean my plate.

At six o'clock in the evening, I am startled awake from a nap with another round of contractions. I call the nurse and she tells me that Dr. Reddings will be in to see me shortly. Ten minutes later, he examines me.

"Nina, this baby is due. I am going to do a C-section. It's taking too long for the baby to come on its own."

My hand visibly shakes as I pick up the phone and call Bob to tell him the news and ask him to hurry back to the hospital. After a few minutes, my contractions increase dramatically but they still are not occurring at regular intervals.

"Bob should be here any minute. Any minute now, Nina. Hold on," I tell myself.

Dr. Gilbertson walks into my room. "What are you doing here?" I ask. "I thought you left on vacation?"

"I did, but the car broke down, so we're leaving tomorrow. I understand that Dr. Reddings wants to do a C-section. Nurse," he calls over to a nurse who has just entered the room, "I want to examine Nina." The examination is so painful that I am having everything I can do to hold back the tears.

"Nope! I am not going to do a C-section. Your labor is progressing. I expect you will be having this baby tonight. I still think it's at least a few weeks to a month early."

Bob enters the room and looks at Dr. Gilbertson, confused, as I explain what is happening.

By eight o'clock, I have dilated to seven centimeters, where I hover for a while before, once again, the pain and contractions stop. At ten o'clock, I tell Bob he should probably go home and wait. For the third time, he leaves the hospital.

"Can I have some water? I'm so terribly thirsty," I ask a nurse.

"I'm afraid not. You might go back into labor and deliver this time. I don't want you to get sick."

She leaves my room and returns with ice chips. "These will help your dry mouth. Also, I have put a fan in here. It's so hot and stuffy tonight." She sits beside me and slips a few in my mouth. It feels so good and soothing.

"Look!" I announce to her, observing. "My legs are jumping up and down, and I'm not doing anything. They're moving all by themselves!"

The expression on her face turns to one of panic. She runs out of my room without saying a word, and seconds later, several nurses and the resident doctor place me on a gurney and wheel me rapidly down the corridor.

"Your doctor is on his way," someone says to me as I fall asleep.

In what seems like five seconds later, "Wake up, Nina," another voice demands repeatedly. "Open your eyes, Nina! Open your eyes. You've had a baby girl!"

I can hear the words, and I feel excited, but I cannot respond.

"Come on, lady! You have had a lot of anesthesia. We need to wake you up." I open my eyes and close them again. I am too tired to hold up my eyelids. I can feel someone putting pillows behind my head and making me sit up in my bed. I feel like a rag doll as my arms flop alongside me, hanging over the sides of the bed. I cannot pull them up and really, I do not care to do so. I just want to go back to sleep.

"Oh no, you are *not* going back to sleep! Your husband will be here in a few minutes. You *do* want to see your baby, don't you? Your delivery was at about eleven o'clock this evening. You were heavily sedated, and we told your husband that you would be sleeping until morning and that he should go home and get a real night's sleep. Neither of you has had any sleep for almost two days," the nurse says.

"Okay," I groan, annoyed. "It hurts! My bottom is so sore!"

"I'm afraid you will be sore for a few days. You had to have a deep episiotomy. Your baby was coming out shoulders first, so Dr. Gilbertson had to cut and pull. You were too weak for a C-section, as you had gone into shock. He did great! He saved both you and your baby!" the nurse said, proudly.

"Saved us? From what?" I ask, still trying to process what the nurse was telling me.

"Your little girl had a difficult time breathing. She really struggled. We gave her oxygen and she eventually settled down. She never stopped breathing, and she'll be just fine."

This whole situation is so confusing. I am hearing too much information all at once, and I cannot seem to comprehend it all. It has been a very long couple of days.

"Why would she struggle to breathe?" I ask.

"She was in the birth canal for a long time before she was born," the nurse answers.

"Oh, then Dr. Reddings was right after all when he said he wanted to do a C-section. He said I was due and didn't want to wait," I say to my nurse.

"It's best not to question the doctors' decisions, Nina. You and your baby are safe," she reassures.

"I need to use the bathroom," I interject.

"You won't need a toilet for the coming days. We catheterized you. It'll be a while before you heal up a bit."

She leaves the room and Bob walks in to see me. His arms are loaded down with flowers, candy and magazines, and he is beaming from ear to ear. He puts everything down, and I sit up in my bed, so happy to see his comforting face. I grimace with the pain that movement caused. He kisses me and kisses me again, and I melt into his arms.

"How are you feeling, Kitts?" he asks. "The doctor said it was a rough delivery."

"Did you see her?" I ask, ignoring his question.

"Only for a minute. She still had not been cleaned, and they said they needed to give her more oxygen, but that I should not worry. They assured me you would both be fine but that you would not be awake until morning, so they suggested I go home and go to sleep. I called Aileen and she said Brook was asleep in the playpen at their house and that I deserved a night off to get some good rest. I'd been up for almost forty hours, so I welcomed her offer."

"You do look rested," I say to him. "I can't even imagine what I look like."

Just then, a nurse comes in carrying a bundle wrapped in a pink blanket. She lays the bundle in my arms and pulls the corner of the blanket back so we could see our new daughter. We both look at her face at the same time, and then we look at each other, wide-eyed.

Our baby's face and head is black and blue, and her entire body is covered in black hair. To make matters worse, the nurse had combed her two-inch-long hair into a Mohawk. She literally takes our breath away.

The nurse notices the shocked look on our faces and tries to comfort us. She reassures us that in a few days, the hair will fall out, even from her head. She notices that we are both blond and assures us that she will be, too.

Again, we just look down at the baby and then into one another's eyes. Bob bends close to me and whispers into my ear, "From now on, we adopt!" We laugh so hard that we accidentally wake up our new little angel. She cries, whales actually, so hard that I fear she might stop breathing. Brook never cried this hard, so this is a new sound to us.

A nurse brings in a bottle of formula and our baby quiets down long enough to take the small bottle. Shortly after she eats, she begins to cry again, or rather, scream! Brook always took her bottle and went right to sleep, so this crying and screaming really confuses me. I cannot figure out what is wrong. She cries all the way back to the nursery. I assume it must just be a bad day. "After all," I reason, "she had an extremely difficult entry into this world."

But every day afterward is the same. I can tell when my baby is on her way to my room because each time they bring her to me, she screams all the way down the hall from the nursery. I almost feel guilty that the other mothers and babies on the floor must be being jolted from their sleep as my baby comes down the hall.

My new angel also makes a habit of projectile vomiting. I am absolutely a nervous wreck. Our pediatrician checks her from stem to stern in the hospital. He says that, because of the difficult delivery and the stress she experienced when she struggled to breathe after birth, she is very colicky. He prescribes some medicine to aid in her discomfort.

By the third day, she still does not seem to be comfortable. The poor little thing is in so much pain, it just breaks my heart. She just curls up in a ball in my arms or on my lap and screams. Her formula is changed, but her behavior does not. Nevertheless she manages to eat her formula, and she gains weight.

On the fourth day in the hospital my catheter is removed. I can finally go pee in the bathroom again; except that I cannot. I cannot pee. It just will not come out. The nurses try running the faucet in the bathroom to try to trick my bladder, but it does not work. *Nothing* works. Now I'm worried about me and the baby.

On the fifth day, the hospital staff threaten to catheterize me again if I do not pee. It takes that much to scare me into it, but I finally am able to urinate. Then, I learn that I also have to have a bowel movement before I can go home, and I am back to square one. Later in the day, after two apples, a dish of prunes and the threat of an enema, the problem resolves itself. I am so relieved and ready to go home with my precious Sommer, who, despite her incessant crying, has begun to lose the black hair and whose bruises have faded to a yellowish-greenish color. We are finally cleared to go home and I ache to hold my Brook. She is a year and a half old and has no idea what a sister is yet.

Bob arrives to take us home, and the nurses fill rolling carts with all the plants, flowers and gifts our friends and visitors have brought and sent to wish us well. I am already dressed and in a hurry to leave. Bob pushes me in a wheelchair to an elevator and we hit the button and wait. Suddenly, I realize something is missing.

"Oh, my God! Bob! We forgot the baby!"

Everyone stops talking, pauses, and bursts into laughter.

"My God, I'm so ashamed. How could I forget my child?" I say. I am filled with guilt and cover my mouth with my hand. Everyone looks embarrassed for me, but we all laugh it off.

Bob and I abashedly go back to the room and find the box with Sommer's "going home" clothing.

The nurses scurry back to the nursery, returning with our baby who was, of course, crying.

As we dress her, I think to myself, "That's probably why we forgot her. We couldn't hear her!"

As we try to settle back into home life, it is not quite the adventure I envisioned when I was pregnant. Sommer cries all the time. She barely sleeps. Dr. Holloway, our pediatrician, puts her on a heavy dose of medicine to calm her tummy. It does little but add to her misery, giving her several bowel movements a day. The doctor says that usually, her particular stomach problem keeps a child from gaining weight and ultimately requires surgery. However, Sommer continues to thrive in that regard. She screams often and poops often, but she miraculously keeps gaining weight. The doctor has little advice for us but to let her grow out of it and that it may take a few more months.

One thing working in Sommer's, or rather my favor, is that we never have to sit long in the waiting room at the pediatrician's office. Because of her screaming and vomiting we are usually escorted into an exam room as soon as we arrive for our appointment. Her screaming frightens all the other babies and makes them cry, too.

Nothing bothers Brook. She still easily sleeps, eats, and is as happy as a child could be. We spend many a night trying to soothe Sommer. We even take her for rides in the car in the middle of the night to try to calm her. Nothing works until she is so tired that she has no option but to give up and fall sleep.

When Sommer is about four months old, we visit our folks in Chicago. My Dad and brother are invited to dinner with Bob's family, and Sommer is having a fairly good day. There are many arms taking care of her, and of course, playing with Brook.

After dinner, I say goodbye to my Dad and brother, who live only a few blocks away, and Sommer starts to scream. "My poor little baby," I think. "God, she must be in so much pain."

She finally falls asleep and so do we, but in a very short time, Sommer starts to scream again. "It's your turn tonight!" I tell Bob.

He rolls out of the sofa bed in the living room and walks to her crib in the kitchen. I watch him pick her up and I roll over to close my eyes, trying to silence the sound of her crying. I start to fall asleep again when my in-laws' bedroom door opens and slams against the wall. I see Mom running to the kitchen in her floral nightgown and I jump up to watch as she frantically opens the bathroom door, smashing it, too, against the wall behind it and screaming, "What did you do to that child?"

I run to the bathroom and stand behind her. I look over her shoulder and into the bathroom and see Bob sitting on the toilet, silent, doing his best to cover himself with his hands.

"What did you do to that child?" she repeats.

"Nothing!" he defends. "I decided to go into the bathroom with her so you all could get some sleep. After a few minutes, I had to take a leak, so I put her on top of this fluffy, pink rug. She instantly stopped crying. I guess she likes the softness."

Mom and I are unable to speak. After a long pause, Mom says, "I heard the bathroom door close, and Sommer stopped crying so quickly." She puts her hand over her mouth and then blurts it out, as if she cannot control herself. "I thought you drowned her!" We both look at Mom in shock and burst into laughter, continuing until Sommer begins to scream again.

As I lay my head back down on the pillow, I take a deep breath. We have only been here for a day, and even their nerves are shot. I wonder if they have any idea how we feel. Our child is hurting, and only time can help her.

Sommer cries incessantly for the next two months, and then suddenly, it just comes to an end. Now we have to make another major adjustment: a return to normalcy.

Bambi, our Saint Bernard, is old enough for obedience school, and I am the one to train her. She and I enjoy the lessons and practice at home frequently. "You know, that's a good-looking Saint," the instructor comments one day at class. "You ought to show her in conformation classes. She has a fine body."

Bob and I discuss the idea and think, "Why not?"

We drive to Springfield with the kids and enter Bambi in a show. The judge instructs me to stack her, which means I am supposed to place her legs straight beneath her and position her head so she holds it high. Then she tells me to move her.

"Move her where?" I ask, confused.

"Down the mat and back," she says and she looks over her glasses at Bambi and me.

I imagine that she is thinking, "You dumb bunny, where else would you move her?" The judge is right. I am ignorant and do not understand what to do.

"Move her where?" I repeat.

"Up and down the mats," she says as she points to them impatiently.

I run up and down the mats with Bambi. When we stop in front of the judge, Bambi's front legs are crossed and she proceeds to pee. We are both so scared. I feel like peeing, too.

Entering Bambi without having taken lessons turns out to be a huge mistake. We should have attended a show before we entered her. The judge gives me a blue ribbon, first place. But I am not proud - we did not have any competition. I just feel stupid and know how stupid I must have appeared as well. Bob and I decide we need a lot more practice and have a lot more to learn if we want to continue our potential new hobby.

"Kitts, this is fun. It's going to be great!" he says to me. "I'm excited to get started."

"Sure, he's excited," I think. "I'm the one making a fool of myself!"

We continue to attend dog classes between our work and other responsibilities. We practice with Bambi whenever we have time. We enter a few more shows and receive more blue ribbons. Then the awful day comes that we score second place and receive the dreaded red ribbon. It is not until we are awarded a yellow ribbon, third place, that we come to the conclusion that Bambi is a wonderful pet with a fantastic pedigree, but she is not show quality. We decide to breed her to a great Champion in the hopes of raising a Champion from birth.

Months later, Bob comes home with a Doberman Pinscher. "Where did you get that?" I question my husband.

"At the airport," he answers.

"You passed by the airport and the dog was running loose?" I ask, skeptical.

"Not exactly. I bought her and had her shipped from New York. Beautiful, isn't she? Her name is Joy. I was reading *Dog World* magazine and saw the ad. I paid five hundred dollars for her," he confesses.

"What the *hell* were you thinking? You bought a dog without discussing it with me? And a Doberman at that, a man killer!" I say, as I have always thought of them. "What about the children? You spent an unbelievable amount of money, a month's salary, without asking me! Where are we going to keep her?" I am in disbelief. He has never done anything like this before, except when he bought my engagement ring.

"She will stay right here in the house with us. She can run and play with Bambi. She comes from one of the most prestigious kennels in the country, Kitts. She's borderline show quality, but her pedigree is unbelievable," he informs me.

He reaches down and unleashes her and she immediately runs to sniff Bambi and the kids. Bambi sniffs back. I grab Sommer, who is playing on the floor with Brook, and yell to Bob, "Grab her!" It is too late. Joy is already licking Book's face. Much to my surprise, Brook begins to giggle. The dogs playfully wrestle around the room so we let them outside to play in the fenced-in backyard. They get along famously.

I am still shocked that Bob made such a huge decision without me but am pleased to find that Bambi and Joy love everyone and get along beautifully with the children. Despite the fact that our home life is happy and content, I begin to feel a change coming in the air. I sense that our lives are about to be transformed and I have yet to determine how.

CHAPTER SEVEN
DAY SEVEN
IN THE HOSPITAL

I jump at the sound of the telephone ringing.

"Hello," I answer.

"Kitten, I love you," Bob's voice says to me. "Please don't hang up. I can explain everything that happened."

I press the phone harder to my ear and continue listening. The pain is still excruciating but I do not want to miss a word - I need to know the answer. I am having a difficult time holding the phone with my hand shaking so badly.

"My psychiatrist had a lot of tests run on me, both mentally and physically. He's discovered that I have hypoglycemia," he said.

"What is that?" I ask.

"Well, it's sort of the opposite of diabetes, and it's been known to make people do things they would never normally do."

"Really?" I ask, wanting to believe but not ready to accept. Now I am interested. I want an explanation and I want it from him! My heart wants it to be a legitimate medical reason. I want to keep my family together. I want our life back.

"Yes, that's why all this happened. I am sick. This illness can be corrected with medication and diet. We can be a family again," he says. I notice that the tone of his voice makes his statements sound more like he is pleading, rather than just informing.

"Yes! Yes!" I think to myself. "That's the reason. That is an explanation I can believe. He could never do anything like he did if he were not sick. He loves me," I convince myself.

"Please, Kitts. Please -- please give me a chance to get well. I will live somewhere else until you feel that I am better and that you will be safe. I love you. I love the kids. You know me. I could never do this. I *must* be sick."

I do really want to believe him, but I realize that regardless of how I feel about him, I have a lot of thinking to do. I want to find out more about this illness of his.

With all the emotional strength I can muster, I tell him, "Bob, I don't think I could ever feel safe with you again. Besides, I truly believe that Sue is still in your life. I want you to know that I've already contacted my lawyer and I plan on filing for divorce." My strength gives way and I begin to cry. "I don't think I could ever trust you again."

"No! No! Please wait. Talk to my doctor. He says he will see you tomorrow and he will explain my situation. Please, please don't give up on me," he begs.

"I can't talk to you anymore. I don't even know how to process all of this," I say to him through my tears. "I don't know what to say or how to feel. I am confused. We will talk again. Goodbye."

I hang up before he has a chance to respond. I put my head back on the starched pillowcase and sob. I can still hear his pleading and am replaying every word he said. Then it occurs to me. "Strange," I think to myself, "...what happened. 'Everything that happened,' he said. He never discussed what happened, only called it a 'situation.' He tried to explain it away as caused by a medical problem." I'm eager to talk to his doctor tomorrow. I must know

As I think about "the situation" my body shakes all over. I am immobilized by fear and I am so confused. I am somehow still hopeful that maybe this can all be resolved. The thought of separating us as a family numbs me to the core. He tells me he can recover, but if he relapses, I might die next time. I realize I am immobilized both by the thought of staying married and by the thought of splitting up our family.

"Is he going to be a constant danger to me? What if he should forget his medication?" I ask myself. "will he become dangerous again?" The word "dangerous" keeps swirling around in my head when a memory suddenly comes back to me from when we were dating.

I was about seventeen years old. After attending an early movie one evening, Bob came into my house with me to watch a TV show we both enjoyed. The show ended, he kissed me goodnight and he said goodnight to my Mom, who was in the other room having a beer and reading a cookbook. When he came to my house, Mom would go to the kitchen to give us a little privacy; just a little.

After Bob left, I sat back down on the rose-colored frieze sectional to watch a little more TV. I was engrossed in a show when Mom came into the room. She walked over to me and touched my shoulder. "Be careful, my darling daughter. He could be dangerous," she whispered into my ear. She let her hand rest there for a minute and looked deeply into my eyes. "You mark my words," she added just before she left the room.

I silently pondered her warning for a few minutes and then consoled myself by justifying her statements and thinking she had just probably had too many beers. She loved to drink beer. As I lay in my bed that night, a warm breeze drifted through the open window, but I couldn't shake the cold, ominous chill I was feeling. Mom's words played in my head over and over. She had a reputation among her family and friends for having an uncanny instinct for judging character. They often called her and asked her opinion about people they had met. They all valued her insight. "Well, she was wrong tonight," I confidently told myself. "She's just had too much to drink."

I had forgotten the prediction until just now. All these years later, I remember that night and I am haunted by it. I close my eyes to relax, and as I do, I feel her hand on my shoulder again. I know she tried to protect me that awful night of the incident, and she is making me remember her prediction to try to protect me again.

Suddenly, I am startled by voices and someone is cranking up the head of my bed. "Time for lunch," a voice whispers to me as I try to snap back to reality. The nurse leaves the room. I just move my food around my plate without taking a bite. I have no appetite. My mind is overloaded. I keep hearing Bob's plea, followed by my mother's prediction, and my heart literally, physically aches. My food goes untouched, and the tray is removed. "What do I do now, Mom?" I ask her. "Maybe tomorrow when Bob's doctor comes in, he'll help me understand."

I look at the clock and I dial our home phone number. Sarah answers with a lilt of happiness in her voice. "Hi, Mom," I say to her.

"Has Bob called you today?" she asks. I assume that he has already spoken to her, as I can hear the optimism in her interrogation.

"Yes. He tells me he has hypoglycemia and that it explains what he did," I tell her. "I don't know what to think. I need to speak to his doctor tomorrow and find out more about his affliction."

"I asked him if he's seeing that Sue anymore," Mom says, "and he said that he definitely is not. He tells me she is dating a cop and that their affair is long over. She has moved on."

"I know that that's what he's telling you, Mom, but he has been acting very strange for months now. He has been distant, not interested in almost anything. He has been very preoccupied. Thinking back on it, he seemed as though he was in a quandary and didn't know what he was going to do. Now I know what he was thinking about," I say.

"Well, maybe that is because of this disease," she says. I hear the hope in her voice.

"I wish I could feel that sure. I want to believe what he tells me, but I am very apprehensive. I purposely change the subject and ask, "Are the kids home?"

"Sure. Who do you want to talk with first?" she asks.

"All of them!" I reply.

"Hi, Mommy," Eric says. "Are you feeling better? Grandma says you were very sick but you are much better now." Then he whispers, "I don't like Grandma's cooking. Can you please come home soon? Can I sleep with you when you come home? I miss you, Mommy. I don't like that you are not here. Daddy isn't here either."

That alerts me as to the confusion they must all be feeling. Eric has never slept with me. His world has been turned upside-down. He is only five years old. "Of course, you can sleep with me!" I answer him.

"Jon wants to talk to you, Mommy."

"Hi, Mom. When are you and Daddy coming home?" Jon asks. "Grandma says that you were in an accident and that Daddy is sick and that you are in the hospital. Are you in the same hospital as Daddy?"

"No we're not, honey, but we talked to each other today and we're both getting better. Are you getting your homework done?" I ask, as though I do not know.

Jon is always the first to get his homework "over with," as he puts it. He is seven years old and is the terror of the bunch, but when I go to his parent-teacher conferences, his teachers praise him. Just the sound of his voice gives me hope that I will be there with him soon. My God, how much I miss this cocky little troublemaker, always looking for attention.

"Okay, okay," I hear him say. "Sommer is pulling the phone away."

"Mom, Jon is being a brat," my nine-year-old, Sommer, tells me. "He threw my book at me because I wouldn't change the TV station." I laugh out loud and think to myself that it seems like life is normal, at least over there.

"Brook is wearing my barrettes, too. Will you tell her she can't do that?" Sommer yells into the phone over the noise of her siblings. "I sure will, as soon as I talk to her. Are you getting your homework done?"

"Yep, Grandma helped me last night. She is a whiz at math. I miss you, Mom. When are you coming home?"

"As soon as I can," I answer reassuringly, but in all honesty, I have no idea.

"I talked to Daddy today," she tells me. "He says that we'll see him real soon! I love Grandma and Grandpa, but I miss you and Daddy. I am scared, Mom. You are always here and it's so strange without you."

"My turn!" I hear in the background. It's Brook.

"Hey, I wasn't finished talking to Mom!" I hear Sommer yell at her. "You better come home soon before I kill Jon!" she squeezes in as Brook takes the phone.

"Hi, Mama," she says. "Everyone at school is talking about what happened to you and Dad. What really happened, Mom? I hear so many different stories. Grandpa says that you were in an accident. What kind of accident? How come you are in different hospitals?" Brook is almost eleven years old, going on forty.

"I know that you are confused honey, and when I get home, I'll explain it all."

"I heard the teachers whispering to each other. I cannot hear what they are saying, but I hear your name. Some of the kids said that their parents heard about you and Dad on TV." Brook is old enough to know that this is more than an accident. She is asking the questions but I have the distinct feeling she already knows what really happened. She just needs to hear it from me.

"I miss you, Pussycat. I can't wait to hold you in my arms." I close my eyes and quietly cry. "I'll be home with you just as soon as I can. Are Grandma and Grandpa able to feed and water the dogs?"

"Yep, the kennel kids come in after school and do the cleaning and Daddy told Grandpa how much food to give the dogs. He fixes it for them, and the kennel kids deliver it."

We now have seven Saint Bernards, four Doberman Pinschers and three Borzois. Being show dogs, they require special diets. It is quite a job, but evidently, Grandpa and the kennel kids are getting it done.

The kennel kids are teenagers who live in the subdivision across the street. They come every day after school to feed and water the dogs and scoop the poop. Bob usually did that in the mornings, as well. I assume Grandpa is doing it now.

"I help them, Mommy," Brook adds. "Mrs. Daton, our receptionist, is managing the Abby. Colleen doing the dog grooming like always. Grandma tells me Colleen comes to the house every afternoon and has a cup of coffee with her. I love Colleen, Mommy."

"I love her, too. And oh, by the way, you are not supposed to wear Sommer's barrettes unless you ask her. Do you hear me?"

"But she has a lot of other ones–"

"Do you hear me?" I interrupt her.

"Yeah, yeah," she answers.

"Go get your homework done," I order. "I know you. You will wait until bedtime, so don't. Go do it now!"

"Mama," she adds, "everything is different here. I want us to be like we were before."

"I'll fix up everything when I get home. I can hardly wait to touch your soft hands. I can close my eyes and feel them in mine. I love you, Pussycat. Now, let me talk to Grandma for a minute. I'll talk to you tomorrow."

"Love you, Mama."

"Hello, dear," Sarah chimes in.

"Thanks for everything, Mom," I say. "I'll call tomorrow." I set the phone down.

"Oh, my God," I say out loud. "It never occurred to me that this mess might have been on TV, the radio and in the newspaper. I cannot imagine how confused the children must be. I don't know how I'll ever fix their lives, or *our* lives, really."

I reach over to a table at the side of my bed and pick up a newspaper. Every day, someone puts the newspaper there, but I have not had the desire to read it. My vision is blurred, anyway. I look at the day and date. I have been here seven days. Seven days, and today is the first day I feel all of my senses, as if my mind is entirely functional. I am alive. I wonder where I have been for these seven days and how could I have not thought of the kids and what they are experiencing. Yet I have been able to remember back to all the years of our marriage. "How strange," I think to myself.

It is dark outside. It is only five o'clock, but it is wintertime, and while the days are shorter, the nights are long and they give me more time than I need to recall the memories of my married years.

Seven days, seven years. I remember our seventh year of marriage and, as I do, I chuckle to myself.

YEAR SEVEN
OF OUR MARRIAGE

"Green Acres, here we are! City folks out here in the country," I say as I sit on an old lawn chair watching the squirrels, rabbits and birds ignore me as they skitter around our new yard. The girls are napping, so I am trying to catch a few minutes of rest myself. I am exhausted from unpacking boxes all morning and I am afraid I will be doing this for weeks to come.

We move from our house in the city with the college students to a home in the country surrounded by twenty-five acres of woods. Our dream is to build a boarding kennel, but first we need to build a kennel for our present and future show dogs.

Much to our dismay, it takes eight months of fighting with the zoning commission for it to come to a decision about which zoning category, exactly, a dog kennel should be. County officials think it should be in light industrial zoning next to small factories; we, of course, disagree with them, as the land we live on is zoned for agriculture. This goes on for months and costs us a fortune in legal fees. Finally, the chairman of the commission stands up and announces, "For Christ's sake, gentlemen, these are animals, not factories. Use your common sense. Animals *are* agriculture. Farming is agriculture. Breeding of cattle is agriculture. Why should the breeding of dogs be industrial?" And so finally, it passes. After months and a few thousand dollars, common sense reigns.

Our yard is full of giant oak trees, some two hundred years old. I sit outside, listening to the sound of nothing. I have never heard the sound of silence. Now and then, I hear the warble of birds, but otherwise, our land is eerily quiet. Our boarding house is on a busy street in the city, and so was my family home growing up. Neither Bob nor I know anything about living in the country.

I can see a large farmhouse across the street with cattle roaming in the front pasture. There are only a few houses on this road, and they are all on farms except for ours. Our land is not flat like theirs, but is instead covered with ravines and trees. It is beautiful to look at, but it is not suitable for farming.

A few of our acres on the other side of the ravine had been cleared years ago, and the family living here then kept horses in dilapidated barns in that area. We decide not to build our private kennel there, as it is too far from the house. Instead, we find a nice, level spot a few hundred yards behind and to the left of our new home. It sits behind a row of large trees and down a slope, so it is not completely visible from the house, but it is only a short walk from the house.

I enjoy my rest, but I have to go back inside and find the pots and pans. When the girls wake up, we will go grocery shopping so I can make us all supper. Bob is back at work, after taking a few days off for the move, and I have been too busy unpacking to do anything else. Thankfully, the former owners had left the kitchen appliances, which are in good shape. We set up the beds, living room furniture, and washing machine as we moved them in, so all the big things are in place.

I take a second load of laundry to the machine and turn it on, but it is not working. I call Bob, and he comes home to investigate. He checks and everything seems to be in working order, so he calls the people who sold us the house. They explain that we probably used more water that day than the well could produce. The seller tells Bob that they usually took their laundry to a laundromat.

"You have to be kidding! You never mentioned this before we bought the house! Now what the hell do we do?" Bob questions furiously. "We're in one hell of a predicament!"

"You never asked," the previous homeowner quips.

Bob hangs up and calls the realtor. "What are my choices?" Bob asked her.

"Well, do you want to get out of the agreement?" she asks. "You have every right to do that. But I know that some people in the country that do not have a good water supply install a cistern to hold purchased water. I know you are already aware that your county property will be annexed into the city soon. Remember? That is why the zoning committee had a difficult time determining your zoning issue. The city will be installing city water to your area within two years. The construction has already begun."

"Shit, shit, shit!" Bob screams. "After spending all that money and fighting the city to clarify what zone we belong in, we wouldn't find another place this close to the city limits, knowing that ours is scheduled to be annexed soon. Once it is, it will be zoned for commercial, not agricultural, purposes. We need the boarding kennel to be as close to the city as possible while still being able to maintain agricultural zoning, which we fought for and have. We are not going to get that lucky again, and if we are too far out of town, no one will ever find us. I have to get back to the hospital. I'll do some checking around about this cistern idea." He is angry and disheartened.

"I'll find a laundromat this afternoon," I reply.

Four days later, the septic tank backs up. We really are, as the old saying goes, completely full of "it." A septic company has to come to clean, repair, and rebuild our entire septic system. The next day, we have a cistern installed to hold more water. And more money just flew out the door.

That night, as we lie in bed, Bob whispers, "Let's hope that's the end of the surprises. We should have had these things inspected before we moved it. We should sue the realtors. That's their business."

The next week passes without incident.

Bob removes the chain-link fence around the doghouse he built while we were at the college boarding house so he can install it at our new home.

During the day, the dogs can romp in their pens while I work and then come inside for the evenings until we have time to install more dog pens and build more doghouses. When I let the dogs in at night, I notice how dark it is out in the country. Just like the silence, I have never seen such darkness. We always lived in the city and the lights – business lights, streetlights and auto lights – emitted a certain glow, but not here.

One night, we go for a car ride and take Joy, our red Doberman Pincher, with us. When we arrive home, Bob turns the car lights off and we begin to slowly, cautiously find our way to the back door when suddenly, Bob lets out a scream. We stop dead in our tracks and he erupts in loud laughter. "God damn!" he exclaims. "Joy came up behind me and goosed me in the rear. I nearly fainted. It is so dark, I couldn't even see her eyes!"

We all laugh and go inside to put the girls to bed. We turn on the evening news. "Lender Drapery Store is on fire and is burning out of control. It's a total loss," we hear the reporter say. We look at each other, wide-eyed. We truly hope there are no injuries and feel terrible for the Lenders, but we know this could be a blessing in disguise, at least for us.

Lenders made custom drapes for our private living room at the boarding house. We decided to take them with us to our new house and use them temporarily for the twelve-foot bay windows in our new living room. We would prefer a better color for the new room, but we cannot afford new drapes. We took the old ones into Lender's having them redesigned when we moved and they have yet to be finished.

The TV reporter says that Lender's will be back in business in a month but in another location. "Honey," I scream, "we're going to get new drapes! Ones that match!"

The next morning, the phone rings. After I hear the news, I hang up and begin to cry.

"What the hell was that call about?" Bob asks.

"That was Mr. Lender. He was able to save two pairs of drapes from the fire, and ours was one of them. Damn!" I say. "He says it'll be about two months before he will be able to finish altering them. If it weren't for bad luck, we'd have no luck at all."

"Hey, we can get through this," he tells me as he cups my face in his hands and kisses me.

As hopeless as I feel, I know he is right. We have our dogs, our new home, each other, and our girls, our two little miracles. Sommer is a year old and Brook is two and a half.

One afternoon, after putting the girls down for a nap, I walk by the bathroom and notice the mirrored cabinet over the sink is slightly ajar. I open it, and my eyes fall on the bottle of the chewable, orange baby aspirins. The cap sits neatly on the bottle but it is not snapped closed. I look inside the bottle.

"Lordy be," I say to myself. I cannot remember how full the bottle was, so I cannot tell if any are missing. I rush over to Brook, and she is already falling asleep.

"Brook, did you eat any baby aspirins?"

"No, Mommy," she answers, half asleep.

I go back to the bathroom and look at the bottle again, trying to remember how many pills were there. I remember a couple of weeks ago when she climbed up onto the toilet and over into the sink to look into the mirror. I scolded her, as she could have fallen off of the sink. Fear envelops me. I run back to the bedroom and ask Brook, "Did the aspirins taste good, honey?"

"They sure did, Mommy," she groggily answers.

I rush to the phone and call the emergency department of our hospital. They suggest I bring her in immediately and tell me to be sure to keep her awake in the car. I run into the girls' bedroom, grab Brook and put her in the front seat next to me. I run back for Sommer and put her in her baby seat in the back. As we drive to the hospital Brook keeps falling asleep. In a panic, I continue shaking her and singing songs at the top of my lungs, trying to keep her awake. We arrive at the emergency door of the hospital and a policeman opens the door.

"Take her!" I scream at him. "She's taken an overdose of baby aspirin."

He scoops her up and I park the car, grab Sommer and rush into the hospital. The emergency team is readying to take a blood sample. Brook cries and the doctors assuage her with a kiddie cocktail for what the medical team has confirmed to be an overdose. Brook relaxes and enjoys her cocktail which she does not know is actually a medication. Shortly after, she begins vomiting.

Bob leaves work to meet us in the emergency department. "How much did she take?" he questions the doctor.

"Probably half a bottle. It is a good thing that you brought her in. She might not have woken up."

I hold her in my arms as she vomits into a container. "If she had closed the cabinet door, I'd never have noticed anything, and Brook might be dead," I say to Bob.

"Let's look at it this way, Kitts: our luck is changing. We are now the luckiest family in the world!" We smile. Bob calls the head of his department to have someone else cover his patients and we all go home together.

The girls fall asleep in the car on the way home. As I place them into their cribs, I begin crying and shaking. Our world nearly changed forever. When they wake up, I decide, I will kiss them until my lips turn blue. "Dear God, you gave us this miracle child; not just the first day she was put into my arms but, once again today," I pray, so full of gratitude.

Months later, Bob, his Dad, and one of the boys who lived at the college boarding house, Joe, build a beautiful dog kennel for our dogs. It is constructed down the hill and about fifty feet from our back door, hidden behind the trees and bushes. Huge oak trees canopy the kennel and provide shade. There are eight six-by-six rooms inside with a hallway running from one side to the other. The outside wall has two six-foot windows with screens for ventilation in the summer and which will stay closed during the winter. The hallway holds two powerful, commercial fans to circulate the air in the building. Each dog quarter has a heat light to keep the dogs warm during colder months and each has a forty-foot long exercise area made of chain link. Three dog pens are built in the basement to hold females for birthing or show dogs who have been recently groomed for an upcoming show. With all of that complete, we add a couple more Saint Bernards.

Once a week, after dinner, I take one of our Saints, Hans, to dog school to train him for showing. He has to learn to stand perfectly still as a judge examines him. Show procedure is strict. The judge will feel the bone structure of his head and body and look at his bite to make sure his upper and lower teeth line up perfectly and that he isn't missing teeth—a disqualification for some breeds. He or she will ask the handler to run the dog back and forth on the rubber matting to check for proper movement and a smooth gait. Upon the return run, the judge will look for expression, alertness and a pleasant disposition. He will do the same to each dog in that particular class and choose the dog that best represents the standard for each breed. Of course, this is very subjective, as each judge has his or her own preferences. We work hard to make sure our dogs are well-bred and well-trained.

Eventually, we hire a professional dog handler to guide our dogs and to show off their best assets. Bob has not yet learned to do this, but he often goes to the shows with our new handler to learn by helping him groom, water, and run the different breeds he shows. The handler gives Bob lessons on all fronts of the show world and teaches him what it takes to make a dog an American Kennel Club Champion.

While Bob is away showing the dogs, I stay at home, care for the other dogs and the girls, and answer inquiries about the puppies of our pregnant females. I also complete the pedigree forms which tell the history of each dog like a family tree. They go back four generations and take quite a bit of time to complete, but they are a necessary document for each show dog.

I am also the problem resolution expert for the people managing our college boarding house, and it is becoming a pain in the neck. They have free rent and in exchange, all they have to do is clean the house and be house parents to the student residents. I visit unannounced every so often and it sure does not look as polished as I had kept it when we lived there. I expect better from them and it really frustrates me. Sometimes, I pick up the bedspreads and drapes and wash them here to help our tenants, but mostly to make myself feel better. I am particular about our new home, too.

Shortly before our first Christmas in the new home, we decide to decorate the fireplace mantle with live garland. The girls sit on the couch, watching patiently as Bob tries to hang it. He struggles, and the garland keeps falling from where he attempts to hang it. After several attempts, he finally proclaims, "Alas! It's perfect!" As soon as the words leave his mouth, the whole thing falls down again.

"Oh, shit!" Bob exclaimed.

Brook looks appalled and reminds us that Daddy should not have said that. "That's right, honey. Daddy should not have said that. What *should* he have said?" I ask.

Brook stands up, her hands on her hips, and proudly announces, "Sunnabitch!"

Bob points a finger at me and says, "I've told you to watch your mouth!"

She apparently picked that up from me, and boy, was that far from what we expected her to say! We cannot help but laugh. She brings us much-needed comic relief.

CHAPTER EIGHT
DAY EIGHT
IN THE HOSPITAL

"Wow!" I say out loud as I look through my hospital window. The sun is shining, and the day looks beautiful and warm but it is January in Illinois, so I know that it must actually be quite cold. I begin to feel the chill coming through the window and decide to sit further away in one of the lounge chairs. I grab a warm blanket and cuddle up in it. The chair is close to the nightstand where the phone is and I am expecting a call from my mother-in-law.

"To think I have been here eight days," I say out loud.

A couple of days ago, my in-laws made arrangements with some of our friends to take care of our children. Mom and Dad are planning to return to their home in Chicago. They helped Bob get an apartment after his attorney advised him not to return to our home or visit the children until they can determine the gravity of his "illness."

The boys are going to stay with the Datons. Nora Daton is my part-time receptionist at the kennel. She works for me when I am not available. She lives across the street and has a son Eric's age. All three boys attend the same grade school. Our school district is separated into different schools, as the area has developed and outgrown the local school. The girls, who attend another school, are staying with the Sellers, our kennel club friends. They have a child, Allison, who is the same age as my Sommer. They will be in the same classroom, and Brook will be there with them in the next higher grade.

I jump as the phone rings. "We are ready to leave," my mother-in-law tells me. "We've delivered the children's clothes to the homes where they'll be staying and called the schools to make arrangements with their teachers. The boys' teachers will be making arrangements with the bus driver for them. The girls will be living close to their school, so they will walk to and from school.

Then, in a softer tone, "Dearie, please consider the children when making the many, difficult decisions that lie ahead of you. They need both of you. You cannot possibly run both kennels and the raise kids by yourself. You have to believe in your heart, as we do, that this happened because Bob is sick. He will get well and soon you will be a family again. Please do not get a divorce. Take plenty of time. He says he will do anything it takes to fix this up. He loves you. Do not make hasty decisions. Wait until you get all the facts," she begs. "Promise me now?"

"I love you," I respond, avoidant. "Be careful driving home. Please call me when you get there." I am still holding the phone receiver, mulling over our conversation. I move to hang it up, and as I put it into its cradle, it rings again and startles me. I jump back and accidentally knock over the water pitcher.

"Hello," I say, as I shake off the water that spilled on the phone and then onto the floor. "Hello?"

After a moment of silence, I hear, "Hi, Kitts. I miss you." I was not expecting Bob and I am unnerved.

"Mom says you're doing much better. Please, please listen to me. Do not hang up. Please, please hear what I have to say. The doctors tell me it will not take long. With proper diet and medication, I can be normal again. This will never happen again, Kitts."

"Bob, I can't talk to you now. I just cannot handle any of this. I do not know what to believe! Please do not pressure me. I need time to think and to try to make sense of this horror." I hang up without saying goodbye and without any promises.

He knows me too well. He knows how much my commitment to our family means to me, and he is using it as leverage to try to keep me. My heart is breaking into a million pieces. I do not want to end my marriage. With everything inside of me, I *want* to believe him, and yet, everything practical in my brain is telling me it just cannot be. It will not work. It is just too late.

Oh, how I miss him. The weight of this decision is almost too much to bear. I am not ready to make a decision but now I must. Physically, I am feeling much better and taking little medication now. My wounds are healing on the outside, but the inside is another story. I cannot be sure my fear of him will ever subside, or that it should subside.

As the day passes, several groups of our friends have found the courage to come visit me. They have obviously been prepared for what I look like. They give me encouragement.

One of the groups is led by Reverend Gandy, the Presbyterian minister, who counseled us earlier on our marriage problems. His group contained my dearest friends, the Sellers. He begged them to convince me that this marriage is beyond fixing. They all agreed. But I am still not convinced.

After they leave and as I am thinking, my eyes fall upon the covered mirror on the wall facing me. I have not yet been brave enough to remove the towels covering this mirror and the one in the bathroom. I know I must look like a monster. People come to visit me and stand outside my room, look at me, and then step back to check the room number before asking, "Nina, is that you?"

"The time has come," I say as I breathe out a sigh. I have to look at my face so I can deal with what has to be dealt with. I have to look in the mirror and see myself.

I press the call button for my nurse. "Hi, Nina. What can I do for you?"

"I think you can uncover the mirror. I think it's time that I take a look at myself."

As she walks to the mirror, she says in a soothing voice, "Now, just keep in mind that with plastic surgery, you will look exactly as you did before to try to make sense of this horror." I hang up without saying goodbye and without any promises.

He knows me too well. He knows how much my commitment to our family means to me, and he is using it as leverage to try to keep me. My heart is breaking into a million pieces. I do not want to end my marriage. With everything inside of me, I *want* to believe him, and yet, everything practical in my brain is telling me it just cannot be. It will not work. It is just too late.

Oh, how I miss him. The weight of this decision is almost too much to bear. I am not ready to make a decision but now I must. Physically, I am feeling much better and taking little medication now. My wounds are healing on the outside, but the inside is another story. I cannot be sure my fear of him will ever subside, or that it should subside.

As the day passes, several groups of our friends have found the courage to come visit me. They have obviously been prepared for what I look like. They give me encouragement.

One of the groups is led by Reverend Gandy, the Presbyterian minister, who counseled us earlier on our marriage problems. His group contained my dearest friends, the Sellers. He begged them to convince me that this marriage is beyond fixing. They all agreed. But I am still not convinced.

After they leave and as I am thinking, my eyes fall upon the covered mirror on the wall facing me. I have not yet been brave enough to remove the towels covering this mirror and the one in the bathroom. I know I must look like a monster. People come to visit me and stand outside my room, look at me, and then step back to check the room number before asking, "Nina, is that you?"

"The time has come," I say as I breathe out a sigh. I have to look at my face so I can deal with what has to be dealt with. I have to look in the mirror and see myself.

I press the call button for my nurse. "Hi, Nina. What can I do for you?"

"I think you can uncover the mirror. I think it's time that I take a look at myself."

As she walks to the mirror, she says in a soothing voice, "Now, just keep in mind that with plastic surgery, you will look exactly as you did before the area has developed and outgrown the local school. The girls, who attend another school, are staying with the Sellers, our kennel club friends. They have a child, Allison, who is the same age as my Sommer. They will be in the same classroom, and Brook will be there with them in the next higher grade.

I jump as the phone rings. "We are ready to leave," my mother-in-law tells me. "We've delivered the children's clothes to the homes where they'll be staying and called the schools to make arrangements with their teachers. The boys' teachers will be making arrangements with the bus driver for them. The girls will be living close to their school, so they will walk to and from school.

Then, in a softer tone, "Dearie, please consider the children when making the many, difficult decisions that lie ahead of you. They need both of you. You cannot possibly run both kennels and the raise kids by yourself. You have to believe in your heart, as we do, that this happened because Bob is sick. He will get well and soon you will be a family again. Please do not get a divorce. Take plenty of time. He says he will do anything it takes to fix this up. He loves you. Do not make hasty decisions. Wait until you get all the facts," she begs. "Promise me now?"

"I love you," I respond, avoidant. "Be careful driving home. Please call me when you get there." I am still holding the phone receiver, mulling over our conversation. I move to hang it up, and as I put it into its cradle, it rings again and startles me. I jump back and accidentally knock over the water pitcher.

"Hello," I say, as I shake off the water that spilled on the phone and then onto the floor. "Hello?"

After a moment of silence, I hear, "Hi, Kitts. I miss you." I was not expecting Bob and I am unnerved.

"Mom says you're doing much better. Please, please listen to me. Do not hang up. Please, please hear what I have to say. The doctors tell me it will not take long. With proper diet and medication, I can be normal again. This will never happen again, Kitts."

"Bob, I can't talk to you now. I just cannot handle any of this. I do not know what to believe! Please do not pressure me. I need time to think and this happened. Everything that is not perfect can be fixed. Do you understand?"

I think to myself, "Exactly as I was before? There is no way that I can ever, ever again be exactly as I was before. I will not ever *look* the same, nor will I ever *be* the same. Everything – everything – has changed forever."

"Come on over," she says as she pulls down the towel. I do not move. She comes back and takes me by the arm and slowly walks me to the mirror. I imagine she believes that I will need help to remain standing when I see how I look.

I stand up and from afar, I look into the mirror. I look like a bald mannequin.

She guides me closer to the mirror, and I am struck with a full view. I gasp aloud. I do not even know who this reflection is. I have never seen myself without hair. There are multitudes of black stitches sticking out all over my face and head. I look like a patchwork quilt with stitching that needs to be trimmed. And where one set of sutures ends, another begins. I cannot believe how many stitches there are.

"I think I still look like me," I say, trying to convince myself. As I speak, I notice that my cheeks cave in where the stitches are. It looks like the stitches are attached to my cheekbones. When I speak, it feels as though they are sucked into the bone. "Oh, my God, no wonder no one recognizes me," I admit to the nurse.

I notice that I have a nicely shaped head. Under the black threads, my face is yellow and purple, so I can tell the bruising is healing. I ask for a hand mirror and my nurse returns with one. I look at the back of my head, and I notice that a part of it is still bandaged.

"There were large pieces of your scalp missing," she reminds me. "When they removed the heavy compression bandage, they replaced it with these gauze pads."

I try to pull my ears forward to see the backside of them. I see that there is an incredible amount of stitching behind them. They are still red and hurt terribly to the touch so I am unable to take a closer look. "I knew it was bad, but I didn't realize just how bad," I say to the nurse as I hand the small mirror back to her.

"Even with all the stitches and bruising, anyone can tell that you were beautiful before and that you will be beautiful once again," she says convincingly.

"Thank God my children can't see this. They'd be horrified," I say.

She gently helps me get back to my bed, and she leaves me to my thoughts. I think of the deep creases on my cheeks and consider how I will look if the scarring cannot be repaired. I will look like a monster, I decide, and I weep silently to myself.

With a heavy heart, I want to know what I did to deserve this. I want to know why he could not just tell me he does not love me anymore and go about his life. Why did he have to do this to me? I am still numb, processing what I just saw in the mirror. He must be very sick to do this to me, but I still do not know if it could be an excuse for what he did. I wonder if I will ever find a definitive answer.

I spend the day falling in and out of sleep. Friends call on the phone and stop by, and my room is full of the beautiful flowers they bring. My Dad calls often, too. He never gives me advice. He just wants me to know that he loves me.

The staff and helpers at the kennel tell me that everything is running smoothly there. "Thank God it's January," I keep thinking to myself, "the slowest month of our season." I am also grateful that we have no litters of puppies to be cared for and none of our dogs are due to deliver. "Thank you, thank you, God, for that. Thank you, too, for saving me," I add, although I admit to myself that I wonder why he did.

I must be sleeping more than I realize. It seems as if I just saw the sun rising and now the nurse is telling me goodnight. But I cannot sleep now. I have to remember our eighth year of marriage. It starts to come back to me. Oh, what a year that was.

YEAR EIGHT OF OUR MARRIAGE

An hour into New Year's Day, 1967, all the revelers have left the party we hosted at our home. Bob is taking a shower and I am putting away the leftover food. I smile as I think about the wonderful time we had. Our parties are always so much fun and the house is filled with laughter.

Bob has just returned home after taking our neighbors, the Crawfords, back to their house. They had a bit too much to drink. We realized this when Joyce Crawford went to the bathroom, missed the toilet, and landed on the floor, laughing and calling for help. It was the only time anyone ever got that drunk at any of our parties, and it was pretty funny.

I finish putting the food away and excitedly prepare to deliver my New Year's present to Bob. I slip into bed only to find he is already sound asleep. I nudge him, laughing. "Have you had a few too many glasses of champagne and eggnog?"

"Yeah," he replies as he cuddles me up in his arms, falling asleep again. I look at his belly and notice his seems much bigger than mine does. Maybe he should be telling me the news.

"Bob," I say, attempting to shake him awake.

"What?"

"We're going to have a baby," I tell him.

"Ah ha."

It is all I can coax out of him. "Bob, do you hear me? We're going to have another baby!"

"Ah ha. Ah ha."

"Bob, wake up! Wake up!"

"Yeah, yeah. I am up. I'm up!"

"Did you hear me?"

"Uh-uh," he mumbles.

"You didn't even hear me! Now listen to my words. *We are going to have another baby*!" I finally have his attention. His eyes open, and he looks very hard into mine. "Do you hear me?"

"Uh-huh."

"Do you know what that means?" Nothing registers on his face. "We are pregnant!" I repeat.

"We're pregnant? We're going to have a baby?" he asks.

"Yes, next summer."

"I thought you can't have any more," he says.

"That's what the doctor thought. Apparently, he was wrong!"

"We are? We are? We really are?"

"I have a feeling this one's going to be our boy," I say, smiling.

His face lights up and he flashes that gorgeous smile of his. "Oh, Kitts! I love you!" He wraps me up in his arms and holds me close, smiling as he falls back asleep.

"Well," I think. "I better give him the news again tomorrow, just in case!"

We spend the rest of the winter rather routinely, and that routine includes endless plowing and shoveling. Our house sits up a few hundred feet from the main road, and the driveway is not in the best condition. The gravel moves around quite a bit, creating large ruts. The people we purchased the house from had never put enough rocks down to make it good and firm, and despite the fact that we have added quite a bit more, we still have a lot of problems with it.

Sometimes, when snow starts to melt and turns a little slushy, we cannot even pull out of the driveway. The car just sinks in and has to be towed out. A city garbage truck even had to be hauled out once. Needless to say, that was the last time they picked up our garbage, so we had to hire a private company to come by and remove it.

Bob often has to leave the car down at the main road when he arrives home from work, put on a pair of great big boots, and walk up to the house so he will not have problems pulling the car out in the morning. That is, as long as the city plows do not bury it as they plow the main road. The city snowplows usually made their way through our neck of the woods during the middle of the night. Several times each winter, the snow is so heavy that our entire Mercedes is hidden underneath the snow that the plow scoops off the road. From the window in the morning, we find our car by spotting the giant igloo. We just can NOT win. When it is especially bad like this, Bob has to walk down to the main road with his shovel and clear the snow off the car, trudge back up the driveway, change his clothes, and prepare to leave for work. On some days, Bob will return to his car only to find it completely buried *again* by the snowplow. And so the winter goes.

Spring arrives, and with it comes a couple more dogs added to our private kennel. We have such big dreams of "someday." Someday, we are going to own the best Saint Bernards and Doberman Pinschers in the country. We purchase the cream of the crop, the best Saint and Dobe puppies, and breed them to the best champions to establish our own line of champions.

One beautiful June afternoon, after a happy and uneventful spring of being happily pregnant, I suddenly discover that I am bleeding. I call Dr. Gilbertson and he instructs me to come to the office. I ask a neighbor from our old neighborhood to come over to watch the girls while I wait for Bob to come home to take me to the doctor. His office in Bloomington is forty-five miles away. When Bob finally pulls up in the car, we immediately drive to Dr. Gilbertson's office.

The doctor examines me and instructs me to lie down at home with my legs elevated as often as possible. "These are familiar instructions," I think, as I had been told to do this a few times before delivering Sommer.

The next day, I am still bleeding. Dr. Gilbertson admits me into the hospital. Bob cancels his patients' appointments and comes home so we can arrange a sitter for the girls and heed my doctor's instructions as soon as possible. I am six months pregnant so it is critical that I follow medical advice in order to keep my baby and me healthy and safe.

As the day progresses the bleeding slows. Bob leaves the hospital, picks up the girls, and heads home for the night.

He calls me the next morning. "How goes it, Kitts?"

"I'm barely spotting," I tell him. "Take the girls to Aileen's and go to work. I'll call you if anything changes."

Around noon, I make my way to the restroom and notice more spotting. The nurses call Dr. Gilbertson. He examines me again and listens for the baby's heartbeat. He listens and listens, moving the stethoscope all over my belly. He then gently takes my hand and looks sadly into my eyes.

"I'm sorry, Nina. I believe that your baby is dead. I have not been able to hear a heartbeat, either yesterday or today. That is why I had you admitted to the hospital. I thought you were going to miscarry, but I did not want to frighten you with my suspicion. I still cannot find a heartbeat and now your spotting is heavier. I have to assume the baby died. I wanted you to be in the hospital because this far along in your pregnancy, a miscarriage would be like delivering a full-term baby. What you need to do now is get out of bed and walk the corridor. I want you to force yourself to go into labor. If this does not happen, you may have to carry the fetus until its normal delivery date and then deliver as though it were alive. Some people think it's God's way of ending an imperfect pregnancy."

He pats my hand and tells me he will be in later to see me, but for now, he instructs me to walk up and down the halls.

"And why again should I do that?" I ask as if I had just been part of a sad, sad scene from a movie.

"It will be much better if you can begin laboring now as opposed to the alternative. I'll send a nurse to walk with you."

I call Bob, as I cry hysterically. He tells me he will be here as soon as he can. I feel dead inside. I have never heard of anything like this, a baby dying while a mother still carries it. How does that happen?

Every hour, a nurse comes in, and we walk the halls. Soon, our friend, Dr. McGinn, walks into my room. I tell him the terrible news and he sighs heavily. His wife has already told him of my condition. "Come on. I'll walk with you," he offers.

We walk for about fifteen minutes and are about to re-enter my room when we hear loud voices at the other end of the hall. We both turn around and see Bob and a nurse rushing toward us.

"This man says *he* is your husband and only husbands are allowed on this floor. Who are *you*?" she asks, pointing to Dr. McGinn, wearing an indignant look.

"Yes, who the hell are you? I'm her husband!" Bob accosts Dr. McGinn.

The nurse's eyes open wide. The men stand their ground, glaring at each other. Then suddenly they both break into hysterical laughter. The nurse's dirty look fades into one of confusion.

Dr. McGinn explains who he is and tells her he took off his hospital coat before he came to see me. Bob explains that he had already assumed from down the hallway it was Dr. McGinn, so he decided to make a game of it. The guys laugh as the nurse huffs back to her station. It is typical of Bob, finding humor wherever he can.

Dr. McGinn leaves and Bob and I return to my room. He holds me in his arms, and we cry.

The next day, the bleeding stops. I am sent home to await the delivery of a dead baby which I am to expect within 60 days. Every day, I pat my stomach and talk to my baby as though it were alive. "Don't worry, little guy," I say, certain that it is a boy. "Everything is going to be okay. You are not going to have to suffer through life. You will not even have to die. You have already left us in your sleep. We'll see each other one day again, at the end of *my* life." Then I cry. I cry all the time now. Brook hugs me and wipes my eyes every time she witnesses it. Sommer is not even two years old, thankfully too young to understand this traumatic situation.

A few weeks after I return home from the hospital, we are watching TV when I feel a bubble floating in my stomach. A little later, I feel it again. I tell Bob, and he just shakes his head. "Maybe I'm getting ready to go into labor," I say, sullen. And then it hits me and I whisper, "Or maybe the baby is alive!"

"Probably wishful thinking," he says. I have to agree.

Morning arrives, and as I lay awake, waiting for Bob to wake, I again feel what seems like lots of bubbles in my belly. It is the same sensation I had experienced the night before, but more intense. "Bob! Bob, wake up! I think I am feeling the baby. It feels just like when Sommer was kicking."

Bob sits up, suddenly very awake, and says, "Call the doctor as soon as his office opens. See if you can get in right away. I'll transfer my patients to Sally for the morning."

At nine o'clock sharp, I call the doctor. "Dr. Gilbertson wants me to come in as soon as I can," I say to Bob.

As Dr. Gilbertson examines me, I pray like I've never prayed before. Bob watches, and his anxiety is expressed in his eyes. The exam seems to take forever. Dr. Gilbertson puts his mouth to my ear and whispers, "I have picked up a very strong heartbeat." Bob literally jumps with joy.

"How is that possible?" I ask.

"It must have been in such a position that I couldn't hear it before."

"You mean that I walked the hospital trying to deliver a dead baby, and my baby is alive?"

"Sometimes we have no answers," he says. "Rejoice in the news. You're going to be a mother again against all odds *again*!"

On the way home, I say to Bob, "You know, honey, this will be one very strong baby. It truly had to fight for its life while I worked so hard to lose it." I cry with relief.

"I'm speechless, Kitts," he says softly. "I feel like we've experienced a miracle, but I can't help still feeling a little apprehensive. I feel as though God has played a cruel joke on us. I am confused. How can a baby just hide for a few weeks?"

"I guess it's like Dr. Gilbertson says. Sometimes there just isn't an explanation."

Over the following weeks and months, we pat and talk to my stomach constantly. "Don't you dare scare us again, or when you are born, I won't let the doctor spank you. I'll do it!" Bob jokes.

Our baby is not due for a few weeks, but my back has been aching terribly, so I call my friend Patty, a nurse, and tell her how I am feeling. "I'm not having any contractions, Patty. My back is killing me, and I cannot sit down comfortably. My bottom hurts."

"I'll be right over to take you to the hospital. My girls are in school. Call Bob and tell him to meet us there. I'll bring my sister with me and she will take care of the girls," Patty replies.

"Don't be crazy!" I tell Patty. "I only have a backache and I'm uncomfortable sitting. I am not in labor. You are blowing this out of proportion. My last labor was forty hours, and rule of thumb is that labor with the next baby is cut in half. So why should I go to the hospital?"

"Because you can't sit down," she explains. "The baby is in position."

Again, I protest.

"Listen, Nina. We are coming over *now*. Get the girls' stuff packed. My sister will take them to her house while you and I go to the hospital. If it is false labor, I will bring you back home. It's better to be safe than sorry."

Twenty minutes later, their cars pull into the driveway. We load the girls into Jackie's car and I leave in Patty's. "I'm telling you, I'm going to feel like a fool," I say to her as I try to find a comfortable position.

We arrive at the emergency door of the hospital, and the policeman on duty greets me with a wheelchair. "Can I just walk in? It hurts to sit down," I announce to the cop.

"No way," Patty says. "Take her to admitting. I'll park the car."

By now, I am not just embarrassed. I am really angry. The nurse at the check-in asks for the insurance card, and as I hand it to her I complain again about how much it hurts to be sitting. Patty comes back, tells the admittance clerk that she is a nurse, and requests that they take me to an examining room immediately. They agree and wheel me away.

I strip and lie down on the table to be examined by the attending doctor, who takes one look and asks the name of my obstetrician. "Call Dr. Gilbertson *now!*" he orders a nurse.

He looks at Patty with one of those "knowing" looks and says, "I'll be taking her into delivery. Is her husband here?"

"He's on his way," I tell him. "She insisted on my calling him an hour ago." I point to Patty and wave goodbye to her as they wheel me into another room. New nurses arrive and one explains to me that a student nurse will prep me for delivery.

Gail, the student nurse, grabs a razor and goes to work. Suddenly, she stands back. "I can't do it. It's too close!"

"Close to what?" I say. "I'm not even in labor yet!" She does not respond and leaves the room.

Another nurse comes in, completes the prep, and lets me know my doctor is on his way, as if to reassure me.

And I am sure that everyone around here is crazy. I remember Sommer's delivery and know that I am a million miles from giving birth.

The next thing I know, I am looking up at Bob.

"Wake up, sleepyhead. We have a baby boy!"

I feel drugged and hear someone mumbling.

"Come on, Kitts. Wake up!" Bob coaxes me. I do not understand what he is saying to me. I just feel tired and want to go back to sleep. Someone brushes my hair off my forehead. "Wake up, sleepyhead." I look up to the voice I just heard. Bob's face comes back into view. "We have a baby boy!" he exclaims.

"We have a boy? I had a baby?" I ask. "When? I don't remember being in labor." The fogginess in my head begins to clear. "How come I didn't have labor pains?"

"This little guy didn't want to wait for a long labor. He decided it was time for him to make his first appearance a little early," a nurse tells me.

"If I was so far dilated, why didn't you let me be awake for the delivery?"

"Your doctor made the call," she said.

"Oh, well. I guess it does not matter. Our little guy is here! When can we see him?" I ask, finally aware and ready to meet my newborn son.

As I finish my question, a nurse appears in the doorway and puts him into my open arms. Bob pulls the blanket away from his little face so we can look at him. He is looking at us, too, and he is beautiful. His eyes are blue and his hair is blond. He resembles my mother. He is a good-sized baby, about six and a half pounds. We open the blanket to check out his little arms and legs and he just lays there silently, looking at us.

He seems so calm. We were so happy he did not have the difficult journey into this world that Sommer did. I look up towards the ceiling and say, "Mom, he looks like you. I hope he has your spirit and your zest for life."

"You played hide and seek with us, little man!" I say to him.

"I have a feeling he's going to keep us on our toes," Bob says as he caresses his little feet.

A few days later, we return home with our new baby to start the next chapter in our life. We had already switched bedrooms, moving out of the smallest room and into a bigger one. That room was too small in the first place for us, but it is perfect for a child. The girls already share the largest bedroom. We purchase a twin-sized bed for Brook, Sommer stays in the crib that Bob slept in when he was a baby, and Jon sleeps in the one we purchased for Brook, four posters, ruffles and all; except that we change all the pink ribbons to blue.

"What are you doing?" I ask the girls as I stand in the doorway to their bedroom. I notice that they are both sitting on the floor, their underpants off, checking their vaginas. Brook looks up and says, "Mommy, how come we don't have a roller like Jon?"

"He's a boy. That's how boys and girls are different," I explain. They find my answer acceptable, put their panties back on, and go about their business. I laugh to myself and can hardly wait to tell Bob. A "roller," they called it - like a pastry roller, I imagine.

Summer comes and goes. Fall follows closely behind. The girls love Jon and take wonderful care of him.

We also have a new litter of Doberman puppies. One day, I find Brook sitting in the whelping pen with Tanya, the puppies' mother, and Joy, Tanya's mother. My heart nearly stops. It is dangerous for anyone to be that close to a mother dog and her babies. To top it off, the fact that Joy joined them in the pen could be dangerous even if Brook were *not* visiting with them. Brook begins to pet the tiny puppies, and I yank her out of the pen by her arm, in a panic. "Never, ever go into a pen where a Mommy dog is nursing her babies! She might bite you," I scold Brook. My heart is racing as I hold her close.

Then, I watch in awe as I witness something I have never seen. Joy, the puppies' grandmother, begins to lick the puppies' bottoms to stimulate their bowels. Incredulous and nervous, I prepare for Tanya to snap at her. Much to my surprise, nothing happens. I have never seen such a lenient and trusting mother dog.

An hour later, I call the dogs out to go potty. They jump out of the whelping pen and exit the house. When they come in, they eat, drink some water, and to my amazement, both jump back into the puppy pen. Tanya lies down and nurses the puppies and Joy lies down close by and cleans them. They do this for three weeks. Many of our fellow dog enthusiast friends come over to witness the unimaginable situation.

Our dogs tolerate all kinds of moderate torture from our kids, never even growling at them. However, one day when one of the girl's friends hit Brook, Tanya growled. Now, when other children are present, all dogs are put into their pens. The dog was just protecting her family, but it is not worth risking a child being hurt.

The next morning, Bob leaves for work and I am making the beds when I hear a moaning noise. I follow the noise and find Jewels, one of our Saint Bernards. She is lying in the middle of the kitchen floor and Brook is sitting on top of her. Jewels groans but makes no effort to get up and move. Sommer, who is two, is sitting by the dog's head, playing with a bucket of toys.

"Jewels, are you okay?" I call to her. She picks up her head, and I notice something hanging out of her mouth. I walk over to her and open it to reveal clothespins pinned to her tongue. Evidently, Sommer had pulled out Jewels' tongue to put the pins on it. All the while the dog never moves, and Brook remains sitting on her back, reading her book. I remove the clothespins from the poor dog's mouth and scold Sommer. Jewels just gives her a big lick, as if to tell me it was no big deal.

These dogs are our children, too. Some of our kids have pointy ears, some slobber everywhere, and some weigh as much as a grown woman, but they are our babies nonetheless, and we are all one big, happy family.

CHAPTER NINE
DAY NINE IN THE HOSPITAL

"Today's the big day!" a nurse calls to me from the doorway.

"Right on!" I reply from my bed.

She enters the room, followed by Dr. Smith. I watch as they prepare a towel on my bedside table and proceed to remove some of my stitches. It takes nearly an hour to complete the job. The removal of the ones behind my ears is especially painful. I do my best not to complain.

"There, that's the last one," he mumbles as he finishes. "There are still a few that are too tender to remove right now. We will take those out in a few more days. There are also many more underneath the skin. Those will dissolve by themselves with time. Time will help erase the scars and soften the memories, too," he adds softly as he puts a comforting hand onto mine. "A little plastic surgery and no one will ever know." Dr. Smith leaves. The nurse folds up the towel and follows him.

I reach for the mirror when the phone rings. "How's it going?" my Dad asks me.

"The doctor took out most of the stitches today," I tell him.

"That's great news! Have you made any decisions about the future? I hope that you give it some time." Dad loves my husband, but then, Dad likes everyone.

Uncharacteristic for my Dad, he begins to ask me questions. "How are you going to manage everything by yourself? You barely have time to get all the work done with the both of you there to do it! I talked to the kids last night. They look forward to your coming home. Do you have any idea when that will be?" he rambles.

"No, Daddy. I have no idea of anything. I am still so baffled about everything. Do you think I can forgive and forget? It's just way too much, isn't it?" But then I stray from the subject before he can respond. "How's your new snow blower doing?" I ask.

"I love it! Yesterday, I cleared off the sidewalks halfway down the block," he says proudly. "The lady living in Jackabowski's house gave me a tie for Christmas. Sometimes, she makes me cookies, too."

"Well, Dad, it sounds like she has a thing for you. Go for it! After all, it's been over five years since Mom died," I tease.

"No, no," he insists. "Your Mom never liked her, anyway." He laughs. "She was sure a beauty, wasn't she?" he asked, wistfully.

He then tells me about all the local news and how my brother is doing. "My Dad and my brother," I think to myself, smiling, "a marriage made in Hell." I just cannot imagine the two of them alone together again.

My brother went to medical school for a time, but his professors decided it was not his forte. He is brilliant at chemistry, though, so he became a pharmacist.

We wrap up our conversation. "I love you, Dad," I say to him. "Goodnight. I'll call you tomorrow."

I am not ready to talk about the decision that I am not even ready to make yet.

As I lay my head back down on my pillow, my mind wanders all over the place. I talk to the kids at least three times a day, and they are truly anxious about me and my situation here in the hospital. Bob's psychiatrist tells me he is not a danger to the children. They now have permission to visit with their father. They tell me they are confused. They love him but wonder if he will still love them. I have no idea what to tell them.

The phone interrupts my thoughts. "Hi, Mom," I say to my mother-in-law. I love her and my father-in-law so very much. I feel terrible for them. As parents, I know they feel at least partly responsible for the actions of their son. Still, they never admit that. They blame his obscure illness instead. They have to hang onto something, I guess.

Sarah asks how I am feeling and proceeds to give me a pep talk about how everything will be just fine. When we say goodbye, I start to wonder how it will ever be "just fine."

Life can never be normal again. I am afraid of him and I wonder how I will feel when I see him. When he talks to me on the phone, he assures me that, someday, it will all be like "just a bad dream." I wish it were just a bad dream, but in reality, it is a horrific, living nightmare. I do not know that I can make myself believe this was an accident or the result of an obscure illness that he never showed signs of previously. He tells me he loves me, He had been so affectionate and so loving in the weeks preceding the incident.

And then, for the first time, a thought goes through my mind that burns a truth I cannot ignore and I will never be able to forget. "He must harbor a deep, deep hate and resentment to have done this -- he tried to *kill* me!" I suspect, with horror, that he was trying to get rid of me so he could keep the business, the property, the show dogs and the kids. I realized, if we split assets in a divorce, he could lose more than half of all of our assets. The twenty thousand dollars we used as a down payment for the kennel came from a settlement for the injuries I sustained in the car accident we had in our ninth year of marriage. Now I have questions -- more and more and more questions. The more I think, the more confused I become, talking myself into and out of what should be obvious at this point.

I close my eyes to rest and feel myself falling asleep when, suddenly, I see his eyes looking down on me, cold and emotionless, like they were that horrible early morning. I scream, "Bob, what are you doing?" He does not answer. I sense his mind working though. He continues his attempt to eradicate me from his life with those cold, emotionless eyes.

"Nina! Nina! You're having a nightmare," someone yells in my face while shaking me.

I jump at the sound of the nurse's words, and she apologizes. "Calm down, dear," she says. She sits down beside me and squeezes me in her arms.

My body shakes uncontrollably and then suddenly goes absolutely limp.

I hear a voice. "Nina, you are safe! Look around you. Do you know where you are?"

I look around and answer, "Yes." I am feeling so cold, and my hands are visibly shaking again. I pull the covers up high around my head as though to protect me rather than to warm me.

"I will give you something to calm you down," my nurse informs me.

As I nod off in response to the medication, I continue to work through everything in my head. In the forefront of my thoughts is the recurring question: "Why does Bob never talk about what happened that night?" He never apologizes. He never says he is sorry. He never acknowledges the gravity of what he did.

The night is slipping away from me as I try to find the answer. I look for it in our ninth year of marriage.

YEAR NINE
OF OUR MARRIAGE

"Where am I?" I ask.

"You're in an ambulance," a voice tells me. "You were in an automobile accident. Do you remember it?"

"No, no, I don't," I say. As I turn my head, I can see that Bob is lying beside me. His eyes are closed, and he is not talking. I can hear the children crying, and Bob begins to moan and mumble that he cannot feel his legs.

"The blood, Mommy, the blood!" the girls cry out to me.

"Don't be frightened," I whisper to them. "Brook, remember months ago when you split your head? It bled and bled, but it was only a little, tiny cut. Remember, honey?"

"Yes," she whimpers weakly.

"My baby, Jon, where is he?" I ask.

"I have him here in my arms. He is fine. All the children are fine. We'll be at the hospital soon," a deeper voice tells me.

I feel as though I am in a tunnel. Voices keep fading in and out. I cannot understand what they are saying, and I am so sleepy.

I call out to anyone who will listen. "Please call my husband's parents in Chicago. They need to know why we are not at their home yet. I cannot seem to remember their number. Why can't I remember their number? I know it as well as my own," I say as I try to keep myself calm.

"Is Jon alright?" I ask again. "He isn't crying. I don't hear him."

"No, he isn't crying. He is just looking around. He is alert, and his eyes are clear," a reassuring voice relays to me. I fall into a peaceful place.

"Wake up! You've got company," someone says in a loud voice into my ear. I look up to see my mother-in-law.

"Mom, we were in an accident," I tell her.

"Yes, dear. I know," she says.

"How did you get here so fast?" I ask.

"Well, I don't think it was so fast," she says. "It's four in the morning."

"Four in the morning?" I try to comprehend the time discrepancy, but I cannot.

"The children, Mom, are they okay?" I question.

"Yes. They have had full X-rays and have been released from the hospital. Your friends from Bloomington, the landlords of your first apartment, the Burns, have taken them to their home for the night. We'll pick them up and take them to your house, where we'll be staying until we know more."

"Is Bob okay?" I ask.

"He will be. He has injured two discs in his back and he will have to wear a brace for a while. He also has whiplash and a broken finger. It was caught in the steering wheel. He will not be able to go to work for a month or so, they tell us. He cannot even take care of the dogs, but his injuries are reparable. He will be released any minute. We'll take him home when we pick up the children."

"Mom, does anyone know what happened? How did we get into an accident?" I ask. "The last thing I remember is that we were driving on Route 29 headed for your house to attend Uncle Riley's funeral."

Mom answers, "Two policeman greeted us when we arrived here at the hospital and they explained what happened. They said that they witnessed the accident from a restaurant they had just exited across the street. They heard tires screeching, looked up and saw a car rounding the bend in the road. One of the cops said to the other one, 'He is going way too fast to stop at that flashing light!' The driver of the car tried, but he could not stop in time.

"Your van was hit as the cops watched. The driver hit you broadside, tearing the door on the passenger side - your door - completely off. The impact sent your van spinning across the road to the other side. You were thrown out and bounced on the pavement like a ball, they said. They thought surely you were dead. The force of the impact caused Jon to bust through the wooden bars of the playpen. He was also thrown from the van and landed on the street in the path of a moving semi, directly between the front wheels. The driver did not run over him but he thought he might have and even after reassuring him, he had to be taken to the hospital by a police officer due to shock."

This explanation helps me put the pieces together, and I begin to awaken. "How is Jon?"

"He's fine," Mom comforts me. "Calm down, dear. I told you they are all going to be okay. Miraculously, the only injury he sustained is to his lower legs. The accident scraped a good deal of skin off them. Nothing is broken, but his legs are heavily bandaged. He won't be able to crawl for a while, so he'll have to be carried for a few weeks."

"The girls. The girls, Mom. How are they?" I ask.

"They'll be okay. They were knocked unconscious on impact. They told the hospital staff that they never saw the accident or heard a thing. They woke up in the car. They have severe whiplash and their necks are all black and blue, but they will be okay. I just spoke with the Burns and the girls are sleeping now. Jon had a bottle of milk that was retrieved from the car and is also sleeping."

"Are they allowed to sleep after being unconscious?" I ask.

"The Burns wake them all up periodically to make sure they are okay. We will pick them up soon and take them home. Right now, we have to make sure *you* are okay," Mom says cheerily.

"Me. Am I okay? What am I still doing here?"

"You suffered a terrific concussion. Your right ear was nearly cut off. Other than some terrible bruising, though, they tell us you appear to be fine. However, they are going to keep you for a few days, just to be sure. Dad is with Bob. Try to get some rest. You are all so lucky. We'll call you later," she says before she gives me a kiss and leaves.

I lay my head on the pillow.

"Wake up. It's nearly nine o'clock," someone sternly says.

I open my eyes and look around, remembering that I am in the hospital. I feel sore all over.

"How about my helping you sit up?" a nurse asks.

"Thank you. I'd love that," I reply. She raises the back of my bed. I cannot move my eyes without becoming dizzy. "You know what?" I say to the nurse, and before she could answer, I say, "I need to get to the restroom. Can you help me? I'm a little unsteady."

"Sure, swing your legs around to this side of the bed. I will help you. Now, stand up. Give yourself some time to get your balance."

As I put my left foot down on the floor, pain shoots up my leg and seems to reach my brain. I try the other foot, and the same thing happens. "I can't," I tell her, "the pain is unbearable!"

"Let me help you back into bed. I'll get you a bedpan and call your doctor."

I sob helplessly. I cannot walk. I cannot even stand up. "Maybe I'm paralyzed!" I cry.

Another nurse comes in with a bedpan and assures me that if I were paralyzed, it would not hurt. I accept her response with relief. A few hours later, a man in hospital garb informs me he is taking me for x-rays, and I am wondering why they have not already been taken. After they are completed, I am returned to my room. Just then, two people come to my door.

"Boy, you look great. I cannot believe it. Look at you now!" The man says as they enter. They both walk toward me. The man extends his hand to shake mine. "I'm Jim Marcusson, and this is my wife, Lily. Do you recognize our voices?"

I shake my head, indicating that I do not.

"We're the people who were in the ambulance with you," he says. "It's a brand new one. Our ambulance company just purchased it, and we had just picked it up from the dealer hours earlier and decided to take it on its with Bob. Try to get some rest. You are all so lucky. We'll call you later," she says before she gives me a kiss and leaves.

I lay my head on the pillow.

"Wake up. It's nearly nine o'clock," someone sternly says.

I open my eyes and look around, remembering that I am in the hospital. I feel sore all over.

"How about my helping you sit up?" a nurse asks.

"Thank you. I'd love that," I reply. She raises the back of my bed. I cannot move my eyes without becoming dizzy. "You know what?" I say to the nurse, and before she could answer, I say, "I need to get to the restroom. Can you help me? I'm a little unsteady."

"Sure, swing your legs around to this side of the bed. I will help you. Now, stand up. Give yourself some time to get your balance."

As I put my left foot down on the floor, pain shoots up my leg and seems to reach my brain. I try the other foot, and the same thing happens. "I can't," I tell her, "the pain is unbearable!"

"Let me help you back into bed. I'll get you a bedpan and call your doctor."

I sob helplessly. I cannot walk. I cannot even stand up. "Maybe I'm paralyzed!" I cry.

Another nurse comes in with a bedpan and assures me that if I were paralyzed, it would not hurt. I accept her response with relief. A few hours later, a man in hospital garb informs me he is taking me for x-rays, and I am wondering why they have not already been taken. After they are completed, I am returned to my room. Just then, two people come to my door.

"Boy, you look great. I cannot believe it. Look at you now!" The man says as they enter. They both walk toward me. The man extends his hand to shake mine. "I'm Jim Marcusson, and this is my wife, Lily. Do you recognize our voices?"

I shake my head, indicating that I do not.

"We're the people who were in the ambulance with you," he says. "It's a brand new one. Our ambulance company just purchased it, and we had just picked it up from the dealer hours earlier and decided to take it on its at that flashing light!' The driver of the car tried, but he could not stop in time.

"Your van was hit as the cops watched. The driver hit you broadside, tearing the door on the passenger side - your door - completely off. The impact sent your van spinning across the road to the other side. You were thrown out and bounced on the pavement like a ball, they said. They thought surely you were dead. The force of the impact caused Jon to bust through the wooden bars of the playpen. He was also thrown from the van and landed on the street in the path of a moving semi, directly between the front wheels. The driver did not run over him but he thought he might have and even after reassuring him, he had to be taken to the hospital by a police officer due to shock."

This explanation helps me put the pieces together, and I begin to awaken. "How is Jon?"

"He's fine," Mom comforts me. "Calm down, dear. I told you they are all going to be okay. Miraculously, the only injury he sustained is to his lower legs. The accident scraped a good deal of skin off them. Nothing is broken, but his legs are heavily bandaged. He won't be able to crawl for a while, so he'll have to be carried for a few weeks."

"The girls. The girls, Mom. How are they?" I ask.

"They'll be okay. They were knocked unconscious on impact. They told the hospital staff that they never saw the accident or heard a thing. They woke up in the car. They have severe whiplash and their necks are all black and blue, but they will be okay. I just spoke with the Burns and the girls are sleeping now. Jon had a bottle of milk that was retrieved from the car and is also sleeping."

"Are they allowed to sleep after being unconscious?" I ask.

"The Burns wake them all up periodically to make sure they are okay. We will pick them up soon and take them home. Right now, we have to make sure *you* are okay," Mom says cheerily.

"Me. Am I okay? What am I still doing here?"

"You suffered a terrific concussion. Your right ear was nearly cut off. Other than some terrible bruising, though, they tell us you appear to be fine. However, they are going to keep you for a few days, just to be sure. Dad is maiden voyage to Minonk to show it off to my brother. We had only been at his house a few minutes when we heard the crash.

"We jumped back into the ambulance and ran to your aid. When we saw you, you were rolled up in a ball on the street with a pool of blood under your head. At first glance, we thought you were probably dead. People who were already on the scene directed us to a semi-truck driver, who was screaming that a baby was under his truck and that he ran over it. Sure enough, there was your son, lying on the pavement between the tires, not under them. He did not make a sound when we grabbed him. His legs were bleeding but he did not cry at all. We presumed that he was in shock. We wrapped him in a blanket and gave him to someone close by to hold while the police helped us assist the rest of you.

"We went to check on the driver, your husband, and found him unconscious. That is when we discovered the two girls in the back of the van, also unconscious, but they began to stir as soon as we opened the door. We then ran over to you and discovered that you were still alive, but your pulse was very slow. We placed you in the ambulance and then placed your husband next to you. The girls had woken up by then, so we squashed them and the baby in front with us.

"Ideally, it would be better to have two ambulances to evacuate all of you, but the closest ambulance couldn't get to our rural area for thirty minutes. We knew that in that amount of time, we could have you in the hospital. We are here to see how you all made out. I never expected to see you still alive, let alone sitting up in bed. I feel like I'm looking at a real-life miracle."

Lily says, "When you were in the ambulance, you would regain consciousness now and then and comfort the girls because they were terribly frightened and crying. Your head was soaked with blood, so we wrapped it in a towel, but it seeped through and traumatized them. You would speak very calmly to soothe them, reminding them that sometimes the tiniest of cuts bleeds like crazy and that you were all going to be fine. Then you would pass out again.

"Your husband woke up about halfway to the hospital and instructed us to call some friends of yours, the Burns, who lived in Bloomington, where the hospital was located, and also to call his parents in Chicago. Then he passed out, too. I do not think I have ever witnessed a more memorable emergency than this one. Looking back at the scene of your accident, I'd have guessed there to be at least one fatality, but, well, look at you!"

I thank them for their kindness. They wish me good luck and leave.

A doctor comes in with my x-rays and tells me that my pelvis is broken completely in half. It is a very clean break, so with complete bed rest, he is confident that it will heal itself without surgery. He says they will take new x-rays in few days to check the progress. He tells me to plan to stay for two weeks, at which point they might move me to a hospital in Peoria.

I settle in and try to absorb it all, but my thoughts keep going back to the day before, when we were loading up the van for the journey. Bob arrived home from the hospital late, as he did often, always explaining that his patient load was getting heavier. He began loading our things into the van. He jammed a twin mattress into the far back for the girls, allowing room for Jon's wooden playpen to sit in front of the mattress and immediately behind us in the front seats. I helped the girls up into their quarters and placed John into his playpen.

"Oh, dear! Bob, my seatbelt has fallen behind the seat and is under the playpen. I'll get Jon out so you can find it," I said.

"Like hell! If you think I am going to tear this shit out, you have another thing coming! You will just have to do without it. Get your rear in the car. We are late. Let's go!" he demanded.

"What the hell is wrong with you?" I yelled back at him. "We wouldn't be in this rush if you weren't so late coming home from work *again*!" That dialogue plays inexplicably over and over again in my head.

"Well, you are all alone here now. Your family just left the hospital," a nurse, tells me.

Bob does not come to say goodbye to me or, as a matter of fact, come in to see me at all. I assume he just has too much on his mind, but it still hurts my feelings.

"Thank you, Mama," I say, my face to the ceiling. Even though my Mom passed on a few years ago, I still feel her presence whenever I am stressed. She could not prevent the accident, but I know she woke me in the ambulance to comfort the children. I feel her hand caressing my face, as it did in her living years. "Thank you, Mommy, for giving me strength." I feel myself relaxing, knowing that I am not alone.

"Breakfast time! Rise and shine!" someone calls to me. I look up and see a nurse who throws open the shade and cranks up my bed. She pushes a tray in front of me and leaves the room.

I close my eyes and try to remember what the hell just happened. It quickly comes back to me. I remember where I am and why. I reach for the cup and smell it, that delightful morning scent of coffee. I drink that cup, push the call button for another and proceed to eat my meal.

As my tray is taken away the phone rings. It is my husband, and he tells me that my in-laws decided to take the children with them back to their home in Chicago, where other family members can help care for them. Three young kids is quite a handful for two grandparents, especially when one child must be carried everywhere.

Bob explains that he is not able to lift anything and cannot do any work. Friends of friends we do not know well have come forward to offer their help. Employees from several area kennels come over and pick up some of the dogs to board at their kennels until we recover. Other friends make up a schedule to feed, water and clean for the next month. Amazing people surround and support us.

Two weeks after the accident, I am still in the hospital and Bob is able to return to work with a very restricted workload. Instead of moving me to a hospital in Peoria, I am moved to a hospital bed in our living room. My in-laws bring the children back and Mom stays to help us for a week.

The day after I return home, Dr. McNamara comes to check up on me in my new quarters. Mac is an orthopedic specialist, but because he is our family friend, we have asked him to be our family physician until we recover from the accident injuries.

"Hi, Nina. I'm here to check up on you, lady," Mac says. "Okay, let's listen to your heart and lungs. Loosen up your pajama top," he instructs me.

As I unbutton, his face breaks into a cocky smile and pointing to my small breasts, he looks up to my husband and says, "Well, Bob, I see that you must have married her for money!"

"Damn you, Mac!" I say, and we all laugh.

A week later, I am up and going, and two weeks later, Bob is back at work full-time. Only four weeks after the accident, our life returns to normal. All the dogs are brought back and our friends are more than happy not to have to scoop poop anymore. Bob and I have finally healed, and our children are flourishing.

Brook is four and a half. She is the only one of us with brown hair, which is beautiful and hangs to her waist. She has blue eyes, just like the rest of us. Sommer is three and a half. She is tall and willowy, soft and gentle. Jon is one and a half. He is cute and spoiled and demands everyone's attention. All it took was two and a half weeks of being carried around for him to learn that traveling from one set of arms to another is the best mode of travel. He has become a "Mommy's boy," as Bob calls him.

We feel that God has blessed our family richly and beyond anything we could have ever imagined. We lived through a situation that many would not have survived and I just hope we can do justice to the opportunities we have been given. Life is good.

CHAPTER TEN
DAY TEN
IN THE HOSPITAL

"Ahhh," I say as I open my mouth as wide as I can. Dr. Perry, our family dentist, is looking inside to see if he can discover the source of my pain. My face and the inside of my mouth have been hurting, and so far, no one can locate the problem. Dr. Perry has been advised that I have severe fractures in many of my facial bones, so he expects that I will experience a substantial amount of pain for a while. However, with each passing day, the pain should be subsiding. Instead, it is becoming worse.

"Nina, for the life of me, I can't locate any problems. None of your teeth are missing. I checked the x-rays that you had taken this morning and see no dental cause for your discomfort. As soon as you are released, I want to see you in my office. I have more powerful x-ray equipment there. You may have lateral fractures of the roots and those are damn hard to see. I will prescribe something for your pain. Hopefully, it will keep you comfortable until your appointment. Call my office as soon as you know when they are going to release you."

He pats my hand and leaves.

"Hey, girl! Looks like you are back on the pain meds," a nurse says as she places a pill onto the palm of my outstretched hand.

"I hope this helps," I say. I watch the nurse leave and notice that her silhouette looks fuzzy, like a camera out of focus. The vision in my left eye is still not focusing properly, but with each day that passes I notice a slight improvement.

I close my eyes, waiting for the pain pill to do its job. Maybe it will also dull the pain I am still experiencing on the backside of my ears. I cannot lay my head down on either side while I am sleeping. When I do, I am jolted awake with excruciating pain. Almost all the stitches have been removed from behind my ears, but there are places that are still oozing fluid, and they are very, very sore. I can barely touch them.

The phone rings and again, I jump. "Hi, Kitts," Bob whispers. "I've been released from the hospital. They have decided that I am mentally healthy and am not a danger to anyone anymore. I have to watch my diet carefully. You had better believe that I will definitely do that. This disease, hypoglycemia, can make people do irrational things. My doctor also tells me I can spend time with our kids, too. Please give me time. You will realize I am healthy. You will feel safe with me again and we can be a family again. Doesn't that sound wonderful? I am not pushing you, hon. I know it will take time. You can go back to live in our house when you are released and the kids can come visit me in the apartment. I will keep it until you feel safe, no matter how much time it takes. I miss the kids, and I miss you. Soon, this will all be over. I love you, Kitts."

"I don't know what to say," I answer. And that is the absolutely truth.

"I love you. Think this over. I need you and the kids," he repeats and hangs up.

My tears make my vision worse than it already is.

"This will all be over," I say quietly out loud. I repeat his words again and again. "How can this be over?" I ask myself. "This *what*? He has still never admitted to anything!"

And now my mind is going again: "His psychiatrist assures him he is no longer a danger to me and especially to the children, but I do not understand how he can know that. I am worried about what will happen if he does not follow his diet. He has seen some doctor for ten days, and that is all it takes for him to determine he is safe and that this illness caused this tragedy. I have known him for almost twenty years, and he sure fooled me. He also fooled his lie detector test. His doctor clearly does not know the whole story, only Bob's side of it.

"I am scared. I am scared to death. I can hardly even talk to him. I do not know how I can ever live with him again. I will be terrified to turn my back to him. I wonder, if I do not take him back, if he would hurt the children to get back at me? The Bob I thought I knew and loved with all of my being is gone. Our life, as it was, is now over. I cannot imagine life with him again, but I also cannot imagine life without him. I am terrified of my best friend, my lover, my entire life.

"I am afraid of everything now. I am even afraid to be alone in my room. I have to leave the bathroom light on and the door slightly ajar so I am not completely in the dark. I have never been like this in my life. I have never been frightened of the dark."

I start feeling the effects of the pain medication and I welcome the relaxation and calm. Before I fall into the deep sleep that has protected me for these ten days here in the hospital, I force myself to focus, to recall what happened in our tenth year of marriage.

Ah, yes. I remember.

YEAR TEN
OF OUR MARRIAGE

Several weeks after the car accident, I return home from my check-up and make dinner for my family.

"How did Mac say you were doing, hon?" Bob asks me as we clear the dinner table.

"He said that I was healing beautifully. I asked him when he thought it would be possible for us to have sex again. He told me anytime we think we're ready."

Bob laughs, puts his arms around me, and whispers, "What about tonight?"

Afterward, we lay on the bed, exhausted. A few minutes later, Bob snuggles up to me and says, "It'll be a long time before I try that again!"

"You better believe it!" I add as we laugh.

After another month, I begin to wonder if our healing bodies have caught up with us yet and we are ready for a little romance, again. I am thankful to not be on my period when I realize that I have not had one since the car accident. I brush it off and assume the trauma caused me to be irregular.

As Bob walks into the house from work, I mention it to him. "It's too soon to call Dr. Gilbertson, anyway," I say. "I'll wait a couple weeks and see what happens, or doesn't happen for that matter."

Two weeks later, my period still has not started. I make an appointment with Dr. Gilbertson, who confirms that I am, indeed, pregnant again. All it took was that one time.

Bob can hardly contain his excitement. "Only once, and I did it! I'm a baby making machine!" he gloats.

Dr. Gilbertson sends me to an orthopedic surgeon to make sure my hopefully healed pelvis will hold up under the stress of a pregnancy. "Hell, how should I know? I haven't delivered a baby since I was an intern!" he barks. "Your obstetrician is more capable of making that judgment than I am."

It is difficult to feel secure about my pregnancy when I leave his office. I am already in my third month, and the veins on my legs are blue and as large as fingers, protruding from under my once smooth skin. "Most of the time, those veins go away after delivery. Every once in a while, they don't," my OB informs me. "I still can't believe you're pregnant. That little bit of an ovary I left in you sure is potent!"

The months pass slowly and it is difficult this time. I am in and out of the doctor's office and have at least a dozen emergency room visits. First, it is the usual spotting, and then comes the toxemia. I am swollen like a blowfish and experience regular cramping. I feel like my body is threatening to abort our baby. My doctor sends me to two other obstetricians for their opinions about delivering with my pelvic condition.

My doctor is the chief of obstetrics at the hospital, and even *he* is sending me for second opinions. I find these consultations alarming and unsettling. On top of that, I am so very busy that I cannot even imagine how I will be able to handle another child plus the two kennels and all the other responsibilities I am handling that surround the dog showing and breeding business.

As I sit at the kitchen table with a glass of Kool-Aid for a couple minutes before I get back to it, I think back to ten years before, when my main concern was the type of designing job I would find. Then the winds of change blew me in an entirely different direction. I never even thought about having children. I was always so goal-oriented. I was willing to put my dreams aside temporarily, but temporarily has turned out to be forever. I do not have regrets. Everything just fell into place so naturally, and I fell right in line with it. I really love being a Mommy.

"*No more* children for you, little lady. The toxemia, the bleeding, and the veins are telling us to pay attention to what your body is saying. And it is saying, *no more*," my doctor warns.

I am due Fourth of July weekend, 1969. By the week of my due date, my shoe size has shot from an 8.5 narrow to a 10 wide. The only shoes that fit me are slippers. Bob's parents come into town on the third in the hopes that they will be here when the baby arrives. The fourth, Friday, comes and goes with no labor and no baby. Saturday, the fifth, does the same.

On the night of the sixth, I awake, realizing I am lying in a puddle of water. It is four in the morning, and my water has broken. "Mom, Dad, wake up! My water broke and made a mess on the sheets. will you take them off and put them in the washing machine, please? We're going to the hospital," I ask my in-laws.

My labor pains are close and hard, very different from my other pregnancies. As soon as we rush into the hospital the pain becomes constant. The nurses prep me and I cannot hold back the groans but try.

"Shhh, shhh," Bob whispers.

"I'm barely making a sound!" I say to him, incredulous at his insensitivity. "Listen to the other women in labor. They're screaming!"

"I'm sorry, Kitts," he whispers. "I'm just not used to you making any noise while you're in labor."

Dr. Gilbertson enters my room and examines me. "Looks like you are just about ready." He nods to one of the nurses in the room. Suddenly she arrives with a cart.

"Are you able to slide onto the cart?" the nurse asks.

I do as she asks, and a few seconds later, I feel the bumps between the floor tiles as we pass over them. "Hey, is there no smoother floor?" I yell, in pain and irritated.

We finally enter a delivery room. A mask is strapped to my face and I relax.

I open my eyes. I am no longer in pain. I try to sit up, but I cannot. The room is spinning around me as I focus on the ceiling.

"You did great, Kitts! You did it!" I hear as Bob squeals into my ear. "Another boy! Now we have two of each, a perfect family!"

"I had a boy?" I ask Bob as I continue to awaken from the anesthesia. "Is he okay?"

"Yep. He is *huge*; nine pounds! He has a cleft in his chin just like mine and he looks just like me!" he boasts. "I love you, Kitts." He kisses me as a nurse places a big baby wrapped in a blue blanket into my arms.

I pull back the top and look into his beautiful, round face with the Bob's deep clefted chin. He is sleeping peacefully. We decided months ago to name him Ericson. I smell him. I love the smell of my newborns. I notice his hands are so much longer than my other babies' were. He wiggles as I touch them and quietly goes back to sleep.

Bob runs a hand over Eric's blond hair. "I sure can't deny him. Look at that chin! Dr. Gilbertson said Eric was delivered easily and with no complications. He then cautioned me we should not even think of more children. We won this battle and might not be so lucky the next time. I could hear the relief in his voice when he told me everything went smoothly. I guess he was worried about you and the baby. He is right. Why have any more? We are perfectly balanced now, two and two!

"I'm going back to the house so that my parents can head back to Chicago. They were supposed to leave this morning but when you went into labor, they offered to stay and take care of the kids. It's late afternoon, so I'm going to skedaddle home, call the babysitter, and see them off. I am sure they will be stopping here to check out our newest before they leave Peoria. Go back to sleep honey," he whispers to me. "Soon sleep won't be easy to come by." He kisses me and leaves for home, and the nurse pops in behind him.

I rest my head on the pillow as she picks up Eric to take him to the nursery. "I'll bring that big, beautiful boy in to see his Mommy again in a few minutes," she announces in a singsong voice and leaves with him.

I drift off into the remnants of the anesthesia. It seems like only a few minutes later that I feel something on my chest and wake up to Eric in my arms. He is sleeping, so I close my eyes, too. We are both safe now that he has been born. It has been a very long, hard nine months. I am exhausted.

"Hello, Mama!" a voice says to me. I looked up to see a smiling Dr. Gilbertson. "Well, we made it! The delivery went smoothly. However, I did have an orthopedic surgeon standing by just in case I ran into a problem with your pelvis. We did not experience any problems, though. I must remind you that you are <u>not</u> to get pregnant again. This pregnancy was dangerous for both of you. Frankly, I am surprised that you both made it to term. Thankfully, both of you are healthy. *No more babies for you!*"

"All right; all right," I say and nod in agreement. I am sick of hearing it. I am also tired of the doctor and hospital visits and never knowing if I will miscarry or deliver too soon. He does not need to worry about me getting pregnant again. I've had enough.

"You know, one of these days when I retire, I'll write a book. I will devote one chapter to you, and it will be about how a woman can get pregnant so many times with a dwarfed and tilted uterus, severe endometriosis, and only a quarter of one ovary. It is mind boggling, but you had three babies!"

His face turns solemn. "From now on, I only want to see you for regular, yearly visits. Do you understand?"

And I understand, completely. I shake my head in agreement.

He continues, "You will probably not beat the odds next time and you don't strike me as a foolish person. We are going to keep you in the hospital for about a week. I want to make sure that your pelvis is strong enough to handle the demands of the other three children. I'll write up the orders and see you tomorrow." He softens up, smiles at me, and leaves.

The week is full of phone calls to and from the kids, Bob and our friends. I feel like a queen. My baby is always brought to me so nice and clean. I give him his bottle and then we take a peaceful, restful nap together.

I think of my kids at home. I miss them so very much. Brook is preparing to attend kindergarten when school starts.. Sommer is a year and a half younger and is loving, gentle and obedient. Jon, who is two, even bosses her around sometimes.

Despite my desire to see my other children, these days in the hospital are going by way too quickly. It is wonderful not to have to cook or do dishes. I am able to order all my meals from a menu, and order I do - extra-large portions of everything. The bad news is that I eat it all. One day, supper comes in on three trays and I realize I am over doing it. But boy, am I enjoying it!

I love the quality time with my new son, too, just the two of us. I cherish the hours I spend cuddling him, kissing him, and whispering into his sweet, tiny ears. I realize we will never have this volume of quality time alone together when we go home.

"This scale can't be right!" I tell the nurse. "Take me to another one." I step on the next one and shock everyone once again. I delivered a nine-pound baby last week, and I am leaving the hospital weighing one pound more than when I was admitted. I smile sheepishly at my nurse thinking, "I'll bet she tells the entire hospital of my gluttony. It'll take me six months to take the pounds off, I'm sure!"

On my last day in the hospital, the phone rings, and I answer the call from our friend Dr. McGinn. "Hi, Jack," I answer. "I'm not even home yet and I'm already dreading those late night feedings after listening to the demands of three other little people all day."

"Well, a baby that size doesn't even need a night-time bottle. Just put his bassinette into a room far away from yours. When he wakes up, he will cry for a bit and then off to sleep he will go. We do it all the time," he tells me. As a doctor and a father of six, I assume he must know this business well.

"I can't believe we never heard of this method before!" I say to Bob. On our first night at home, we push the bassinette into the kitchen. "I'm sure I'll hear him cry," I say to Bob, and we retire in our own bedroom for the night.

It seems like only minutes later that I sit up in bed, realizing it is morning. I see the sun shining and peeking through the shades and instantly panic. "Oh my God! The baby!"

We both rush into the kitchen. Eric is sleeping like an angel. "My God! It worked. We'll do it again tonight," Bob says.

We do it every night for a week, and then we move him back into our room. He never wakes up during the night after that. A couple of weeks later, I call Dr. McGinn to thank him for his advice. He listens silently on the other end of the line. "I was only kidding with you, Nina. We never did that our kids! I cannot believe that you did that! Holy shit!" he laughs at our stupidity. Hey, it worked for us!

The next two months fly by. It is time for Brook's first day of kindergarten. "Mommy, Mommy, here it comes!" she cries out, pointing to the yellow bus approaching. She is so thrilled. Her blue eyes are dancing with excitement.

My heart pounds so loudly that I am sure it can be seen pulsating through my sweater. My first baby is going off to school. I am giving her up to the world, to strangers who I have to hope will guide and teach her properly and safely. It is my first experience of letting a child go. And it is breaking my heart.

The bus door opens, and she climbs up the stairs. She has been looking forward to this day. She turns to me and blows me a kiss. "I love you, Mommy!" she sings to me as she runs to a seat and the bus pulls away. Tears flow from my eyes as I watch the bus until it turns a corner and disappears from sight. With no need to be brave any longer, I openly sob. As I walked the long driveway back up to the house, I pass a bush, and a bird flies out of it. I timidly peek into the bush and notice a nest. It is empty. I imagine that a few months ago, a mother bird had to let her babies take their first flight, as my Brook did today.

As I reach the house, I race to answer the ringing phone. "Well, did she get off okay?" Bob asks. I begin crying so hard that I cannot speak. "It'll get easier every day," he reassures me.

A few months later, Brooks' teacher calls me on the phone to tell me about what Brook had done minutes earlier. It is show and tell day and the students took turns sharing stories about the items they brought to class. When it was Brook's turn, she stood at the front of the classroom empty-handed. At first, her teacher thought she forgot to bring something to share. But then, Brook put her hands on her hips, she addressed her class:

"I just want you all to see what a special child looks like. *I* am a special child because *I* am adopted. Your parents had to take what they got, but my parents *chose* me!"

I laugh and laugh. It is so like Brook to be so confident and assertive, and it makes me so happy that she is proud to have been adopted. She does not really know what it means, but it makes her feel so special. She is secure in our love.

I pour myself a cup of coffee and reflect on the past year. My brother, Joe, is attending a prestigious college in Chicago. It is a forty-minute train ride from home but he lives on campus. He comes home on weekends often. Joe plans on becoming a Doctor of Medicine. He is so spoiled that Dad won't even let him have a summer job. He might hurt his hands. Give me a break! I had to work 2 jobs!

The kids are all doing great and love to play on their new outdoor playground equipment and the old semi-truck tire we filled with sand. The messes, laundry and baths are all worth it.

I look to the plot of land next to our home and watch the architects scurrying around with their pads of paper, sketching blueprints for our next project. Our big dream of owning and running a modern and beautiful boarding kennel is finally coming true. The Abbey will be equipped so that each dog will have its own indoor and outdoor quarters. A plexiglass door will open with the pull of a chain, permitting the dog to go outside for cleaning purposes or just to leave the window open to allow them to run in and out, as they please. It will be air conditioned and heated; even the floors will have heat coils under the concrete. It will have upper berths for the small dogs and lower runs for the large breeds and will be, we decided, the *best* kennel in the United States. We hope to build early next year. The twenty thousand dollars we settled on from the car accident, mainly due to my injuries, will be the down payment. The plan is for me to manage it. I will have to hire full-time help at our home to babysit and keep the house clean while I work next door at the kennel. Since I will only be fifty feet from the house, I can run back and forth, as I am needed.

These days, our show dogs have been taking home quite a few big wins in the show ring. Bob attends the dog shows with our professional handler, Clint Gander. They enter mainly in our part of the country, the Midwest. Weekends usually find me at home. We hired high school kids to help us with kennel cleaning, so I try to find time to enjoy the kids.

"Hey, Mom! You can't do that!" Jon yells at me.

"Yes I can!" I yell back as I enter the house carrying third base with me. "I just stole third base, and I'm taking it with me. I'm done playing for today."

I played three games of whiffle ball with Jon and the girls while the kennel kids worked. Their shift is over now, and I have housework to do. I have to feed the dogs and then find the time to fill out certified pedigree papers for the owners of our new puppies, always a tedious job. On especially busy days, I also have to interview potential new owners of our puppies and then clean our house and cook for four children. It is starting to become overwhelming and I am running out of energy. I feel like I am a hamster on a wheel and I cannot jump off of it. I cannot even remember the last time I read the kids a book, let alone played with them or spent real quality time with them. I immediately put that thought out of my mind because the hamster wheel must keep spinning.

We now have six Saint Bernards, two adult Dobermans and two Dobe puppies, which we kept out of the last litter. They are about two months old now. It is time they need to be trained for the show ring. I have no idea when I am supposed to find time to do that, but I know I will.

One day, as I scoop the Dobermans puppies' poop, I notice that they have diarrhea. I go back to the house, grab some Kaopectate, and pour it down their unwilling throats. Diarrhea could be an indicator of several health issues, some serious, so I figure it is best to be safe rather than sorry.

"Tomorrow, I'll take a stool sample to the vet to make sure it's not a serious problem," I think.

These two puppies are the product of our own beautiful Doberman, Joy. We drove her to Ohio to be bred to the top Doberman Champion in the country. The stud fee was enormous, but we had a litter of seven. We kept two and sold two of them for show possibilities as they had exceptional bodies. The other three do not have the same promise but many a dog breeder has made the mistake of selling a pup as pet quality only for it to turn into a great Champion. At this age, it is a calculated guessing game.

Bob arrives home late from a dog show. "Honey, the Dobe puppies have loose stools. I'm taking samples to the vet in the morning," I tell him. "I'm worried."

The next morning, Bob comes into the house with a concerned look after scooping and feeding at the kennel. "Their stools are bloody," he says. "I'll run a sample over to the vet and leave it at the door so he can check it right away."

The veterinarian calls shortly after eight. "Can you bring the pups in?" he asks me. "It doesn't look good."

I load up all four children and the pups, and we are at the clinic within an hour.

After checking them he announces, "They have distemper."

I freeze, and the word "distemper" rings in my ears. "Distemper is usually a deadly disease," I say to him. "Are they going to die?"

"It looks serious," he replies in a soft, low voice.

"They had their shots two weeks before their ear cropping. Wasn't that enough time for immunity?" I ask. "You were supposed to vaccinate them a couple of weeks earlier, but you said you were out of the vaccine. You said that there was still plenty of time to spare for the shots to be effective. What happened? Are they going to die?" I demand an answer.

He does not answer and says he does not know. I start to cry, which makes the girls cry in turn. We leave the clinic with medicine to administer in hopes of saving them.

After dinner, Bob calls the new owners of the other Doberman puppies. They are all experiencing the same symptoms. Over the next few days, we remain in daily contact with all of them. Every day and every night, we cry with the families about those poor puppies, which all must each be euthanized, including ours. We assume that when we drove all of them to Chicago to a specialist to have their ears cropped, they were exposed to the virus.

I have seen quite a few litters of Doberman puppies. We thought this was the *one*, the special one. Their heads and bodies were elegant and strong. "Truly a miracle litter," I had said only a month ago.

We refund all the fees and pay all the vet bills. Our reimbursement expenses are tenfold the purchase price of each puppy.

We talk to an attorney about the possibility of suing the veterinarian who surgically trimmed their ears and gave them their shots, along with the drug company that manufactured the serum. He tells us that each of them is pointing fingers at each other and even at us. We do not pursue it, but instead switch veterinarians, both general and specialist.

Our hearts break for the losses suffered by the poor families who bought our puppies. It feels as if a part of our hearts has died with them. We did all the right things, yet it went so very wrong.

Bob is worn down with grief. Somehow, we both know that the magic this litter promised is something we will never see again.

CHAPTER ELEVEN
DAY ELEVEN
IN THE HOSPITAL

"Ah," I say as the liquid flows down my throat. "This is what the doctor ordered." I laugh. "How did you get permission to pull this off?" I ask Ann.

"I had Jack call and ask Dr. Smith if it's okay. He told me that even though you are still on light pain medication, you are not to be driving anywhere. One martini won't hurt."

"Remember when I started this tradition, Ann?"

"Yep," she answers. "I think it's been about eight years now."

"I started it, you just remember that," I brag. "You were in the hospital with one of your bronchitis attacks and were going to be released the next day. I called your husband and asked him what he thought about my idea. He said that you were off the heavy stuff, so it would be fine as long as I was not caught. He gave me the number of your friend and head nurse, Katie, so she could help. I planned with Katie to arrive at five o'clock for happy hour. She would be ending her shift then and wanted to join us. I arrived on time and tapped on her desk, signaling that I was ready.

"I entered your room with a round bud vase holding a beautiful red rose. You told me it was the most beautiful rose you had ever seen. I told you it was not just beautiful, but medicinal. You looked confused. Just then, Katie entered the room with three plastic drinking glasses and a water pitcher full of ice.

"I removed the rose from the vase and told you it wasn't water in the vase; it was martinis! We filled the glasses with ice and martinis and Katie and I told you how we pulled off the caper. We talked and laughed for about half an hour until your dinner arrived." I reminisce.

"How many times have we pulled this off?" Ann asks me.

"Maybe eight," I answer. "Those were the days." We enjoy our martinis and giggle as we fill the empty vase with water and put the rose back in it.

We talk about everything except the reason I am here. We laugh a lot. Ann goes home an hour later to feed her brood of six and her husband. I am served my dinner. I eat and as I finish my meal, I notice that the calming effect of the drink has worn off, and I am no longer at ease.

I am emotionally back in the real world and in my terrifying reality. I feel so lonely in this large, empty room. I should be home with the love of my life, reminding the kids to make sure that their homework is finished. Bob should be laughing and teasing me. Instead, we are *all* lonely and frightened in our own ways. Bob is in some empty apartment. The children are separated and not living in their own home. I realize that we will never know that sound of home and happiness again. And I am overtaken with the need to connect with someone safe.

My hand, almost automatically, picks up the telephone receiver. I dial Andrea. "Hi, Andrea," I say. "How are the girls?"

"They're fine," she answers. "They went out to the drug store with Bob to pick up a prescription and some ice cream. Would you like me to have them call you when they get back?"

"Not if they still have homework to do. Have them call me tomorrow before they leave for school. I can't thank you enough, dear friend," I say.

I call Joyce Crawford, who is taking care of my boys next. We see much more of Andrea's family because of our common interest in dogs than we do of Joyce's. I know that the boys are having a more difficult time because of that and the fact that they are younger than the girls. I have never been away from any of them for longer than three days. It has been eleven, and the doctors tell me it could be several more before I am released. I realize how frightened they must be and I am so heartbroken for what we are all going through emotionally.

I hope that by the time I am released, the bruises will be gone. My head is bald and my hair definitely will not be back by then. One of my friends has offered to loan me a wig with hair the color of mine own, but it hurts when I wear it even for just a few minutes; the wounds are still too fresh. I will have to wear a scarf. I know the children will be frightened when they see me. I honestly am not sure how I will handle that. As I imagine that moment, the phone rings and I answer it.

"Mommy, I want to come home right now," Jon demands of me. "We've been here too long."

"But you always love playing with Doug!" I tell him.

"I'm tired of him!"

"What did you have for supper?" I ask, changing the subject.

"Fried chicken. Mrs. Crawford makes real good fried chicken."

"I can't come home for a few days yet. You can last that long, can't you?"

He does not answer but instead asks me if he can sleep with me when I get home, like Eric will.

"Of course. I will keep you very close to me," I reply.

"Will Daddy be home, too?" he asks.

"No," I answer, "but you'll get to see him and sleep with him, too."

"Let me have the phone!" I can hear Eric as he tries to pull the phone away.

"Let it go," Jon says.

"Jon, please let Eric talk to me, too."

"Hi, Mommy," Eric's little four-year-old voice whispers, "I love you, Mommy. Can Mrs. Crawford fix chicken for you when you come home? It's real, real good!"

Evidently, Joyce overheard their conversation. She shouts to Eric, "Of course I'll fix chicken for her!"

"I heard what she said, baby. I can almost smell it from here."

"Give me back the phone!" Jon yells as he grabs the phone back. "Mommy, can I read a bedtime story to you on the phone?"

"No, because you still have to take a bath, but when I get home you can read to me, okay? I love you."

Nighty nights are exchanged and I lay the phone down in its cradle. I know that the boys do not understand our situation at all. They are just too young. The girls are older and they know what happened. I do not know that I will even be able to make any of them feel secure again when I do not even feel secure myself.

I wish I were tired enough to sleep, but instead, I lie wide awake, thinking, thinking, thinking, and remembering our eleventh year of marriage.

YEAR ELEVEN OF OUR MARRIAGE

"Cars are already in the parking lot," I say to Bob, who is just finishing up with some final touches in the grooming room, while I excitedly peek through the drapes covering the new kennel window.

It is finally the big day. The Abbey Boarding and Grooming Kennel is open for business, and it is the classiest and most modern pet kennel in the area. The local newspaper has already been here earlier this week to do a feature on our new business, devoting almost an entire page to the kennel which they deemed homey, sanitary, and "as close to home as a kennel can be." We had billboards erected announcing the opening a month ago and thankfully, it looks like people have seen them.

"Welcome! Come in. Please look around," we say as we usher potential customers into our fabulous building.

I can hear Bob explaining to a family, "Of course, you may bring his bed and toys. Let me also point out that the floors are heated. There are heating coils inside the concrete floors. During the winter, none of the animals lay on cold concrete. The temperature is not hot, but warm, just enough to take away the cold and dampness. During the summer, it is air-conditioned. We use power equipment to clean and sanitize the walls and floors. Music is playing all day and night to aid in relaxation."

"Hell, I'm staying here, honey. You take the kids and dog on vacation!" a man jokes to his wife.

The open house is a huge success and we are proud of making yet another dream come true.

Each day, before the kennel opens for business and before the children wake, I run next door and pull the chains that open the Plexiglas doors to allow the dogs to go outside to play and exercise while I sanitize the inside. I give them fresh water and run back to the house to ready the girls for school. Then, while I am dressing the girls, Bob cleans, feeds, and waters our own show dogs.

I send the girls off to school on the school bus, dress the boys, and wait for Mrs. Flory to arrive. I hired her to be a housekeeper and babysitter from nine in the morning until five in the afternoon daily. Sometimes, she starts supper for me, too.

By the time she arrives at nine, The Abbey has been cleaned inside and out, and I am dressed and ready to open for the day. Mrs. Flory is so excellent at keeping the house in order and seems to love her job. There are days that when she arrives, she stands in the doorway to the kitchen, and yells, "What have you done to *my* kitchen?" I laugh and explain that if I could keep it perfect, I would not need her.

At nine o'clock, I open the doors of The Abbey for business. "Let me see," I say, talking to myself as I look for the frozen chicken for just one of the many dogs. "Smoky is in number eleven, and he gets stewed chicken mixed with his special dry dog food blend."

Some dogs we board require special diets, and I always abide by those rules. Once I have the animals fed, I begin to prepare the chicken and eggs I cook every few days to be added to the dry mixture for our show dogs. One of our friends works for a dairy, and he has to take the eggs and cottage cheese off of the shelves of stores if they have not been sold by the date stamped on the carton. He brings the old products to us to add to our dry dog food. Although the products are out of date for humans, they are still safe for our show dogs and are an important part of their diet.

I cook the eggs and mash them, shells and all. It gives them beautiful coats of hair. I then over-cook twenty pounds of bone-in chicken every couple of days in a pressure cooker, mash it and add it to the eggs and dry food formula. We also add calcium and cod liver oil to boost nutrition. Our show dogs, which by now total twenty, eat like the Champions we want them to be.

One day out of the blue and with no prior communication, a woman named Nora Daton walked into the Abby and said she needed a job. She lived right across the street and she could be available as soon as her kids left for school. I looked up to the sky and said "Thank you, God, I need a part-time receptionist." I hired her on the spot. Nora is a gift! Now I will have time again to work on pedigrees, cleaning, sales, etc. I may have a little time to breathe.

"Hi, Terry," I say as I welcome her. Terry is our dog groomer. To say she is quite eclectic would be an understatement. She is a full-figured lady and I use the term, "lady," loosely. She is as wild as her bleached, white-blond, punk rock hair, which looks as though she put her finger into an electrical socket. It stands on end. Having said that, I must admit that she is one of the best dog groomers in the country!

As I walk through the food storage room, I glance at the sulky we made for our Saint Bernards to haul little children. As part of one of our advertising programs, we welcome field trips of kindergarteners from area schools. We introduce them to our Saint Bernards and sometimes permit them to bottle-feed new puppies. We give all of them, two at a time, a ride in the sulky pulled by one of our gentle giants. The children love their visits and usually deliver albums of pictures they drew of their special day when they return to school. I save each one of them as a remembrance to look back on years from now.

I look at the clock, and it is almost three, time for the girls' bus to bring them home. I can't believe the days are flying by as quickly as they are. As I enter my immaculate house, Mrs. Flory tells me the boys are still napping. I look in on Eric, the sweetest and gentlest baby. He never cries. Our pediatrician tells us he may be seven feet tall, my gentle giant.

Jon is still napping, too. His blond curls lie on his pillow, and they look like corn silk. They hide the retractable horns he exhibits at will.

"Hi, Baby," I address Brook as she bursts through the door, sweaty from the long run up the driveway. She is a bit chubby and full of life. Secretly, I hope that her natural mother never comes back into her life. I cannot share her. She *is* me. She is my life, and I could not love her more.

Sommer follows her into the house. "Mommy, look at my drawing. Can I go in the woods to collect bugs? I'll put them into a jar so I can see them better and then I can draw them." She is my little artists and loves to draw.

After the girls have a snack and change into play clothes, they go into the yard to play. Jon wakes up at their rustling and wants to go outside with them. "Girls, keep an eye on Jon so he doesn't wander off," I ask as they run into the yard. There is not anywhere that they can go, really. We are out here with acres of trees and no close neighbors, but he can still find trouble if he wants it badly enough.

"Hi, sweetie," I call to Eric as he finally wakes. "Would you like to play in your playpen?" He just smiles. He agrees to anything. I put him into the playpen in the yard with the other children.

I usually return to the kennel and feed the remaining pets that need feeding until about five o'clock, when the babysitter leaves. Bob arrives home at about the same time and goes directly to the kennel to relieve Nora and, at six o'clock, to lock up for the night.

He is a huge help at The Abbey. He loves being a physical therapist, all of his patients love him, too. He has such a great sense of humor. He remembers every joke he has ever heard and can repeat it funnier than the first time it was told, which helps his patients relax and focus less on their pain.

Even with his full schedule, he still attends many dog shows with Clint but he now does much of the handling himself. He plans to be a professional handler and the owner of a kennel that produces great Champions someday.

To be an American Kennel Club Champion, a dog must win a total of fifteen points in the show ring. Points are based on the number of dogs of that particular breed that are shown and on past entries for that particular breed. Breeds that are more popular have a higher quota to attain. In accumulating fifteen points, a dog must acquire at least two "major wins." Major wins are those shows where the entries are large enough to win a three-, four-, or five-point win. It cannot win a series of one or two point shows to total fifteen. It must come up against major competition at least twice.

This year, Clint finished our first Saint Bernard, who became Champion Missy of Cold Creek, (the name of our personal breeding kennel). At one show, he was showing our male Saint Bernard, Hans, and the show judge was checking his teeth when Hans let out a low growl. Bad temper is never acceptable. The judge backed off a bit and said to Clint, "Did I hear that dog growl?"

"No, sir," said Clint. "He was just clearing his throat to say hello."

The judge laughed. He was not fooled, but Clint ended up winning a five-point major. A few months later, Bob handled Hans himself and received the necessary points for Championship. Champion Hans von Harry of Cold Creek was his title, and he was featured on the cover of the *Dog Digest* magazine as the official standard for the breed. We are so very proud of that accomplishment.

I am able to attend some shows, but my primary job is to keep our home and kennels running smoothly. I smile to myself as I remember back to our local dog show the month before.

The day of our local dog show, the kids and I attend to watch Bob show one of our Saints. Happy wins the show and earns the point necessary to make her an AKC Champion of Record. Bob is so excited that the entire audience hears him exclaiming as he leaves the show ring, "I won! I won! And the dog didn't do too bad, either!" The crowd laughs with us.

We advertise our puppies in a national dog magazine, so we ship them all over the country. One day, I sell one to a Mrs. James Cantrell of Ocala, Florida. "Do you know who I am?" she questions.

"I'm sorry, Mrs. Cantrell. Should I recognize your name?" I ask.

"Have you ever heard of Cantrell Convertibles Furniture?" she replies.

"Why, yes. Indeed, I have. I have seen some semi-trucks with that name written on the side. Is that the same Cantrell?" I ask.

"Yes, indeed," she answers. "And have you heard of the Cantrell cattle ranches in Ocala, Florida?"

"No, I'm afraid not."

"We raise cattle that roam over thousands of acres," she boasts. "I'm interested in purchasing a quality Saint Bernard puppy, not for show, but just to be our pet."

We then discuss the one puppy that I have for sale. She agrees to buy him, sends me a check for two hundred dollars, and we make plans to fly the puppy to her.

A week has passed and the day is here to ship the puppy to his new home in Orlando. I drive to the airport, with the puppy in a cage.

The puppy will fly in a cargo plane called "Major Air". We have used this procedure before when shipping our pets and it has worked well. When the plane cargo lands in Chicago, the pilot, himself takes the puppy to the designated airline and flight.

"Hi, Jim. Here is the puppy. His final destination is Florida. He has a reservation on Western Air Lines flight 3042. All the information is here in this envelope," I explain to the owner of the cargo airline, based in Peoria. Through previous shipping experiences, we have determined that the puppies receive better care on this private airline, than the small planes from major airlines that fly from Peoria to Chicago. In Chicago, the dogs are transferred to a major airline to be delivered to their new owners.

"We'll take good care of him," he tells me. "I called Chicago, and Western tells me they'll take him if the temperature outside doesn't reach ninety degrees, and it's a hot one today. The cargo department is pressurized but not air-conditioned." I agree to the plan and leave for home.

A couple of hours have passed when, the phone rings. "Nina, this is Jim from Major Air. I am at the airport in Chicago. Western Air Lines says it is too hot to ship the puppy today. The temperature is supposed to be cooler tomorrow, but they cannot keep him overnight. I guess I'll have to bring him back to Peoria on my next flight, which is very soon."

"Okay, Jim. We have no choice. Bring him on home!" I agree. I then make plans to pick him up, back in Peoria and return him the next morning.

I pick up the phone to call Mrs. Cantrell. I know she is planning on picking up the puppy in Orlando this afternoon. "We have a problem shipping the puppy," I tell her and explain the situation.

"No, no!" she says. "You can't do that! We're having a cocktail party! And he is the guest of honor!"

"No kidding?" I laugh. "Really, you are having a party for this puppy? Well, if that doesn't take the cake!"

"We absolutely must have the puppy back here! Do you think Jim Albright could be a help?" she asks me.

"I don't know," I reply. "Do you mean Jim Albright, the president of Western Air Lines?"

"Yes, my dear. He is coming to the party. Maybe he could get the airline to bend the rules a bit and get him here in time."

"Well, if anyone can do it, the president of the airline would definitely be the one!"

"I'll call you back," she says. Thirty minutes later, the phone rings.

"Nina, where is the puppy now?" Mrs. Cantrell asked.

"He is in the air on his way back to Peoria."

"You must send him back immediately to Chicago. It will be cooler in the evening and we have him scheduled for a flight to Orlando. I'll have my driver waiting for him at the airport, and he'll bring him home to the party."

"You actually got permission to put him on a Western flight?" I ask, amazed.

"Jim Albright made all the arrangements himself," she says smugly.

I call Major Air to explain this new development, and they tell me it is the craziest thing they have ever heard. Jim agrees to call Western to confirm the arrangements before they take the puppy back to Chicago on the next flight, which is the last flight of the evening.

"Nina, guess what? She was right. The pup is scheduled on a flight this evening. I still cannot believe it. Here is what we will do. Jim should be back here with the dog soon. We'll let the puppy run around a bit and give him some water, put him back into his cage, put him on our last flight to Chicago, and take him over to Western Air as soon as we arrive."

Later that evening, Jim calls back. "You're not going to believe this one. When I landed this buggy in Chicago, I could not find anyone to take the pup over to Western. I waited for about a half an hour and then decided to run him over there myself, but not until I checked the time the flight was scheduled to take off. It looked like we could not make it in time, so I called Western, and they told me that the flight had been delayed. I ran with the puppy and the attendant at the gate called the pilot who told me to bring him onto the plane. The plane doors were closed.

"I knocked on the door, and a stewardess had me put the cage and the puppy in first class. She whispered to me they delayed the flight for an hour *just* for this one bit of cargo! Can you imagine how crazy those passengers would be if they knew why they were delayed? I guess power talks. I'll never stop telling this story Nina. Never!" We laughed and laughed.

At midnight, Mrs. Cantrell calls to tell me how much the guests enjoyed the puppy. We breed our dogs with the hope that they will continue to reach celebrity status, but we never dreamed that one would be treated like royalty and fly first class.

CHAPTER TWELVE
DAY TWELVE
IN THE HOSPITAL

I feel limp, as if my body is falling to the floor. I hear a voice in the distance. Someone lifts me and places me in a wheelchair and then onto my bed. I look around and everything is fuzzy. I cannot seem to focus my eyes. "What are you doing?" I ask a nurse, who is taking my hospital gown off of me.

"You fainted, Nina. Sometimes, when people faint, they lose control of their bladder. That happened to you, so now we're getting you freshened up and putting a new gown on you."

"What happened?" I say, still feeling fuzzy.

"You were standing at the window. I walked up behind you and tapped you on the shoulder. You jumped at my touch and then gently fell to the floor. I am so sorry. I did not mean to frighten you. After what you have gone through, I imagine it will be a long time before you feel safe. Are you okay?" she asks. "Did you get hurt?"

"Hurt?" I say, in a haze. "I don't know." After a few seconds of trying to assess whether I was hurting, I said, "No, I don't hurt."

The nurse moves my arms and legs, checking to see if they were injured in my fall. "Nina, again, I'm sorry to have startled you. I'm so glad that you aren't hurt." She gives me a hug and leaves the room.

I cannot believe I fainted again. "Am I going to keep doing this?" I wonder. I hope it never happens again, especially in front of the children. I reach over and find my rosary on the nightstand. I just want to hold it. It gives me great comfort just to have it in my hand. "What is becoming of me?" I ask myself. "Am I going to be afraid of everyone and everything forever?"

The day turns to evening, and the phone rings. It is Brook, complaining that she does not like what Mrs. Sellers fixed for supper and that the Sellers boys are annoying brats, carrying on as young girls often do. My children are not whiners. Bob always told them, "If you're going to whine, I'll give you a reason." Now, they whine almost every time they call me.

"Pussycat, you thank Mrs. Sellers for dinner, even though you didn't like it. She does not know all of your likes and dislikes. It is very difficult to fix a meal for her four children and her husband and please you and Sommer, too. Before you hang up, put Mrs. Sellers on the phone. I love you, Brook," I say.

"Hello! What's up?" Andrea asks.

"I hope they're not causing you any problems, Andrea."

"Oh, heavens no," she says. "As a matter of fact, I just don't pay any attention to any complaints from the kids, yours or mine!" She laughs.

"Thanks, Andrea. I owe you. Have the girls call me tomorrow. Oh, wait! Let me talk to Sommer."

"Hi, Mommy," her sweet little voice says.

"Are you behaving?"

"I guess so," she answers. "Guess what, Mom? We are going to have a surprise birthday party for Brook next week. Mrs. Sellers and I are planning it. It will be a "backwards party." That means that everyone has to wear their clothes backwards. She says that maybe you'll be coming home that day."

"Oh, what fun, Cooser!" I exclaim. "If all goes well here, I may be discharged earlier on and maybe even be there in time for her party. Won't she be surprised?" "Cooser" did not come from anywhere in particular or mean anything. It is just a nickname for Sommer that I happened upon one day. Earlier that day, I had been told that I might be able to go home on the day of Brook's birthday party. "It'll only be a few more days, and I'll be home. Now get to bed. I will talk to you tomorrow. I love you, Cooser," I say before we hang up.

Every time I speak to the children, I cry. I feel so sorry for them, and for me, but then I smile and think to myself that I must be getting better. I am worrying more about them than I am about myself. I am so longing for my babies. Until now, I had been so self-absorbed that I had not heard their hearts hurting. I had not noticed how brave they are trying to be, how hard they are trying to exist in the situation in which they find themselves as they await the day of my homecoming.

"What would have happened to them if I had died?" I wonder. I look up and pray out loud, "Dear God, you gave me back my life. Now, please give me the courage to face the many heartbreaking decisions that lie ahead of me."

There is no sense in trying to sleep. I stay awake, wondering if Bob is still up, too. And if he is, if he is thinking about me and the children.

I walk to the window. It is cold and dark outside. Cars pass idly by the hospital. Normal people driving normal cars as the live their normal lives. They make me wonder what "normal" will be for us. One of the streetlights sways with the wind, and rays of its light fall on the chrome trim of an automobile like flashes of fire.

Fire. That takes me back to our twelfth year of marriage.

YEAR TWELVE
OF OUR MARRIAGE

"Hello," I answer the ringing phone at The Abbey. "Of course we have room for Sparky. February third to what date? We'll see you on the third!"

"Thank God for business," I think. "We need it."

January and February are the slowest months of the year for our boarding and grooming business. Few people travel because of the snow. Those who go south for the winter usually take their pets with them. People are reluctant to get their pets groomed in the deep of the winter, as well.

It seems as if only my mother-in-law calls these days, and at least once a month, she reminds us that four children is enough for anyone. "You are both being careful, aren't you?"

"You bet we are," I say. "Four is definitely enough. I gave all the baby stuff away, and we can't afford to buy it again."

She also constantly harps at us about having too many dogs. When she and Steven visit, she shakes her finger at Bob and says, "You better not be ignoring me." He laughs it off and passively acknowledges her, but it is not enough. She stands on her soapbox and lectures us, telling us we have too much to do, and, "You, Nina, you are burning the candle at both ends." No one knows that better than I do.

One day, while they are visiting us for Christmas, I overhear a conversation between Bob and his mother. As I pass our bedroom, I notice that the door is closed. I can hear both of their voices but they are muffled. I stop walking and creep quietly back toward the door. It is not typical that they are in the bedroom together talking alone.

"You make sure you don't get her pregnant, damn it! She cannot take on any more responsibilities. She looks like hell! And if I see that yellow dress on her one more time when we go out, I will scream. She buys beautiful clothes for you to show the dogs and doesn't spend a cent on herself."

"Hell, the only time we go out is with you guys. She says that if she needed more clothes, she would get some. So get off my back!" he snaps at his mother. "She has decent clothes to greet customers at the kennel and she tells me that's all she needs."

Sarah retorts, "This dog showing and kennel is taking every minute of your lives. If she gets pregnant again and runs into trouble like she did the last time with the pregnancy, you will lose it all. You can't possibly afford to hire the help it would take to do all that she does."

"Jesus Christ, Mom! Get off my back. I know, I know, I know. The doctor cautioned me, too." As Bob becomes more irritated, the conversation grows quieter. I cannot hear what they are saying, so I go back to the kennel.

I'm thinking about what Mom was saying when I snap back to reality, open my desk drawer, and take out a check for five thousand dollars from Prospect Bank, which I have to deposit today. We have officially begun robbing Peter to pay Paul. The boarding kennel has not established enough of a reputation yet, and this time of year, we have almost entirely expenses and little to no income.

Bob and a friend, Tom, are preparing to participate in the Texas dog show circuit. We cannot afford the expenses of such a gamble, but the men already planned their vacations, and the entry fees were paid before we found out how badly the kennel would be doing this time of the year. There are seven shows in seven days. The guys plan to take two days to drive there, stay at a cheap motel, and come straight home after the shows. We hope to win at least two of them so we will have our first ever Doberman Champion.

We did not realize just how much the closing of the plants at Caterpillar, the machinery company headquartered in Peoria, the last two weeks of July impacted everyone in the community. With thousands of employees on vacation at the same time, bakeries, restaurants, doctors, lawyers and other local businesses also closed their doors. During those weeks, our kennel was filled beyond capacity, with cages even in the bathroom. We remained three-quarters full through the rest of year except for January and February, which have proven to be less than lucrative.

We miscalculated big time. We talked to owners of boarding kennels all over the United States about their busy and slow seasons, but none of them were located in an area where vacation time is so limited. We still have a long way to go, though. The rule of thumb is that it takes five years for a business to show a profit, and this is only our first year in business. I hold the check in my hand and wonder how long it will help us survive before we have to pay it back in six months. I sigh and begin to work, hoping for a miracle.

The next day, Bob and Tom leave for Texas with huge hopes of winning the necessary points to make Tanya, our first Doberman, a Champion. Bob calls me every day.

"We made it in two days," Bob tells me. "The trip was fine, and the dog traveled well. We are here in Houston. We stopped and visited with Dorothea. Boy, she has a beautiful home on the outskirts of town. Her home is the nicest one in her black neighborhood. She has a very high, wrought iron fence all around it 'to keep out the riff-raff,' as she tells us. She fixed us a meal, or should I say a feast? Her daughter is beautiful, too. She said that she sure misses Wilson, her husband, since he recently died.

"We checked into a motel a few minutes ago, and now we are getting ready for bed. I am so glad that we drew a late show time for this first show so we can sleep in. God knows I need it! Love you, Kitts. Wish us luck!"

I surely wish them luck. Tanya has all the small points she needs towards Championship, but she still needs her major wins. Her breed has a huge entry, making it that much more difficult to procure.

I close my eyes and cross my fingers as I slip into bed. It feels odd to be in our big bed alone. I lie there, remembering back to our life in Houston,

Texas and the time we spent there. I miss my Dorothea. I remember feeling her tears on the collar of my coat as we pulled away to start our new life here in Peoria.

After we left Texas and moved back to Illinois to settle down, Dorothea told me she and Wilson decided to adopt a baby girl, too. They had a son who died as an infant because of a heart problem, but after hearing all about our adopted baby and how wonderful and beautiful she was, they decided that, even though they were in their mid-forties, they had a hole in each of their hearts that needed to be filled. Not long after the adoption, Dorothea wrote to me that Wilson had suddenly died and that God must have sent her the baby because He knew that she would need her. Money was not a problem. Wilson provided well for their future.

I close my eyes and can still hear her calling me "Miz Nina" and see her shaking her finger at me, saying, "You are too skinny. Ah needs to fatten you up!" Every day, she brought me something extra for my lunch. "Dorothea, I miss you," I say out loud, pretending she can hear. "It's unlikely I'll ever get to see that beautiful smile again. Our life is so busy, and a thousand of miles separate us."

Each night, Bob calls me with sad news. Tanya goes Reserve Winner's Bitch. That means second best and no points toward her Championship. It cost a lot of money and we lost. We do not win a single show on the circuit. Second place every single time. Two tired men and a beautiful dog come home defeated, with empty pockets and heavy hearts.

March finds the kennel still empty, and we have to use the remaining three thousand dollars from the loan to pay the mortgage and purchase tons of dog food for the coming busy season, which is just around the corner.

The girls begin ballet lessons in April, and somehow, just by attending their classes, I am talked into joining the Peoria Ballet Board of Directors. I honestly feel that I need something to take me away from the house and business. I am assured that it will only be for one evening a month, so I agree. At the third meeting, I am suckered into taking on the chairmanship, or position of president. Secretly, I am proud of the honor, but afraid of the time commitment. It works out well, though, and it is a welcome departure from my normal daily routine.

Our life is interrupted for a weekend this Spring. Bob's younger brother, James, is getting married. It's a beautiful spring day and his bride is lovely. Brook, is a flower girl. My in-laws are still having a problem with their Polish Catholic son marrying a German Lutheran soon-to-be daughter-in-law, an out-cross marriage these days. We just laugh it off. James and his fiancé are happy. She comes from a good family. We hope God blesses them with nothing but good fortune.

Bob still continues to participate in dog shows when he has a break from work at the hospital. Once in a while, he takes Jon. Bob tells me he never feels sleepy on the road because Jon talks all the way to the show and all the way back home.

One evening in May, Bob comes into the kitchen and announces, "You are going to a mobile home convention with Martha! Billy Bolden called me at the clinic and told me that Martha, his wife, does not want to go because he spends all his time talking sales and purchasing new samples, so she is all alone. He wants to know what I would think if she asked you to go along to keep her company. I told him I would run it by you. It would do you good to get out for a few days; a mini-vacation."

"Are you out of your mind?" I ask him rhetorically. "Who's going to take care of the children? The kennel? I'm not leaving here just so Martha isn't lonely."

"Look at it this way, Kitts. You need a break. Mom is after me all the time because you work day and night. This would give you an opportunity to fall apart. No responsibilities, just fun."

"I have no clothes," I say as a thought hits me. "You know, Vanessa might have some clothes I can borrow. Since she got into real estate, she has been doing a lot of clothes shopping."

I look at Bob. "What am I thinking? Somehow, I have made up my mind that I am going. I cannot believe this, a married woman, alone without her husband and out for fun. It sounds wicked. I don't know," I giggle. I am excited, but in the back of my mind, I am beginning to feel uneasy. I am not comfortable with the idea.

"Yes, you do," Bob demands. "I'll call Billy with the okay."

We make the trip without any problems. We spend the first day at the pool drinking lemonade and then attend a welcoming cocktail party that evening where Martha introduces me to Pete Jones. "He is a sales representative for Billy's biggest wholesaler," Martha tells me.

He comes on strong and very flirty, and he sure is handsome. "I can't believe that your husband let you come here alone," he teases as he sizes me up. "Won't you ladies share a table with me? Hey, hey, Billy! Over here," he yells.

We sit down and enjoy a fantastic dinner I secretly like the attention he lavishes on me. He is my dinner partner for the next couple of days, along with Martha and Billy, of course. He tells me he is married and has a son with a baby on the way. He is a smooth talker and definitely strikes me as more of a ladies' man than a married man. But I soak it all in and really enjoy it.

As I dress for dinner in my friend's clothes, I look in the mirror and say, "You know, Nina, you look damn good!" I have not fussed over myself in years. I always look good, but these past couple of days, I feel glamorous. I like the feeling, and I intend to keep it.

After the convention, I return home to a happy family with open arms. Glad to have had the break and glad to be home.

A few weeks later, the phone rings. "Say, Nina, I will be in Peoria in a couple of days. How about meeting me for a cocktail?" Pete Jones asks.

I can feel myself blushing as I timidly answered, feeling a little guilty, "That may just be possible. I have an exercise class Wednesday evening. There is a bar across the street called Charlie's. I would love to have a drink with you. How does eight o'clock sound?" He agrees.

Wednesday arrives and I am a nervous wreck. As I exercise, I anticipate the moments until I see Pete. I fantasize how we will begin this meeting and I feel excited – even invigorated.

As I enter the bar, he comes up to me and gives me a nice hug and a light kiss on the cheek. I feel flushed and nervous. "I hope you don't mind," he says. "I ordered for you. A martini, I believe, is your favorite." We sit and chat for about thirty minutes.

"Will you allow me to take you out to dinner?" he asks.

Then it hits me. "No, no Pete. I have already lied to Bob. I told him I would be a little late because I am going to do some shopping. But now I realize I am just not cut out for this sort of clandestine life. Our fun times at the convention enlightened me to the fact there is more to life than children and dogs, but I can't live in the shadows," I tell him.

"Well, I don't mean that we would do anything improper, Nina. Why don't I invite your husband, too?"

"No, no, no Pete. This kind of life is not for me. I cannot tell you how wonderful you have made me feel. The flattery you've paid me has helped me rediscover myself." I kiss him innocently on the cheek and walk out of the bar.

I walk to my car, shaking and ashamed, wondering if anyone I know saw me. I consider how I might have felt if Bob had done what I just did. I silently thank Pete, though, for making me feel alive again. On the way home, I decide that we are going to get out of the house and out of the kennel. Bob and I are going to find time for us.

By June, the kennel is filled with boarders. I work harder than ever. I find myself easing up on everything and just laughing more. I even feel sexier - and Bob likes it.

"I'm editor of *Dog Gone News!*" Bob announces as he enters the house after a kennel club meeting.

"Like hell you are!" I shout. "You don't have time for that! You do not have time to spend with the kids now. You never play with them. The only time you see them is when they help you carry out the dogs' food and water. Jon has been taking swimming lessons for months and you have never even had the time to watch him. Not even once! *Dog Gone News* comes out once a month. From what I have heard, it is quite a time-consuming job gathering the reporters' stories, deciding what to print, and putting it all together. When in the hell do you think you can find the time?"

"Well, it's done! I told them I'd accept it, and that's that," he retorts nastily. And he is pissed.

Instead of congratulating him on this appointment, I rave like a madwoman.

I can't stand it anymore!" I yell at him. "Do you need to feel more important? You cannot handle any more responsibility! You don't have enough hours in a day to donate to such a position!" I storm away, leaving him standing alone.

As I lie in bed that night, a chill comes over me. And while I don't understand why, I am afraid. I'm afraid that Bob is taking on way too much, and it is getting out of control. He is looking for recognition within the kennel club membership and I already anticipate what will happen. That job will take more time than he has to give, and I will have to help. He is being careless is decisions as they relate to our time and our family. I recognize he disregards sensibility and is aggressively competitive in the show ring. In the past, he congratulated other dog handlers, even if they beat us. Lately, he walks away bitching about his losses. He seems angry. He is no longer the jovial, fun-loving man I married. What is happening to him?

Several weeks after he accepted the title of editor, the first edition of *Dog Gone News* is being put together at The Abbey. I look at the clock and realize it is ten o'clock at night. So I go next door to check on the progress.

"How's it going?" I ask Bob.

"We have a few more kinks to smooth out," he replies.

"I'm going to bed," I inform him. "It's already ten. I told you this would happen."

"Once we get a system figured out, it'll run smoother," he tries to convince me as he gave me a peck on the cheek.

I go to sleep and am awakened to the sound of a door slamming. I look up to see Helen Fare at my bedroom door. She is one of the reporters that has been working on the paper with Bob. "I have to pee," she tells me, "and one of the guys is on the john at the kennel. Sorry, I didn't mean to wake you up."

I look at the clock, and it is two in the morning. "Damn! I knew this would happen," I say to myself.

The next morning, Bob is running late for work, just as I expect. He looks exhausted and I am really, really irritated.

Spring and summer prove financially profitable at The Abbey, but they are still not good enough to repay our loans. I sit at my reception desk at the kennel, and a car pulls up to the door. We designed the kennel to look like a Swiss Chalet. The driveway, as it comes up to the building, curls around under a covered area so the dog and its owner will be protected in inclement weather. The double glass doors open.

"Nina, I don't know how you do it!" our client says as she drags her dog into the building. "You always look so beautiful and polished sitting at that desk. You should be a private secretary instead of the welcoming lady at a dog kennel."

I smile and think to myself, "You should have seen me earlier, when I was hosing down the dog pens in my old boots and torn blue jeans, my ripped blouse, no makeup, and tousled hair."

After I check her dog in, I return to my desk to determine my next move. I have to obtain another bank note from a different bank to repay the other one which is now due. When I talked to Bob about it this morning, he said, "You'll figure a way. You always do," and left for work. Sometimes, his Pollyanna attitude is none too helpful.

By September, we are still hoping the money we need will find its way to our kennel. Several litters of puppies are due and we can sure use the extra income they will bring. As I am thinking about it, Bob calls me into the basement.

"Nina, come downstairs! Beauty is having her puppies!" I hurry downstairs.

"Clean this one off," he says as he hands me a wet, somewhat slimy newborn puppy. I notice that he is helping Beauty by gently pulling out a puppy that seems to be stuck. We deliver the puppies until late into the night. We take turns running to the kennel, doing the chores, and taking care of our children in the process.

"This makes nine," he says. "Nice litter."

I give the last pup mouth-to-mouth resuscitation. The last puppy born is often in the birth canal too long because the contractions are weak. When that happens, the puppy struggles to breathe and often dies if it does not receive assistance. I rub her gently with a soft towel to rev up her circulation. I open my mouth again, put the puppy's mouth into it, and gently blow to try to open her lungs. "I think she's going to make it. She is not struggling to breathe anymore. Let's find a place for her to nurse," I say as I look for a nice nipple on Beauty.

We never let our dogs deliver their puppies without our being there to assist. After all, each puppy means hundreds of dollars, and one of them could be our next Champion. Sometimes, when too much time passes between puppies and the mother is straining to deliver, we give her an injection to stimulate a harder labor in hopes of forcing the puppy out before it drowns. It is often its only chance at life.

Our entire basement is partitioned off into spaces for delivery rooms or, as they are properly called, whelping pens. After the delivery, the mother and babies stay in these pens for six weeks. The mother goes up and down the steps many times a day to go to the bathroom, spend time outside, and relax without the pesky puppies.

Sometimes, a mother does not have enough milk, so we help by bottle-feeding the puppies. If a puppy is too weak to nurse, we have to put a feeding tube down the puppy's throat, which we fill with formula we mix in bottles for premature babies. We repeat this every four hours in the hopes that, after a few days, the affected puppies will be strong enough to nurse on their mother.

For every puppy we sell at two hundred dollars, we probably spend three hundred for food, showing expenses, veterinarian bills and other expenses. It is an expensive hobby, and I wonder if it will ever pay its own way. Bob applies for and is accepted as a professional dog handler, so he also begins to handle other people's dogs for extra cash, leaving him with even less time than he had before, which was close to none.

Meanwhile, the reputation of The Abbey is growing and our breeding kennel, Cold Creek, receives praise from our competition. We have proof of the quality of our dogs by the numerous victories they win in the show rings.

"That's a great idea," I say to Bob's mother. She just offered for all four children spend a few days with them in Chicago, giving us some time to actually relax. Bob takes part of his vacation time from work, and we drop off the kids at his parents' house in Chicago. We ask Nora and some of our other kennel workers to add some hours to their schedule and line up a list of our own home projects. The number one project is to replace the bathroom carpeting.

"No! No! No! No more green!" Bob asserts. "We have enough green carpeting in the kitchen and the dining room." We continue walking through the aisles of carpeting rolls.

"I just can't make up my mind, honey. Let us think about it for a day or so. Nothing is jumping out at me, and it's almost time for us to be at the Venettis' for dinner so let's shelve it for the moment," I say.

"I remember the year it took me two hours to choose a Mercedes-Benz, and it took you two weeks to choose the color. That is before we got into all of this dog business, when we actually had money!" We both laugh.

"Dinner was wonderful, Mary. You are a fantastic cook," I tell her.

"It's just too bad that I eat so much of what I make," she laughs as she put her hands over her large stomach. Dan, her husband, brings in her famous Italian dessert when the phone rings.

"My God, are you sure? Holy cow!" Dan looks at us, his face suddenly drained of color, and yells, "It's your receptionist. Your house is on fire!"

None of us says a word. I grab my purse and rush to the car with Bob. Dan jumps in his own car and follows behind us.

"Thank God Nora remembered where we were going for dinner," I think. "Careful, Bob! You're going too fast!" I caution him as we round the corner. As soon as the house comes into view, we see three huge fire trucks, two on the front lawn and the other at the north side of our home in the driveway. Firemen are running in all directions, yelling orders.

"Get out of the way!" a fireman screams at us as we run up to the back of the house. We stop, frozen in disbelief.

"My God, Bob! The puppies!" I scream.

"They are fine! The puppies are all okay. They're next door at the boarding kennel," a voice yells to us. I look up to see one of our high school kennel boys. He is out of breath and sweat is rolling down his face.

"How did they get there?" I ask hysterically. "How did *you* get here? What are you doing here? How did you know about the fire?" I shoot the questions at him faster than he can answer.

"Rob and I were just going out to get some ice cream. We pulled up to the stop sign as we were leaving our subdivision across the street, and something caught my eye across the street. I realized it was fire. Fire was shooting out of the roof on the south side of your house, the side facing the kennel. We turned the car around and went to Nora's house. She called the fire department. She left her kids with her husband and climbed into our car and we drove over here.

"The back door was unlocked. The stairway to the basement was filled with smoke, but the door going into the house was closed. That is where the fire was. We did not see any fire downstairs, so we all rushed down there. We opened all the pens, and the mother dogs all ran out and stayed at the back door. We scooped up as many puppies as we could and put them into empty galvanized washtubs we found in the dog kitchen and piled them, one on top of another. We ran them over to The Abbey and put them into empty pens. We rounded up the mothers and put them in with their own puppies.

"But we're not sure we put the puppies with the right mothers. We just were finishing picking up the remaining puppies on the second trip when the firemen arrived and they yelled at us for being in the house. I told them about the puppies and that we had rescued all of them from the house. I still had one in my hand that was having trouble breathing, so a fireman brought out a small oxygen mask and put it over his little head. I think he will be okay. While we got the second load of puppies, Nora entered the house and opened the kitchen door. The house was filled with smoke. The only fire she saw was over the electric range," he explains.

"I saved the children's portraits off of your living room wall and your red velvet bedspread!" I hear an exasperated woman's voice interject. I look over as Nora runs up and hugs me. "I took them over to the kennel. I know how much you treasure those things. A fireman came in and practically dragged me out, so I could not get more. I told them that there was not any fire in there, only smoke. He told me that the fire was in the attic and that I needed to leave the house," Nora adds.

My body convulses as we all walk around the house, surveying it. Suddenly, the firemen on the roof pull out hatchets and open a huge hole in the south wall of the house near the attic. As we walk around to the front of the house, they use an axe to break through the double dining room windows and throw out some kitchen cabinets, which they have pried away from the walls. They land at our feet. My beautiful fine china and crystal comes spewing out of them, breaking into thousands of pieces. The flames in our house burst through the holes in the roof.

"Get *away* from here!" a fireman demands.

I look into Bob's eyes and they express his silent shock. I take him by the hand. "Let's check out the puppies," I say to him, and we run to the kennel.

We pick up the puppies one at a time and examine them. They all appear to be okay. "Tomorrow, we'll take them to the vet and then we'll have to keep a close eye on them for the next few days," Bob says.

"Let's get our portable exercise pens. We'll set one up in the cat room, one in the grooming room, and one in the reception room for the time being." Bob suggests. "We'll put a litter and its mother in each pen. The kennel boys and Nora can help us."

"Put the cats and their cages into the feeding room," Bob tells the boys. "Thankfully, there are only a few cats here right now."

"I'll call the McGinns and the Sellers," I say to Bob.

"Where are you going to stay?" Ann McGinn asks.

"I guess we'll go to a motel. The firemen are still here and probably will be for a while yet. Thank God, the children are in Chicago. I'm so thankful they weren't here."

"Let us know what we can do to help!" Ann says. "I'll call you tomorrow."

Not a minute later, the phone rings. "I have a great idea," Ann says. "We've just returned from our vacation. Tomorrow, we will bring our motor home to your house and park it in the backyard. You and the kids can live in it until the house is fixed."

"Ann, that could be months," I tell her, hesitant to accept.

"Don't worry. We are through with it for the season. It sleeps eight. We will call you at The Abbey tomorrow and make arrangements to deliver it. You will have to clean it up. I haven't had a chance to do that yet."

I tell Bob while Ann is still on the phone and he accepts gratefully.

"Thank you so much!" I say to Ann.

"What a wonderful coincidence," I say to Bob. We put our arms around each other. We cannot even cry.

"It looked like the fire started between the walls, maybe a short in the wiring behind the electric range. We will know more tomorrow when we can inspect it closer in the daylight. Don't enter the house tonight or tomorrow until we make sure it's safe," the fire chief tells us. The firemen finish up, and the trucks pull away for the night.

"We haven't called our folks, yet," I remind Bob. "Let's not wake them up. We will call them in the morning. There isn't anything they can do at this hour."

Exhausted, we fall into bed at the motel. "What the hell happened to a few days of relaxation?" I ask Bob.

He does not answer. He fell asleep on his way down to the pillow. I close my eyes and I hear Dr. McGinn telling me a favorite, familiar saying of his:

I say, "God, let me tell you what my plans are for my life."

Then God replies, "Now, let me tell you my plan!"

"Dear God, where do we go from here?" I ask as I fall asleep.

Morning comes all too soon. We shower and put on the same clothes we wore the day before. We drive home and see the devastation in broad daylight. We exit the car and walk to the back of the house. The windows are busted out and the white vinyl siding is black near the roof. We walk around to the south side of the house and see that the window had been torn out. That entire side of the house is black. There is a gaping hole above the window, and as we step back, we can see the hole in the roof, too.

We enter the house through the back door. It smells heavily of smoke. The smoke, along with fire, has damaged everything. Amazingly, the brass chandelier and its glass globes, which sat in the midst of the flames, are intact despite the fact that the brass and wooden pieces are blackened. The sofa and the covered chair in the living room are water soaked and smell of smoke. The draperies are torn and wet. Everything in our bedroom is just as it had been before the fire except for the smell of smoke and wet ashes everywhere. All of our family albums and pictures seem to have been left undamaged.

As we walk back to the kitchen, I notice that one cabinet is still attached to the wall. We open it to examine the contents. There are only a few red crystal goblets left; one dinner plate, which is cracked; and two salad plates, all from our beautiful Sascha Brastoff China collection.

We open the lower cabinet, and behold, our crystal stemware, which is trimmed in Sterling Silver, is still in place. "They are all here!" I exclaim. "And in perfect condition." I pull one out and hold it up to show Bob, but I notice he shows absolutely no emotion.

I put the glass back quietly and we go downstairs. There are a couple inches of water covering most of the floor in the dog maternity ward. Thankfully, however, the fire did no damage to the wood of the dogs' whelping pens.

"We'll ask our kennel boys to come over here to help us mop up the water. It will take days to dry out. Nothing is ruined. It is just very wet. We will put some fans in here to help dry it up and then re-paint. With some luck, we can move the mothers and their pups back into here in a week. It's still going to be a long time before the house is ready for us to move back in, though," Bob says.

"I guess if we have to look for a silver lining, this is one. The dogs and mothers are okay, and the kids were not home. No one was hurt. The objects can be replaced. We're all okay," I say to Bob.

I take him by the hand and we walk next door to the kennel. He looks utterly and completely defeated.

"Hi, Victor. This is Nina. We had a fire at the house last night," I inform our insurance agent and friend. He tells me he already knows about the fire; he saw it on the ten o'clock news. He says he and an adjuster will be here in about three hours.

We hang up and call Bob's parents and my Dad and brother to give them the news and tell them we will call them later with an update. We all marvel at the fact that the kids were not at home, the dogs were safe, and I no longer have to worry about the green carpet, as it is all gone.

The kennel boys arrive, and we all begin the cleaning process.

"Hi, Victor!" I say as our insurance agent arrives.

"This is Mark Michaels. He is one of our adjusters. We'll both take a look," he tells me. They walk around the house and take notes.

"We'll have to replace the entire roof, the windows and the kitchen wall behind and over the range. The appliances, drapes, sofa, chairs, mattresses, and most of the carpeting, if not all of it, has to be laundered or cleaned, but probably mostly replaced," Mark says. His list goes on and on.

I leave all the men and go over to the kennel to open for business. As I unlock the doors, Nora and Terry pull up. Nora feeds and cleans the cat areas while I explain to Terry, the groomer, who is clearly confused by the setup in the kennel, what happened. I take her to the house, and she looks around as I speak. "Looks like the firemen caused as much damage as the fire," she comments.

"I guess they have to make sure there is no fire lingering behind the walls, so they have to get into them. We have an excellent policy, so hopefully, most of our expenses will be covered," I say.

"Get at least two estimates from contractors. Also, give us a list of items that were ruined," the insurance agent tells me. "We'll give you a housing allowance to live at a hotel or to use any way you wish. We will issue you a check right away. You might want to take the clothes to the cleaners and only bring back to the house the items you will be wearing. I suggest you leave the remainder at the cleaners until the smoke smell has dissipated. I will be in touch with you regularly. Call if you have any questions." Victor gives me a hug and they leave. He and his wife are good friends of ours. "Jane said that she'll call you later. She wants you to come over for dinner tonight."

Bob says, "Since we'll be living in the motor home, we'll add the temporary housing money to the money they give us for furniture to purchase the things we need. I'll call work and let them know I won't be in for a few days."

He adds, "I'll call Mom and Dad now and see if they will ask Aunt Elly if she can help them take care of the kids for a couple more days. They'll just have to miss some school." I am thankful he is becoming engaged again.

After his phone call he says, "It's all taken care of. Mom, Dad and Aunt Elly will care for the kids. They will bring them back next weekend. I will call the phone company and have them put a phone into the motor home when it arrives. I'll call an electrician over to hook the power back up in the house so the puppies stay warm."

We usually keep a heat lamp hanging over the whelping area to keep the puppies warm if they wander away from their Mommy, but they do not have one in their temporary quarters. We turned down the temperature of the air conditioner to accommodate them. We are not comfortable, but the puppies are safe.

One of our kennel boys and his helper approach me after they had finished cleaning to ask me what they should do next. I can't believe it! To think you were passing by the house and spotted the flames was perfect timing in itself. Then, not only did you have the fire department notified, but you also had the courage to go into the house knowing that all those puppies and their mothers were trapped in the basement. You were brave to go down those stairs time after time retrieving the puppies. We are so lucky. If you had not been the ones to see it, there is a good chance the puppies would not have made it. Entering a burning house wasn't very wise, gentlemen," I say, smiling.

"We didn't think the back door would be unlocked, but we thought we'd try it. When we opened the kitchen door, we peeped inside and saw the flames over the stove, so we closed the door and ran downstairs. There was no fire down there so we just grabbed as many puppies as we could handle. By the time we were done, we could not see them anymore because the smoke was so thick. We counted them to make sure we had them all," Patrick says.

I hug them both and send them to the boarding kennel to help there. They help Nora with the responsibilities she took over for us while we continue to work on the house repairs.

"How very brave those teenage boys were," I think, and then, "How stupid! They could have been killed!"

I go back to The Abbey and finally thank Nora for saving my prized pictures of our four children and my custom silk velvet bedspread. "I'll keep the pictures at my house until you're ready for them. The bedspread doesn't smell of smoke, so you probably won't have to clean it," she says.

We send the boys home when their work is complete and head back into the reception area to the ring of the phone. "Good Morning, this is The Abbey," I answer.

"Are you open for business?" a voice asks. "I heard you had a fire."

"The fire was next door. We are open for business. Are you calling to make a reservation?" I ask.

I make the reservation and realize I will probably receive a lot of calls over the next few days. People may be confused as to whether the kennel was on fire, as the news story mentioned the puppies.

By mid-afternoon, the basement is clean. We disinfect everything with Clorox and set up huge, commercial fans to help dry it faster. Every now and then, a drop of water drips on our heads from the wet floors upstairs, but we are making good progress. It is nearly four o'clock when the McGinns pull their motor home into our yard. "We'd have been here sooner, but we had to clean it a bit," Jack tells me.

We show them the damage the fire did to our house. We thank them again and again before they leave.

"We are the luckiest people in the world." I say to Bob. "This will work out great. Here are the keys. Let's check out our new home." As we step in, we look at each other and burst into laughter. It is a mess! We joke that it is worse than our fire-ravaged home. "I'm glad they cleaned it up," Bob says sarcastically.

"Just remember what our kid's rooms looked like when they left and remember that they have two more kids than we do. I think we will spend at least one more night in the motel. Cleaning this will be a full day's work, if not more, and I'd like to bring the children here to sleep when they come home," I say.

"Weren't you just saying how lucky we are?" Bob say. "I think our luck just ran out!" We laugh, and it is the first smile I have seen on Bob's face since the day before.

Two days later, the motor home is clean and ready. We stock the cabinets and ready it for a new family to move in for a while.

A contractor is hired by the insurance company and the work began on rebuilding our home. All too soon, Saturday arrives, and with it come Bob's parents delivering our bundles of joy. By now, we really miss them.

We show Bob's folks the damage and the motor home. They do not even stay for lunch, saying they have a lot of work back home and they need to get to it. As they pull out of the driveway, we wave to them, as always. Bob looks at me and starts to laugh. "I'm surprised they even stopped the car long enough to let the kids out! They looked exhausted. Four kids for a week. I bet they never offer to take them for a vacation again!" Bob says.

The kids handle the new situation well. They think living in a motor home is pretty cool. I am proud they are all so flexible.

It has been two weeks since the fire, and our kennel club is hosting a celebration on Peoria's riverboat, called the Julia Belle Swain, to honor our two kennel boys who saved our puppies. Each boy is given a medal of honor presented by the president of the Illinois Valley Kennel Club. Dinner is served on the boat and reporters from the newspaper and the TV are invited. The boys take home medals and pictures from the newspaper and see themselves on the evening news. Most importantly, they leave with the feeling of being heroes.

We choose new appliances, carpeting and cabinets for the house. The bedroom carpeting is cleaned and deodorized, and every wall in the house is re-painted. Aside from my regular daily obligations, I also have to oversee the remodeling. Bob is back at work, so the most time we spend together as a family is at dinner each night. We are both working constantly. However, on the weekends, he is able to escape by going to dog shows while I, as usual, stay behind at home. I'm beginning to become jealous and a little resentful.

After six weeks, the remodeling is completed and we move back into our home. I am not feeling well and assume I am just overtired or my period is due. I suddenly feel a flash of heat run through my body and stop, paralyzed with fear. It has been six weeks since the fire and I have not had my period. "Oh my God," I think to myself. "I could be pregnant. My cramps are getting stronger. I better get to the bathroom." I look at my panties and see a few drops of blood. "Oh, thank God. I must be late because of all the chaos."

Days later, the cramping continues, as does the light bleeding. It was not a regular period. "Bob, I think I'm pregnant," I say to him on the phone at his office.

"What are you talking about?" he questions, alarmed.

"I've missed my period. I thought it started a couple days ago, but it never kicked in. I am having terrible cramping. Are you sure you pulled out in time?"

"Of course I did. I told you that night. We have done that before and I always pull out in time. Gotta go," he says as he hangs up in a hurry.

I remember the one and only night we made love in the motor home, before the kids came back from Chicago. We knew we would all be too close to each other to do it when they returned. I told Bob it was not a good idea because my birth control pills were ruined in the fire, so I had missed them for a few days. I had so much going on that I never even thought of them until that night. He told me he would be careful and pull out in time.

Later that night, after dinner, I say to him, "I'll call the doctor tomorrow. I cannot get pregnant again. You promised to pull out in time. You said you would be careful. Dr. Gilbertson warned me never to get pregnant again. I cannot spend months in bed. Who will run the kennel and how will we afford to hire that much help? We will lose it all: the kennel, possibly the baby, and maybe even me. How could you put me in this situation?"

"I'm sorry, Kitts," is all Bob says.

The next day, I call Dr. Gilbertson. He gives me the number of a new independent laboratory in town. They perform a new and accurate urine test that can give a false/positive reading three weeks after a missed period. I make the appointment for two days later, pick up the bottle, and take it home.

I turn my sample in and then sit at my desk, dreading and waiting for the call. I jump every time the phone rings.

Finally, the lab calls. I am pregnant. I drop the phone into its cradle and look around, grateful that none of my kennel helpers is there. I bawl, terrified. "Maybe I'll miscarry," I hope to myself, "but what if I don't? It's starting over again, just like the last pregnancy. First I have cramping, next is bleeding and then the toxemia will follow. I can't do that again."

"Bob, I'm pregnant!" I yell at him over the phone.

"I'm so sorry," he replies, sounding genuinely remorseful.

"Sorry for what? For being irresponsible?" I ask. "I've made the decision to have an abortion. We will go to New York. It is the only place I can have one. I have an appointment with Dr. Gilbertson tomorrow. I'll discuss it with him."

"Are you sure you want to do that?" he whispers.

"I'm sure I *don't* want to do that. I am sure, however, that I *have* to. I have a family for whom I am responsible. How am I going to take care of them? I have a responsibility to them. What if I die this time? Who will take care of my children?"

"I'm so sorry, Kitts," he repeats, whispering. "I don't want you to have an abortion, but I'll do whatever you decide. I'm here with you."

I hang up, scared and angry. No, I am not scared. I am petrified. I go to see Dr. Gilbertson the next day. "Well, Nina, I agree with the urine tests and believe you are pregnant."

"It was an accident," I explain to him.

"You'll have to start hormone pills immediately and get off of your feet."

Before he can say anything more, I interrupt him. "I want an abortion."

"Are you sure? You have time. Why don't you think it over," he suggests.

"I want an abortion," I repeat firmly. "You know my chances of carrying this baby are not good, and how am I going to care for my other children? The kennel is so far in the red that we cannot afford to hire help. I may have to be in bed the next seven months." My lips quiver as I speak, and I am crying so hard that my nose is running. Dr. Gilbertson hands me a tissue and pats me on the shoulder.

"I don't condone abortion. However, in your situation, I can understand your dilemma. Why don't you wait a few more weeks? With the bleeding you are experiencing, you just might abort naturally," Dr. Gilbertson says hopefully.

"No, no, I don't want to wait. This pregnancy is starting out just like the last one. The longer I wait, the more difficult it will be to do it."

I tell Bob that Dr. Gilbertson signed the form confirming my pregnancy and gave me the information, the location and the cost to have an abortion. We will have to fly to New York early in the morning. Peoria now has a direct flight to New York, so we can arrive in the morning and return in the evening. The entire procedure will last only minutes, but I will have to stay at the clinic for a short time to make sure I do not hemorrhage. Then, we will fly back home. I explain all of this to Bob.

"How are we going to afford it?" he asks.

"It's five hundred plus the airfare," I tell him. "We'll call your parents. Your Mom knows we are in over our heads. She keeps reminding me of it."

"Oh, yeah, 'No more children. Be careful. It's that time of the year when you get pregnant,'" he reminds me and laughs about her aggravating phone calls.

"Bob, you ask them to loan us the money. They loaned us money before to purchase the house in Peoria and we paid them back. I am sure they will be agreeable. We need a money order for half of it and it has to be sent to New York in order to hold the appointment. No refunds. We'll also need the money for the airfare," I state.

"What do you think she'll say?" he asks.

"We'll find out. Call them tonight," I reiterate.

"Why me?" he asks.

"Because they are *your* parents," I snap.

That night, Bob picks up the phone and calls. His Mom answers and he explains. "I'll make the airline reservation immediately," he says. "Yes, I'm going with her." He remains on the phone for quite a bit longer, but he does not say much but to agree with whatever she says. I imagine she is scolding him for our stupidity.

"Mom wants you to call New York tomorrow and make the arrangements. She never questioned the decision or the money," he tells me. "She knows we're about to fall off a cliff." He lowers his head to his knees, looks up and says, "They'll be here next Thursday night so we can fly out on Friday."

I feel so strange, as if I am making a simple business decision. I am not crying, but I am not relieved. I feel dead inside. I do not even feel guilty and I wonder if I eventually will. I remember back to the day when I miscarried and ended up in the psychiatric ward. I have no idea how I will live with this decision. I do not even know who I am anymore. I do not understand the type of person I must be to do something like this and not to be feeling great emotion. I cannot even ask God to watch over me through this, so I decide instead to confide in my best friends.

The next day, I call to share with Ann and Andrea. They both say they understand. Ann does not want me to do it but loves me anyway. Andrea says it is a decision she is happy she does not have to make.

The following Thursday, Bob's parents arrive. We tell the kids that Bob and I are going out of town to look at a new show dog. The kids are happy that Grandma and Grandpa are there because they always bring presents.

The alarm is supposed to ring at six. At three in the morning, I wake up to heavy bleeding and severe cramping. In the middle of the night, I call Dr. Gilbertson and he instructs me to go to the emergency room immediately. He tells me he will meet me there. He has just been called in for a delivery, anyway.

"Don't sign in to be admitted. Just sit in the waiting room and wait for me," he orders.

We arrive at the hospital and sit for only a few minutes. "Nina, come with me," Dr. Gilbertson instructs me.

"Bob stands up and kisses my cheek. I follow Dr. Gilbertson into an examining room. I disrobe and notice that I am bleeding even heavier. I lie on the examining table and assume the position that all women hate: legs spread, feet in the stirrups. I feel the cold speculum enter me and inhale deeply.

"You're either miscarrying now or you're about to. We are going to let nature take care of it. I will keep you here in the emergency room for observation. Should you start bleeding heavily, I will do a D and C if need be; however, it's so early in your pregnancy, that I think you'll be just fine. It should be just like a very heavy period. I thought you were going to get an abortion?" Dr. Gilbertson inquires.

"I was. We were going to fly to New York today," I answer.

"Really? I'm so glad you have been spared that decision, Nina," he says.

In my heart, though, I know that I had an abortion. I did not start the medication I should have taken days earlier, and I did not comply with the bed rest order to stop the bleeding. It's the same as if I had gone through with the abortion.

A nurse brings Bob into the room and I explain. "I'm miscarrying," I tell him with great relief in my voice. We hug. A huge burden has been lifted off of our shoulders.

Before we left the house that morning, we wrote a note for Mom and Dad telling them I was bleeding and that we were going to the hospital. We told them Bob would call them when he knew more. Bob finds a pay phone and called his parents to explain. They agree to stay a little later. When we return home, they never say a word about the deposit or the money for the airfare that they loaned us. They leave shortly after we arrive.

Oddly, I still feel no emotion. I am neither ashamed nor proud of my decision. Over the following weeks, when Bob and I talk about it on occasion, he says that since I did not start taking the hormones immediately when I discovered I might have been pregnant that we, in fact, did create the abortion. He feels some guilt about the decision I made that he reluctantly agreed. But I know that even if he does not agree with my decision, I had no choice. I was backed into a corner.

His parents never mention it again, each of us living with the part we had almost played in the decision to have an abortion and lived with it in our own ways.

Several months later, I am at my desk at the kennel. My mind drifts to the miscarriage, and it reminds me of the story my Mom told me about my own birth. She and my father broke up and got back together again and again. They married because she was pregnant with me. It was not a good marriage. They both drank far too much. When they were both sober, they were happy, but those times were uncommon. Dad always loved Mom more than she loved him, but they stayed together, and she died shortly before their twenty-fifth anniversary. However, I am sure that if abortions had been available at that time, I would not be here now to remember the chain of events that led me to this moment.

I stop thinking about what could have been and continue to play the game of borrowing from one bank to pay back the other, trying to stay financially afloat. The boarding kennel is generating more clientele and money these days, and I only hope that we can succeed before the wolf comes to the door.

CHAPTER THIRTEEN
DAY THIRTEEN
IN THE HOSPITAL

"Mmm, this tastes good.

Enjoy these last meals, Nina. Soon you'll be back in your own kitchen. And back to the daily grind," I say, and I smile as I savor every mouthful of my breakfast.

A figure appears in the doorway. It is Sister Mary Margaret. "Hi, Sister!"

"With a smile that bright, you don't need the room light on," she says, and we both laugh. "Do you have a few minutes to spare for me?" she asks.

"I always have time to hold your hand and say a prayer with you, Sister," I say, agreeing to our almost daily routine.

"I'd like just a few extra minutes today," she says as she pulls a chair up to the side of my bed. "Well, pretty lady; it seems that you'll be leaving us soon." Her plump, pink cheeks puff out with her smile.

"Isn't it wonderful? I can hardly wait! I have not touched my children in such a long time. It seems like a million years ago. My heart aches for them," I say.

"It's only days away. I'm going to miss you," she tells me.

"I'm probably filing for divorce, Sister," I say as I look into her eyes. "Does that upset you?"

"No, Nina, no. That needs to be done. Sometimes there are things that cannot be fixed. This is one of them," she reassures me. The expression on her face grows serious as her brows furrow, and it takes a few moments before she speaks again.

"Nina, I've been the head of nursing here for twenty-five years. I have seen a lot of happiness, a lot of sadness and a lot of death. A young woman died the very day you were admitted. Her husband beat her. Her injuries did not look as serious as yours did, but the damage inside her brain was much worse. We actually prayed for her death, because she would have no quality of life had she lived - she would have been in an irreversible coma. God listened to our prayers and took her home. The damage to your head was some of the most serious I have ever witnessed. Are you aware that all of my colleagues call you our miracle child? Well, God has spared you for a reason, child. Do not be afraid. He has a plan for you, Nina. He will take you by the hand and show you the way. Let's say a farewell prayer together."

We pray aloud:

Hail Mary, full of grace, the Lord is with thee. Blessed art thou among women, and blessed is the fruit of thy womb, Jesus. Holy Mary, Mother of God, pray for us sinners, now and at the hour of our death. Amen.

Sister Mary Margaret continues, "On the days you feel yourself questioning your decisions or the days you are troubled, remember this old nun telling you you have been given your life back and that God will be there to help you. He must love you very much. He must feel that your family needs you much more than He needs you. When you are done with your mission here on earth, He will set a place for you at His table." She takes my folded hands, wraps hers around them, and says, "I'll be praying for you," and leaves my room.

I watch her float down the hall until I see only a dot of black and then nothing. I notice that my hands are still folded, and I put them down into my lap. I do feel scared to be going out there out into the unprotected world, but I know that I must.

My meal no longer appeals to me, so I push my tray aside. I lay my head back into my pillow and think back to the thirteenth year of our marriage.

YEAR THIRTEEN OF OUR MARRIAGE

"Hi, Kitts. We have been invited to the Bellows' for dinner Friday night. What do you think?"

"Who?" I ask.

"My nurse, Sue, and her husband, Carl," Bob says.

"Are you sure that's a good idea, honey? Remember a few years back, you were denied a promotion because you were too buddy-buddy with your staff, and they thought you would not be able to command respect from them? Remember how upset you were?" I remind him.

"That was when I was at the institute," he snaps. "I'm not there anymore. I am here at the clinic. The atmosphere here is much more relaxed."

"Well, it's okay with me," I say to him. "See if Lucy can babysit."

"Great!" he says.

Sue is one of Bob's nurses at the clinic. He talks about her all the time. He is happy to have her in his department because he says she is very efficient.

The dinner at the Bellow's is wonderful. We have a great time. I meet Sue, Chuck, and their three children. We laugh a lot listening to Sue's and Bob's funny stories from the clinic.

"Goodnight! Thank you," we echo as we leave their home. Bob opens the car door for me. He is always such a gentleman.

"That was so nice. I am glad we came. I wonder how she manages to work full-time and still keep her house in perfect condition," I marvel.

"Oh, it's not always like that. Sometimes it's really messy," he says.

I look at him and off-handedly ask, "You've been here before?"

Silence.

Finally, he answers nervously, "A couple of times. Her husband couldn't pick her up, so I drove her home."

"I don't remember you telling me that," I say.

"Well, it wasn't that big of a deal," he says.

I am sure Bob has probably done that for many people because he is such a nice guy, but something just does not sit right. His answer. His stammering. I feel a chill and shiver, so I bend down and turn on the heat.

As we make our way home, I notice that it is a beautiful fall night. The gentle wind blows the autumn leaves, and I watch them scurry down the street. A sudden gust of heavy wind blows them across the front of the car, and they appear to dance on the hood and then float off, waiting to be carried away by the night wind.

And then I hear my mother's voice: *"An ill wind blows no good."*

We say nothing more the entire way home.

As I lie in bed that night, I think about this last summer. In June, we decided to take our first vacation in ten years. We took our children to Florida for ten days.

A smile creeps across my face when I think back to our visit with our friends, the Heinzes. They moved to Florida several years ago and invited us to visit their home on our trip. Margaret and Terry are both nurses who we met in Peoria years before, married, and had a son. We love their constant arguments. They never agree on anything, but they always laugh off their differences. When we arrived at their home, we found them participating in a new adventure. They were running against each other for mayor of a small town. It was a wonderful visit, and we shared many memories from previous years. "I wish we could stay for their formal debates!" I said to Bob as we left.

From there, we took the kids to Disney World. My heart beats faster as I remember one particular day while we were at a Disney gift shop. I saw Bob buying post cards.

"You're buying post cards," I announced, surprised.

"Yep, I thought I'd send some to Lucy."

"You? You are going to write and mail post cards? I cannot believe it. You must be turning over a new leaf. This is definitely not like you!" I laughed.

Lucy is Bob's elderly nurse's aide. He loves her. She worked in one of the senior citizen nursing homes that he serviced while he worked for the institute. They enjoyed each other's company, so when he took the job at the clinic, he brought her with him and saw that the clinic paid her well. I have not thought of those post cards again until now. I wonder if some of the cards were sent to Sue. I never saw him writing on them, just mailing them, it occurs to me. I push that thought out of my mind, shaking my head as I do.

Our trip was wonderful, but we came home to a disaster. Shortly before we left for Florida, we had to fire our groomer, Libby. We discovered that she often used drugs. We never knew if she was going to show up for work, and she started to handle the dogs roughly if they did not behave perfectly. That, we could not accept. We hired a friend of hers, Jake, who sometimes helped us if she had booked too many dogs, called in "sick," or more recently, showed up to work high.

The day we returned from our vacation, Jake informed us he was leaving us and going into business for himself. We soon discovered that while we were gone, he notified all of our grooming clients - the business that we had worked so hard to cultivate and maintain - that he was leaving and where he was opening his shop. He took many of our clients with him and we had to look for a new groomer.

We discovered that money was missing from the kennel and from our home, as well. The next week, we discovered that our housekeeper, Mrs. Flory, played an instrumental part in our groomer leaving. It was she who led him to the building he rented. So we fired her, too, but the damage had already been done. We did hire another dog groomer, but it will be a long time before we have a thriving dog grooming business again, I think. I fall asleep remembering the misery of this summer.

When I wake, Bob is still sleeping beside me. He looks different, somehow. I study his face and wonder if he has really changed or if I am just making too much of the Sue situation.

It's been several days since our dinner at the Bellows'. But I still feel apprehensive. Something just is not right but I cannot put my finger on it. We do not discuss the dinner with the Bellows again.

Weeks later, in the middle of the night, I turn over in bed and notice that Bob is not there. I get up to look to see if he is in the bathroom, but the bathroom is empty. I search the house. He is nowhere to be found. I walk around, looking into each of the rooms, calling softly. As I walk around the corner of the kitchen again, I bump right into him and scream. I startle him, and he yells, too. He is fully dressed and has come in from outside.

I turn on the lights. "Where have you been?" I ask in a panic.

He stutters a bit and then says, "I was so upset about Jake going into business and taking our customers. I thought I'd go and burn his buildings down."

I gasp. "You were going to burn his business down? Oh, Bob, you didn't do it, did you?"

"No, I didn't, but I sure thought about it for a long time," he responds sullenly.

"What is happening to us, Bob? How could you ever think of doing anything like that?" I cry as I hug and kiss him, and I think, "My God, he is going to pieces. What is happening to him?"

We go to bed, but I do not sleep the rest of the night.

Days later, it happens again. I can't find Bob in the middle of the night. I peer out the window and notice a car, our car, coming up the driveway with its lights off. I wait in the dark for Bob to come into the house. He quietly unlocks the door. As he turns to enter the kitchen, I flip on the light switch. He jumps back.

"Where have you been?" I ask, calmly this time.

"I couldn't sleep, so I went for a drive," he stammers.

"You went for a drive? You have never done anything like that before. Why would you go for a drive?"

"I thought I might get tired, you know, de-stress myself," he says.

"Why were the car's lights off?" I ask.

"I thought maybe if the shades weren't pulled down low enough in the bedroom, the lights coming up the drive might wake you," he answers.

"What's happening to you, Bob?" I scream.

"I don't know. I don't know," he says as he sits down and puts his head between his knees.

"You are scaring me to death!" I yell at him.

"Don't worry. I'll get ahold of myself," he attempts to reassure us both.

Again, I cannot sleep the rest of the night.

Within just two days, it happens a third time. He is not in bed, so I peek out of the window and notice the car is still here this time. As I walk softly out of the bedroom, I can hear him talking in a hushed voice on the phone in the kitchen. The lights are off and I silently walk up behind him.

"Who are you talking to, Bob?" I ask in a strong tone of voice.

He drops the phone, clambers to pick it up, and says, "The weather. I was calling to check on the weather."

"It's two o'clock in the morning! Why on earth do you need to know the temperature?"

"I just couldn't sleep. Listening to the temperature over and over again makes me sleepy," he answers as he hangs up the phone.

This happens a couple more times, too, but on those occasions, he pulls the phone cord out as far as he can so he can see me coming. He hangs up the phone quietly and then he denies he was ever on the phone. He rants and raves and tells me I am losing my mind and imagining things.

Even after all of this, I just now begin to question, "Could he be talking to another woman?" I have to smile at the foolishness of that thought. It would be more likely for me to have an affair than for Bob to have one. He is the All-American guy, good father, devoted husband. But something is still very wrong. I feel I am walking down a frightening path, but I cannot put my finger on the source of the fear. Is he that stressed over the betrayal of those we thought were trusted friends and employees? Or is it something else? I cannot make sense of my husband or my world but I have too much to do just to get through the day, so I push my fear to the side for now.

We look forward to taking a few days off from work to visit our parents and do some sightseeing in Chicago. It will be the first time we share "our city," the one in which we were raised, with the kids. We visit one of the museums. As we rest on a grassy area outside enjoying the view of Lake Michigan and the Chicago skyline while eating peanut butter and jelly sandwiches, Brook says, "Mommy, my legs hurt so bad!"

"Mine are, too," I answer. 'We've done a lot of walking today. Bob, how about getting the car and picking us up? We are all really tired."

Brook continues to complain about her legs into the evening.

"I think we're just overtired," Bob says.

"She's complaining about the joints in her knees and her feet," Mom interjects. "My brother had the same symptoms when he was a kid and he had rheumatic fever,"

"Bob, that's it. I could not think of the disease, but that is it. She could have rheumatic fever," I say excitedly.

"Jesus Christ, Nina. There you go again," Bob roars. "Over-dramatizing every situation!"

The next morning when we wake, Brook continues to complain and tells us she does not feel well. We give her some aspirin, which seems to help. We drive home and settle in for the evening.

The next morning, Bob and I are pouring our first cups of coffee when I look up to see Brook crawling out of her bedroom, pulling her body along the carpet with her elbows and forearms. Mommy, I can't walk," she cries.

Bob runs to pick her up and I run to the phone to call Dr. Holloway's answering service. He calls me back immediately and tells me to take her to the hospital right away.

"Could it be rheumatic fever?" I ask.

"It could be, but it could also be arthritis. It could be a number of things," he says. "I'll meet you at the emergency entrance."

We call Nora and ask her to stay with the kids. We rush to the hospital, where a nurse takes us to an exam room to draw blood for tests. While we are waiting, I see that the skin on Brook's knees and around her ankles is else? I cannot make sense of my husband or my world but I have too much to do just to get through the day, so I push my fear to the side for now.

We look forward to taking a few days off from work to visit our parents and do some sightseeing in Chicago. It will be the first time we share "our city," the one in which we were raised, with the kids. We visit one of the museums. As we rest on a grassy area outside enjoying the view of Lake Michigan and the Chicago skyline while eating peanut butter and jelly sandwiches, Brook says, "Mommy, my legs hurt so bad!"

"Mine are, too," I answer. 'We've done a lot of walking today. Bob, how about getting the car and picking us up? We are all really tired."

Brook continues to complain about her legs into the evening.

"I think we're just overtired," Bob says.

"She's complaining about the joints in her knees and her feet," Mom interjects. "My brother had the same symptoms when he was a kid and he had rheumatic fever,"

"Bob, that's it. I could not think of the disease, but that is it. She could have rheumatic fever," I say excitedly.

"Jesus Christ, Nina. There you go again," Bob roars. "Over-dramatizing every situation!"

The next morning when we wake, Brook continues to complain and tells us she does not feel well. We give her some aspirin, which seems to help. We drive home and settle in for the evening.

The next morning, Bob and I are pouring our first cups of coffee when I look up to see Brook crawling out of her bedroom, pulling her body along the carpet with her elbows and forearms. Mommy, I can't walk," she cries.

Bob runs to pick her up and I run to the phone to call Dr. Holloway's answering service. He calls me back immediately and tells me to take her to the hospital right away.

"Could it be rheumatic fever?" I ask.

"It could be, but it could also be arthritis. It could be a number of things," he says. "I'll meet you at the emergency entrance."

We call Nora and ask her to stay with the kids. We rush to the hospital, where a nurse takes us to an exam room to draw blood for tests. While we are waiting, I see that the skin on Brook's knees and around her ankles is

"You went for a drive? You have never done anything like that before. Why would you go for a drive?"

"I thought I might get tired, you know, de-stress myself," he says.

"Why were the car's lights off?" I ask.

"I thought maybe if the shades weren't pulled down low enough in the bedroom, the lights coming up the drive might wake you," he answers.

"What's happening to you, Bob?" I scream.

"I don't know. I don't know," he says as he sits down and puts his head between his knees.

"You are scaring me to death!" I yell at him.

"Don't worry. I'll get ahold of myself," he attempts to reassure us both.

Again, I cannot sleep the rest of the night.

Within just two days, it happens a third time. He is not in bed, so I peek out of the window and notice the car is still here this time. As I walk softly out of the bedroom, I can hear him talking in a hushed voice on the phone in the kitchen. The lights are off and I silently walk up behind him.

"Who are you talking to, Bob?" I ask in a strong tone of voice.

He drops the phone, clambers to pick it up, and says, "The weather. I was calling to check on the weather."

"It's two o'clock in the morning! Why on earth do you need to know the temperature?"

"I just couldn't sleep. Listening to the temperature over and over again makes me sleepy," he answers as he hangs up the phone.

This happens a couple more times, too, but on those occasions, he pulls the phone cord out as far as he can so he can see me coming. He hangs up the phone quietly and then he denies he was ever on the phone. He rants and raves and tells me I am losing my mind and imagining things.

Even after all of this, I just now begin to question, "Could he be talking to another woman?" I have to smile at the foolishness of that thought. It would be more likely for me to have an affair than for Bob to have one. He is the All-American guy, good father, devoted husband. But something is still very wrong. I feel I am walking down a frightening path, but I cannot put my finger on the source of the fear. Is he that stressed over the betrayal of those we thought were trusted friends and employees? Or is it something red and warm to the touch. The areas are so tender that she will not let anyone touch them, crying in pain when we try.

Hours later, Dr. Holloway enters the room grim-faced, bearing the bad news. "She has rheumatic fever. This disease can leave her with damage to her heart. It is not inevitable, but you must be prepared that it is possible. We won't know the answer until the disease runs its course, which takes weeks."

Brook is admitted to the hospital and put into an area for infectious patients. The staff wears masks and gloves. We have to do the same.

Her pain intensifies over the next several days. To change her bed linens, a team of nurses has to pull the sheet under her taut and use it as a stretcher to place her on another bed. They then change the sheets on her bed and repeat the transfer, very carefully pulling the old sheet away from under her, inch by inch. Afterwards, they change her hospital gown and she screams the whole time. Her nurses say that they dread it when she needs the bedpan, but I know they do not as much as she does or as I do. I cannot eat or sleep seeing Brook like this.

Rheumatic fever almost does not exist anymore. Most doctors, even elderly doctors, have never in their long years of practice even seen what it looks like. Consequently, Brook becomes an observational and learning tool for the medical students at this teaching hospital. One day, when I enter her room, I stop short to see her bed surrounded by doctors and nurses. I can't believe my eyes! They are taking turns touching her red areas, asking her if it hurts, and telling the others that the red areas are hot to the touch. Brook is dripping with perspiration and crying.

"Get out of here, you animals! All of you! Get out of here now!" I yell at them. "Call Dr. Holloway, immediately," I scream to a nurse at the desk at the nursing station.

I turn back to the medical team. "How dare you make my child a guinea pig?" I yell, furious.

I put my arms around Brook and press my face against hers. I feel her wet tears on my cheek and cry with her. And then a rage builds up inside me. I run back out to the nurse, boiling with rage. "Get Dr. Holloway here now!" I want the head of this asylum here now, too!"

I run back to the room and assure Brook that if I have to stay here day and night, I will never let anyone touch her again without my permission. I cannot calm down. I cannot leave her side. I feel the anger burning inside of me, and I am ready to claw anyone who comes close to her. I pull the chair up to the bed, and we put our noses together. "I'll never be further away than this again." I promise her.

I rouse from sleep to hear my name from a distance. I look up to see Dr. Holloway. "I'm sorry, Nina. The nurse told me what happened. I've put up a notice that no one is to touch her or examine her except for me," Dr. Holloway says apologetically. "I wasn't aware that was happening. I assure you it will never happen again." He gently examines her and then Brook falls asleep.

I lie on the lounge chair next to the bed. She is suffering and there is nothing I can do to share her pain. I wish for time to pass quickly so this disease will leave her. I pray to God that it will not damage her heart and rob her of a normal life. I stay all night, every night.

On some nights, I visit with our neighbors, who are sitting with their son at the hospital, too. Their boy, Bobby, used to play in the big tree behind our house with our children. He is dying of brain cancer. Strangely, that makes me feel lucky. We have a chance of bringing our child back home alive.

The day finally comes that the redness begins to dissipate. I do not say anything to Brook about my fear of the damage that the disease might have done to her heart. Instead, we celebrate with popcorn and ice cream.

A few days later, we are informed that the disease has left her with a heart murmur. She is lucky that she will probably be able to lead a fairly normal life. She will only have to take a mild dose of penicillin each day for years to come and a heavier dose of antibiotics before any dental procedure and all surgeries. We will go home soon, and I celebrate inside, grateful to take Brook out of this place and heartbroken for the parents of Bobby, who never will. As I leave the hospital this day, I stop at the chapel to thank God for watching over my child's life.

The next day, she is to be moved into a children's ward to share the company of other children recovering from a variety of illnesses. When she arrives, she makes friends with seven other little girls.

"A noisy bunch! Are you sure that you are all really sick and not just trying to get out of going to school?" I joke with them.

Most of them seem to be enjoying each other's company and the couple of hours they have per day to distract themselves from their pain. However, I notice one child who does not ever smile and always turns her back to us. The nurse tells me she is recovering from her third round of skin grafts after being burned in a fire. She never laughs or plays. She just lies there and looks at us. "Her injuries are much deeper than her skin," I think to myself.

Several days later, I have an idea. I run it by the head nurse. "Sounds good to me," she agrees.

I leave the hospital and return later in the day. I pull all of the girls' wheeled beds together to the center of the ward. I have decided to teach them how to play poker. I give each child a roll of pennies and a list of each hand of cards and which hands beat which. After two days, they really get the hang of it. They laugh and scream playfully at each other when one of them wins a hand. They make so much noise that the nurses sternly tells us to keep the door closed. We laugh even louder.

One day, while we are playing, Sister Anne wanders in. Everyone becomes quiet and looks down at their beds. She looks around and realizes what we were up to. A huge smile comes over her face as she does the sign of the cross, looking toward the heavens. She then lightly covers her mouth and whispers, "I hope we don't get raided!" as she leaves our casino.

The kids cannot wait for me to get there every day. The little girl with the burns eventually plays and laughs with us, too. The nurses tell me she has been there for three months and that they have never seen her smile. I wonder, but never ask, why a ten-year-old girl has no visitors. I feel proud, though, that I have helped her find her smile.

I do not visit Brook in the mornings anymore. She is on the mend, and I need to attend to all the things I have neglected over the past few weeks. I call in the mornings and afternoons and visit in the evenings. I do not know if Bob still makes phone calls during the night. I have been so tired that when I finally lay down, I sleep until the alarm wakes me.

Bob visits Brook in the mornings before work. I see him in the early morning. He does his kennel chores and leaves for work. And then I see him briefly at supper before I leave for the hospital to be with Brook. While I am at the hospital, Bob checks the kids' homework and gets them ready for bed. I arrive home just in time to kiss them goodnight.

One evening, as we get ready for bed, I ask him, "Are you still driving Sue home from work?"

"No, her husband's work schedule has improved, so now he is able to pick her up."

We say nothing more, but something is different about him. He seems so emotionally unattached to me, to us. I wonder what is happening to our marriage and begin to feel a sense of loss. "I'm just too tired to even care," I think briefly before I fall asleep.

The next day, I talk to Lucy. "Hi, Lucy! How's it going?" I ask.

"Fine! How is Brook?"

"She's on the road to recovery," I proudly announce. "Lucy, I'm worried about Bob. He does not look good. His complexion is pasty, and he seems very nervous all the time. He is not interested in much of anything anymore. I know this is going to sound crazy, Lucy, but I think he might be having an affair with Sue." I laugh nervously as I try to make it sound like I am joking.

"I know I'm being foolish. Maybe my imagination is working overtime," I add.

"I wouldn't know. I wouldn't know," she repeats after an uncomfortable pause. I detect something unnatural in her voice.

"What can I say?" she says in a very soft voice. "What can I say? I don't know what to tell you."

"Of course you can't say anything to me," I say to her. "I've put you in a terrible position. Thank you, Lucy." I know that she loves Bob and that he is responsible for her being hired into her current position. I cannot expect her to give away much, but when I hang up, I know that I am right. Lucy's response says it all. I decide I will broach the subject with him this evening.

"Bob, are you feeling okay?" I ask.

"Yes, I'm fine."

"You look a little pale. Are you getting enough rest? You worry me. You wake up in the middle of the night and I find you on the phone. You have told me that when you are gone at night, you are out driving, wearing off tension, but you have never done that before. You could be having an affair," I say, attempting to joke. "Maybe with Sue."

"Are you nuts?" he screams at me. "You have quite the imagination. You need to have your head examined." He leaves the room. My husband seems to be living a separate life from me these days. We no longer have a connection.

As I lie down in bed, my mind cannot stop wandering. I abruptly remember something, a comment Lucy made the last time she babysat for us. "Did you know that Sue's husband works the night shift?" she stated. I took it as part of the conversation we were having, but she must have been trying to tell me something. I did not pay attention.

"I hear you now, Lucy," I think to myself.

This cannot be happening. Maybe if it is, it is just a little infatuation. I feel so terribly alone. I need to talk to someone, but I cannot talk. I cannot tell anyone. Anyone I told would think I am crazy. Everyone knows what a great guy Bob is. Sue is not even as pretty as I am, but she is ten years younger and a couple sizes smaller. The last time I stopped in at the clinic to take Bob to lunch, I saw Sue bend over and noticed the outline of her bikini underwear under her white uniform pants. "What a tease!" I thought to myself.

When Bob first started his job, he told me that Sue's Mom worked there, too. He said that Sue's Mom and the administrator of the clinic were involved in a long-time affair and that each of their spouses just looked the other way. I wonder if that is happening with Bob and Sue, too, but I convince myself that it just cannot be. He is such a wonderful man, and I hate myself for having these thoughts. I feel guilty for having these thoughts.

The day arrives for Brook to leave the hospital and we throw a little party for her. I check her out of the hospital and bring her home. The kids are so glad for her return home and for our life to return to normal. We hold off on the party until Bob comes home. He is late quite often now and tonight is no different. He walks in the door and yells to Brook. She comes running into his arms. They hug, kiss, and dance around the kitchen. Our little party brings Bob and I together again, if only for a fleeting moment. It felt good.

After I tuck everyone in, I find myself looking into the full-length mirror. I do not feel attractive anymore, even though I am only a few pounds heavier than I was when we got married. As I climb into bed, I swing my legs up and notice the heavy, ugly veins that appeared when I was three months pregnant with Eric. They were supposed to disappear after he was born, but they never did. I cannot wear shorts anymore. The blue veins are gross.

The next day, I call Dr. Grey, my primary care physician and I make an appointment to see him.

"I think I'd like to have these ugly veins removed," I tell him when he comes into the examination room.

"Well, let's have a look," he says. "It won't be a problem. You are too pretty to have to cover those legs. You will have to be hospitalized for a few days and then take it easy for a few weeks. Can you handle that?"

"You bet. Make the arrangements." The next day, he calls to let me know the appointment has been made for the following Tuesday. Lucy will come to babysit while Bob stays with me.

On the day of the surgery, I look nervously at Bob. "My legs will be beautiful again sweetheart, like they used to be. Remember back to our school years? My nickname was *Legs*. Look at them now!" I laugh. Bob just smirks and that really hurts my feelings.

As I come out of the anesthesia, I can barely see him. "You're fine," he says. "I'm going to the clinic. See you later." I feel him kiss my forehead and hear him leave.

Later in the day, he comes back. "Hi, Kitts," Bob says to me. "Come on, sleepyhead. Wake up."

I open my eyes and notice he is sitting next to me wearing his hospital whites. "I've been here for an hour. I have to get home and relieve Lucy so she can get home. I'll call you later," he whispers, kisses me, and leaves. I fall back asleep.

Bob pops in and out for the next two days. When he is here, it's almost like he can't wait to leave. I convince myself it's because he has so much to do. I sure miss the children, but I must confess that I enjoy having my meals delivered and not having to do the dishes.

I leave the hospital with bandages from my knees to my ankles, but the ugly veins are gone. There are many incisions, each an inch and a half long. They are closed with nasty black stitches. Dr. Grey tells me that the stitches will be taken out in two weeks and the scarring will almost disappear in time.

A few days after I return home, my incisions become red, hot, and irritated. I call Dr. Grey and ask him if he can look at my legs. He tells me to come into the office right away. I call my friend, Patty, and she drives me.

"Are you taking the antibiotics I prescribed?" Dr. Grey asks. "And the muscle relaxers?"

I nod indicating that I am.

As he examined my legs, he said, "I've done this surgery a hundred times and I have never seen a patient with every set of stitches infected. Sometimes, a patient will have maybe one, or even two sets infected, but *all* of yours are infected. Are you keeping off of your feet and staying at home? You aren't working at the kennel, are you?"

"I haven't even been to the kennel since I had the surgery," I assure him.

He cleans the irritated incisions with an antibiotic cream and says, "Well, I'm completely baffled. I want to see you in three days. You will be able to drive yourself by then. Here, apply this cream over the stitches. You should notice a dramatic difference by then."

Three days later, my legs are indeed looking better, so I take a walk over to the kennel to say hello. "Hi!" I say as I smile at Zack, our new dog groomer, and Nora.

"Well, look who's here!" Zack announces.

"I'm checking up on the two of you," I joke. "I'm driving all by myself to Dr. Grey's office, and I decided that if I could do that, then why not walk over here and pester you both?"

I watch Zack groom for a few minutes when I begin to feel a bit shaky. "I think I'll head on back to the house; I'm a little tired," I say. I suddenly feel weak.

As I fall to the floor, I hear Zack's voice. "Are you okay?"

I look into his face above me, bewildered, and ask, "What happened?"

"One minute, you were standing at the window watching me, and the next minute, I didn't see you. Then I heard a thud. From my grooming window, I saw you on the floor," Zack says. "Let me help you back to the house. Maybe you've overdone it."

As we walk into the house, I thank him and send him back to work.

I call Bob and tell him what happened. "Bob, the strangest thing just happened to me. I don't know if I fainted or just got a little shaky in my knees."

"You probably turned too fast and got lightheaded. How are you feeling now?" he asked.

"I'm feeling fine," I answer.

"When you see Dr. Grey, tell him what happened. Call me when you get back home," he says.

A few minutes later, as I pick up the car keys, the phone rings. "Nina," Sue says, "Bob told me what just happened. I do not think you should drive yourself. I'll pick you up and take you to the doctor."

"Don't be ridiculous," I say. "I'm just fine. I will drive myself. Thank you for the offer."

I hang up the phone. "Can you believe this?" I ask myself. "The woman with whom I believe my husband is having an affair has just offered to be my chauffer. Bob is constantly telling me I'm crazy. Maybe I *am* going nuts!"

As I drive to the doctor's office, I replay the last few days in my mind. Bob has been saying that Sue is just a friend. He says he likes that because all of our friends are *my* friends; none of our friends were originally *his* friends. He is proud that Sue and Chuck were *his* friends first. "What an odd and childish response," I think.

"You collapsed?" Dr. Grey asks, shocked. I explain what happened earlier as he examines my legs. "Nina, are you taking any drugs other than the antibiotics and muscle relaxers?"

"No. Nothing."

"Have you had any other episodes like this one? Have you been lightheaded since then? Did you have a problem driving here?"

I shake my head, "No."

"Well, I have to assume that since you haven't had any other episodes like that, maybe you did just get lightheaded because you weren't used to being up. Call me if anything else happens. Here is a prescription for a different antibiotic. Get it filled and start taking it right away."

He takes me by the hand and says, "Laura wants you and your family to stop by the house after church on Sunday to have breakfast with us. We also want you to see our new filly."

"I'd love to," I say.

As I drive home, I remind myself to tell Bob of Dr. Grey's invitation. Bob would love to own a racehorse, but Dr. Grey once told us you only buy a racehorse if you have more money than common sense and if you want your heart broken. He breeds and races horses and takes pride in the fact that he owns the top money earner in the state. His stable boasted some famous names, and then one day a virus hit his stable and wiped out half of his horses, one of them being his top earner. His heart and dreams died with them, and neither he nor his stable ever recovered.

As I pull into the driveway after my appointment, I can hear our dogs barking and begging for my attention, so I walk over to our breeding kennel. It feels so good to run my fingers through their fur, scratch their ears, and rub their tummies.

The last dog I visit is our great Champion, Hans. I pet his head and scratch it only to realize something is wrong. I look more closely and notice that his head feels bony. I step back and take a closer look at him. I run my hands over his body, through his coat and I feel his ribs. His coat is dry. He is wagging his tail so hard that it shakes his body, making it difficult to get a good look at him.

"Hans stop! Hold still!" He finally calms down, and I look into his mouth and notice his gums are pale. He is absolutely emaciated! "My baby, my beautiful boy, our great Champion! Oh, dear God. He must be terribly ill," I think. I open the gate, and he bounces around, runs up to the house, and waits for me to catch up. I open the door, and he runs around the house like a crazy dog, happy to be back inside.

I call our veterinarian. "This is Nina. I am calling about Hans. I have not been out to our show kennel for weeks because of my vein surgery. Yes, I am fine. I have not played with them lately, so I decided to get into the pens with each of them. I discovered that Hans is skin and bones. Bob feeds and waters them. He's never said anything about a problem, so I assumed everything was okay, but I think Hans is very, very sick."

"Bring him in right now," our vet orders.

I open the door to the van and Hans jumps inside. He is used to traveling for dog shows, so he assumes his usual position. He puts his rear against the passenger seat, and I smile to myself because it looks as though he is sitting on the seat like a human. He is the foundation of our kennel and our pride and joy.

When we arrive at the vet and after he is physically examined, Hans is taken in for x-rays.

"I think he has a heart problem. My machine is not powerful enough to get a good chest x-ray of this big guy. I'll call another vet here in town who has the equipment we need to take a good picture."

He calls the other vet and says to me, "Take him right over there. He's waiting for you."

Hans jumps right back into the van, wagging his tail the whole time. He has no idea that he is ill. But I am shaking badly, so angry with Bob. I wonder how this dog has become so thin and how Bob did not notice it.

"Do you think he'll lie here and not move?" the new vet asks.

I'll stand at his head, and he'll be fine. I'll pet him," I say. Hans behaves perfectly, and the doctor takes the pictures. I keep Hans on the table while the x-rays develop.

When the vet returns, he says, "My machine isn't good enough to get a much clearer picture, but what I can see is that there is a shadow around his heart. It looks like fluid. I believe he is experiencing heart failure. If you'd like, I'll make arrangements for you to take him to the University Of Illinois School of Veterinary Medicine."

I agree. "Ten o'clock Monday. Have him there," he says upon his return from making the appointment.

As soon as I arrive at the house, I call Bob and explain what is going on. "How the hell could this have happen, Bob? Where is your head? How could you not notice his condition? He has lost ninety pounds!" I slam the phone down and stand there, unmoving, and just cry.

"What's the matter, Mommy?" the children ask when they notice I am crying.

I explain that Hans is sick and ask Brook to run to the kennel for me. I tell her to ask Nora to close up for me and ask Zack if he can stay a bit longer to help me get Hans into the bathing tub. He will be living in the house for the next few days, and he sure needs the kennel smell washed out of him.

I shampoo Hans and trim his nails, and then I put him into a wire cage and stick the hair dryer arms in the holes to dry him quickly. An hour later, I sit on the floor and brush him. I notice that his coat is falling out by the buckets. "I've failed you, Hans," I say aloud. "I've had so much going on that I've neglected you and all the others who depend on me. I'm sure I'm failing my children, too." My tears fall on his back. He just looks at me, panting and appreciative of the attention.

I cry harder and think, "What is happening? I am a failure in every area of my life. I cannot keep up with both kennels and the children, too. I am failing in all directions, possibly even in my marriage. I am furious with Bob. We need to put our lives back in order, and it must be done *now*."

On Monday morning, I make the two-hour trip to the University of Illinois.

"Hans is most certainly experiencing heart failure," the veterinarian at U of I confirms. "I'll put him on water pills to relieve him of some fluid and make it easier for him to breathe."

From that point on, I keep him in the house but each day, for months, I feel him slipping away from us. On a cold winter day, I hold him in my arms as our vet puts him to sleep forever. He is only five years old and at the top of his career. I kiss him and kiss him and kiss him.

A gentleman who works at the cemetery down the road comes over with his equipment and digs a hole big enough for our giant, beloved Saint

Bernard. I wrap him in one of the blankets with which he slept. Champion Hans of Cold Creek has died. And a piece of our hearts has died with him.

I feel the same cold wind that I felt that day years ago when Mary Kubbiachi read my palm, and I experience a déjà vu. The same foreboding feeling overcomes me.

CHAPTER FOURTEEN
DAY FOURTEEN
IN THE HOSPITAL

I pick up the ringing phone next to my bed. "This is Chuck," the voice tells me. My heart beats faster. I cannot even speak. "Nina, did you hear me? This is Chuck."

"Yes. Yes, I hear you. I just didn't expect to hear from you," I say.

"I understand you are considering reconciling with your husband," he abruptly states.

"Well, I'm thinking about it. I understand that his medical problem, hypoglycemia, could be responsible for his actions. He tells me the affair with your wife has been over for a while now and he hasn't seen her except at work."

"One reason I'm calling is to ask if anyone in the area other than you and Bob sells Sir John's dog food?"

"Sir John's dog food?" I ask. "No one else in the state that I'm aware of. Why?"

"Well, I went to Sue's house yesterday to pick up my children for visitation and I noticed ten new bags of dog food. Ten fifty-pound bags of *that* dog food. So if no one sells it but you, and Bob has not seen Sue, how do you think that dog food got there? And there's no way she can afford to buy ten bags at one time. Seeing those bags of dog food made me realize they're still seeing each other. For me, it doesn't matter. We are already divorced. But I feel I have a responsibility to tell you after all that has happened to you."

After a brief pause, Chuck continues, "But this is not just about the dog food. I have more to tell you. About a year ago, before our divorce, I was sleeping upstairs in our bedroom. My work schedule had been changed and I was on the midnight shift. I must have been in a deep sleep when the phone rang. I think it must have been about 10:00 p.m. I picked it up at the same time Sue picked it up downstairs. Before I could say anything, Sue answered. Your husband was on the other end.

I listened but I was so sleepy, so I sort of only half-listened. When they hung up, I fell right back to sleep. Later that day, I called Sue at the clinic and asked if Bob called while I was sleeping. She denied it. Then I doubted that I overheard a conversation. After all, what they were talking about sounded bizarre. I have thought about it many times over the past few months, but each time I came to the conclusion that I should not say anything to you if I'm not even sure it occurred.

Then when this happened to you, I decided I must say something. And when I saw the dog food and she lied about where it came from, and then I heard you might reconcile with Bob, I knew I had to tell you. Just listen and see if this makes any sense to you. Maybe you will think I am crazy, or maybe not. At least hear me out."

I press the phone hard against my ear, ignoring the pain and I sit up straight. Every nerve in my body is alert. I do not want to hear it but I do not want to miss a word, either. "Go on."

"Sue was yelling at your husband, saying that you could have been killed or killed someone else in an auto accident, and if the drugs were found in your system, he would be in jail. They were talking about your leg injury. Did you have anything like that?" he asks.

"Yes, I had my varicose veins stripped," I answer.

"Did you have a problem, like fainting or passing out?"

"Yes, yes, I did." The muscles in my body involuntarily tense up and I listen even more intently. "Tell me!" I demand.

Chuck continues, "Remember, this is fuzzy to me. Bob told Sue he removed the capsules containing your antibiotics and replaced them with sleeping medication. He thought the sleeping medication mixed with your muscle relaxant would make you sleep sounder and through the night so he could get out of the house to be with Sue.

Sue yelled at him again and said someone would have done toxicology if something had happened and they could have both been blamed. She told him to replace your antibiotic capsules immediately.

Oh, and there is one more thing. Do you remember anything about spoiled tuna making you sick?"

"No, I don't know anything about spoiled tuna." I say.

"Well, I don't remember any more of the conversation. Does any of this make sense to you?"

I am emotionally deflated. I can barely speak. "Yes, Chuck. It makes a lot of sense and explains why I fainted. It explains why my incisions were infected. I think if I had known this a long time ago, I would have called it quits. But I am now enlightened. Their sick relationship existed then and it continues now. Do you remember back to a year ago when I was telling you I suspected this was happening? You thought I was crazy and blew me off!

But thank you, Chuck. Thank you. I know what I have to do. Your phone call just turned my indecision into a definite decision. I'm so glad you found the courage to speak up. You are not just protecting me, but you are also helping me to protect myself. Chuck, I truly hope that God gives you better than what you have had to deal with recently. I think you may have saved my life today."

We say our goodbyes.

I feel as though I am emotionally throwing dirt over a casket at the cemetery. This signifies the finale of the dream that was our marriage. It all makes sense now. I remember the day I first left the house after my surgery. I walked to the kennel and fainted. I thought there was no reason for it, but of course, I did not realize that I had been drugged. How could I have realized that Bob replaced the capsules containing my antibiotics with sleeping medication? How could I have known that Bob, my husband, my best friend, and my lover - the man I slept next to each night - brought those capsules home, knowing I would take them. My God, I was taking sleeping pills and muscle relaxers simultaneously. It is amazing I did not die from that!

My God, he was *drugging* me. I repeat that word over and over again. I do not remember eating any spoiled food, but I have no idea what else they may have tried. Except, of course, the games with the phone. And Bob telling me I must be "going crazy" because he wasn't on the phone.

The dog food, though, is the final blow. Even as I am here, fighting for my life, he is still taking care of *her*. It is not over and it is not going to be over. I must let him go. I may not live through it the next time.

I can hear my Mom repeating one of her mottos: *"When it's too much, even the pigs don't want it."* I know now that it is just too much.

"I still love you, Bob," I say to myself. "But I love my life more."

I pick up the phone to call the man who used to be my husband. "Bob, Chuck just called me with some interesting information." I tell him what Chuck told me.

"He is nuts!" Bob screams. "He's just crazy jealous. Sue is dating some cop, and he wants to lash out."

"Explain the sleeping pills, Bob."

"Chuck's insane! Sue should have divorced him long ago!"

"Explain the dog food, Bob!"

"She called and said she didn't have any money for food for the dog. So I took some of ours to her."

"If the affair were truly over, you would have told her that it was her problem. And ten bags at that? No, Bob. It is not over. I know now that my fainting at the kennel was no accident. I could have died. And this time, I *did* die. I cannot ever trust you again. It all makes sense now. Remember the time at the Vanguards' lake? You never did get permission to go. And then there were all the late night drives in the country. What were you planning? Were you planning to kill me each of those nights as well?"

"Kitts, Kitts, please don't hang up. Please. I love you."

"I love you, too, Bob. I always will. But our love story is over. It has been over for a long time, and I just did not know it. But I see clearly now."

I hang up the phone, lay my head back onto my pillow, and cry out loud. I no longer have a choice. I was reluctant, but I still had hope that this was an accident - or something that it could be explained somehow. Chuck shattered my optimism. Our life can never be put back together.

I confront the fact that all the things that happened these past few years were more serious and deadlier than I could ever have imagined. In the beginning, Bob and Sue were just being sneaky. Then, when they could not successfully drive me to the point of a mental breakdown, Bob resorted to murder, staged as an accident. Mission almost accomplished. He was so desperate to remove me from this life without giving up the kids, the kennels, the land, the house, and especially his parents. He wanted it all - except for me. My God, he must harbor such *hate* for me.

As I lie here, I wonder how Chuck is doing. He was so naïve. I called him and told him of my suspicions early on and he did not believe me. Then, little by little, he must have started questioning the incidents. Before we knew it, he was having marital issues, too.

Devoid of even a glimmer of hope for my marriage, I am finally at peace with my decision to end my marriage. I think back to the fourteenth year of our marriage, in an attempt to bolster what I now know is the terrifying truth.

YEAR FOURTEEN
OF OUR MARRIAGE

I find Bob on the phone in the middle of the night, night after night. He always gives me an excuse, and it is usually that he is checking the next day's weather forecast or the time. He constantly comments on my mental instability, saying that I am imagining things, that I must be having a mental breakdown, or that I must be going through menopause.

The phone calls become incessant. During the day, the calls will come to me at the kennel, and later, they come to me at the house. They are frightening and I am becoming physically agitated and sharp with my tongue. I answer and someone sits at the other end of the line just breathing, not saying a word. "I know it's you, Sue," or "I know it's you, Bob," I say and hang up.

I am becoming more and more distraught, more nervous, and more anxious. I accuse him constantly of my suspicions. One evening I actually accuse him of the phone calls. I do not feel I have anyone in whom I can confide. Bob laughs at me and chides me about how crazy he thinks I am becoming. "I really believe that you are losing your mind," he taunts me. "Maybe you should go back to the mental hospital."

We try not to argue in front of the children, but that has become impossible. My emotions are helter-skelter.

YEAR FOURTEEN OF OUR MARRIAGE

I find Bob on the phone in the middle of the night, night after night. He always gives me an excuse, and it is usually that he is checking the next day's weather forecast or the time. He constantly comments on my mental instability, saying that I am imagining things, that I must be having a mental breakdown, or that I must be going through menopause.

The phone calls become incessant. During the day, the calls will come to me at the kennel, and later, they come to me at the house. They are frightening and I am becoming physically agitated and sharp with my tongue. I answer and someone sits at the other end of the line just breathing, not saying a word. "I know it's you, Sue," or "I know it's you, Bob," I say and hang up.

I am becoming more and more distraught, more nervous, and more anxious. I accuse him constantly of my suspicions. One evening I actually accuse him of the phone calls. I do not feel I have anyone in whom I can confide. Bob laughs at me and chides me about how crazy he thinks I am becoming. "I really believe that you are losing your mind," he taunts me. "Maybe you should go back to the mental hospital."

We try not to argue in front of the children, but that has become impossible. My emotions are helter-skelter.

"I love you, too, Bob. I always will. But our love story is over. It has been over for a long time, and I just did not know it. But I see clearly now."

I hang up the phone, lay my head back onto my pillow, and cry out loud. I no longer have a choice. I was reluctant, but I still had hope that this was an accident - or something that it could be explained somehow. Chuck shattered my optimism. Our life can never be put back together.

I confront the fact that all the things that happened these past few years were more serious and deadlier than I could ever have imagined. In the beginning, Bob and Sue were just being sneaky. Then, when they could not successfully drive me to the point of a mental breakdown, Bob resorted to murder, staged as an accident. Mission almost accomplished. He was so desperate to remove me from this life without giving up the kids, the kennels, the land, the house, and especially his parents. He wanted it all - except for me. My God, he must harbor such *hate* for me.

As I lie here, I wonder how Chuck is doing. He was so naïve. I called him and told him of my suspicions early on and he did not believe me. Then, little by little, he must have started questioning the incidents. Before we knew it, he was having marital issues, too.

Devoid of even a glimmer of hope for my marriage, I am finally at peace with my decision to end my marriage. I think back to the fourteenth year of our marriage, in an attempt to bolster what I now know is the terrifying truth.

Fear has taken over my life, and I cannot shake it. I call Lucy again. "Lucy, is there anything you can do to help me? I really think there is something going on between Bob and Sue and I don't know what to do," I plead.

"I don't know what to say," she repeats nervously, afraid to admit it, I am sure.

"I'm sure everyone at the clinic is also aware of it," I say to her.

"I don't know what to tell you. I wish I could be of more help," she says unconvincingly. I know she wants to help me, but she feels she has to be loyal to Bob.

One night, I create a romantic evening and do my best to be glamorous and sexy for Bob. I feed the children and put them to bed early. I greet Bob in a beautiful negligee and fix a gourmet feast with champagne and candlelight. I am working at making my marriage work and Bob thinks it is funny. He walks in from work, stands there in the kitchen and just laughs at me! I am emotionally devastated.

Bob often calls and says that he has late patients, comes home hours later and goes to bed without dinner. I wonder how this woman with three small children can be having an affair, but as I think about it, I understand that she could be having an affair quite easily. Her own mother has been having an affair for fifteen years. This is the kind of lifestyle that Sue is used to, but it is not the kind of life I can tolerate.

The situation is worsening and I am beginning to crumble emotionally. I just do not know what to do.

This morning, Bob walks into the house after finishing his chores at the kennel and announces that we are going to sell a Saint Bernard puppy to Sue and Chuck.

"Where in the hell are they going to put a puppy? They have almost no yard!" I reply.

"Their yard is small, but they are in the market to buy a bigger house."

I am taken aback. She is taking one of our puppies, which will give him a reason for more contact with her. My fear is unshakable, but I cannot say no, as I have no proof of anything. So, we sell them a puppy.

On the day the puppy is to be delivered to the Bellows, Bob suggests we make it a family event. I feel it is another effort to cram a false friendship down my throat to cover up his lies. "Come with me. We'll take the puppy over to her house together," he sweetly suggests. "We'll bring the kids along, too."

When we arrive at the house, Sue answers the door, surprised to see *me*. "Oh! Come in!" she welcomes us, puzzled. I hand her the puppy that Bob chose for her. My heart is breaking and I cannot believe I agreed to come here. "Why did I agree to this," I wonder.

"She's come a long way since she was born!" Sue says.

My eyes flash to try to catch Bob's, as I realize that he did not pick out the puppy, but that she did. She had to have been to our house sometime when I was not there. I decide not to say anything, at least for the time being. "Come on, kids. Let's get going! I still have to close up the kennel for the night," I say, and Bob nods in agreement.

We do not talk about the slip of her tongue. He must be hoping that I did not notice it. I wish that I had not.

I talk about my suspicions about Sue and Bob's affair with my in-laws. I make sly jokes about his "girlfriend" and complain about the late hours he keeps. Of course, they brush my ideas off verbally, but I know that my mother-in-law believes me. She can see the physical change in Bob, too, and I know she is getting the message.

They came to visit for the weekend. I casually mention my "crazy" uncertainties again while we are all eating dinner. Then I make it sound as though I am only kidding, my usual method of bringing up my suspicions. Bob glares at me with daggers shooting from his eyes. I notice the look on his mother's face. She saw his glare and I know that she realizes this is not a joke.

Over the following months, Mom says things during our phone calls like, "You two need to get out and have some fun." I can hear the genuine concern in her voice as she tries to save our marriage for us. Once, I overhear a phone conversation in the back bedroom between Bob and his Mom. I can hear him telling her quietly, "Mom, she is only a friend. I will talk to her if I want to. Get off my back."

Sometimes when they visit, she asks Bob questions like, "Do you ever visit with them?" or "How is her pup doing?" Bob elaborates on the puppy and tells them she might show it. I look at my mother-in-law and watch her face as she realizes there is definitely a problem.

A couple of months later, I am at the train station waiting for Mom and Dad, who are visiting us again for the weekend. Dad does not drive long distances anymore with his failing eyesight and he loves the train, anyway. In his younger days, he was a conductor on a Pittsburgh commuter line and his love for the train whistle still calls to him.

"How is it going?" Mom asks me nonchalantly when she arrives, but I understand her real question.

"I'm sure they're having an affair," I immediately admit.

"I don't know what he's thinking," Dad chimes in.

"Bob says they're only friends. He says I need a vacation and that my imagination is working overtime." I tell them, hoping they will support me.

"I don't know how you do all that you do," Mom says lovingly.

"She and her family are here visiting all the time," I tell them. "If I don't invite them, he gets nasty. Honestly, it is just not worth the fight. In fact, they're coming over for dinner tonight."

"You are not having that woman in your house!" Mom snaps without hesitation.

"I have to, Mom. He keeps saying that they are just friends. *His* friends."

We arrive home, I ask Sommer, "Where's Dad?"

"He's lying down," she says.

"Lying down?" I repeat, wondering. I look to Mom and Dad and say, "It's Saturday afternoon. He never naps. Maybe he just has a cold. Let's check him out."

We all walk into the bedroom. "Bob, your parents are here."

I walk over to him, touch him and notice he is cold, clammy, and very pale. "Bob, wake up. Bob! Wake up," I yell. I cannot rouse him. "Bob, what's the matter?" I ask him.

He does not respond. His parents wait silently in the bedroom with me, genuine concern on their faces.

"He must have taken some kind of medication. Bob, what is the matter? What have you done?" He does not answer, but I notice a pill bottle on the nightstand. I pick up the bottle and read its label aloud: *Valium*.

"How many did you take?" I scream at him. "And where did you get Valium? And *why*?"

"All of them," he slurs, ignoring my succeeding questions.

"When did you take them?" I am terrified now.

"Maybe a couple hours ago. I don't know." he slurs.

I run to the phone and call the emergency room. "How many did he take? Is he able to speak?" the doctor asks.

"I'm not sure how many he took. He speaks, but his speech is slurred."

The doctor advises, "Get him up and walking. Get some coffee into him. I do not believe that he took all of the pills he claims to have taken or he would not be able to speak to you. If he really took as many as he claims, he would be in a deep coma. Do not question him now. Just be sympathetic. If it looks like he needs it, get him to the hospital or call for an ambulance."

Bob's parents and I begin to walk him up and down the living room. He tells them he is under such stress and is so tired of being accused of this "alleged" affair by me. He insists that there is nothing going on but that he cannot get me off his back. After another two hours, he is more alert and feeling better. We have been so preoccupied with this mess that I forgot Sue and Chuck have been invited for dinner. They arrive with their three children.

My mother-in-law scolds him, "I told you before that this woman is not to be in this house."

Then she orders *me* to tell them to leave. "We're having some problems with Bob," I tell Sue and Chuck quietly. "He took an overdose of Valium. He is very upset and his folks think we better not have company tonight."

She asks how many pills he had taken and I tell her what he had told me. "He couldn't have taken all of them or he'd be dead. I'm sure he'll be okay," she whispers as they leave.

Bob cries for sympathy from his parents. He carries on about how I am falsely accusing him and making him crazy.

When he learns that I sent *his* friends away, he is so furious that he abruptly grabs his coat and leaves the house. He takes off in our car with no word as to where he intends to go. All we can do is wait and hope that he does not hurt himself or anyone else in the process of his tantrum. When he finally returns, we notice the car has a dented fender. Bob insists he does not know how it happened. Still feeling the lingering effects of the Valium, he goes to bed early.

I prepare and serve the dinner I had planned to make for them and our company. After dinner, his folks and I sit up, watching television and glancing quietly at each other, frightened of what is happening, of the known and unknown alike. We do not know how to deal with the situation.

They leave the next day instead of staying an extra day, as they had originally planned. They realize the enormity of the situation and do not know how to respond or how to help. Before Bob's mother parts, she says to him, "I don't want that woman in your house again."

On Monday morning, the children leave for school. I am headed to my friend Andrea's house. She will babysit Eric so I can drive to the University of Illinois to have a few puppies examined. I go downstairs to scoop up the puppies, but as I come upstairs, I unexpectedly bump into Bob. I had assumed that he had already left for work and evidently, he had assumed that I had already left to go to the kennel or to Andrea's. He is holding two of the children's sleeping bags and looks like a kid caught with his hand in the cookie jar.

"What are you doing with those sleeping bags?" I ask him.

"I, I, I had to go to the closet, and I noticed that they needed repair," he stammers.

"You saw the sleeping bags and noticed that they needed repair? Where do they need repair? Show me," I snap.

This is coming from a man who would not notice if the roof was coming off the house, let alone that the sleeping bags need repair. He never uses the kids' sleeping bags. They are kept in their closet, so there is no reason for him to come across them. My heart beats like crazy. I grab them from him and he leaves without another word, surely as shaken as I am.

My mind races. I know that he had planned to put them in the car for his afternoon rendezvous. I am so humiliated, and my heart breaks to think he chose that ugly duckling over a class act like me, as I imagine myself. I surely do not feel like a class act anymore, though. He is choosing a skinny, homely woman who wears bikini underwear he can see through white uniform pants over me, his wife who has stood by his side all these years. I try to regain my composure. It is important that I take the puppies for their exams, so I carry on with my plans.

I am shaking so badly I have difficulty putting the puppies into their cages and trouble unbuckling Eric's seatbelt when we arrive at Andrea's house. Noticing this, Andrea asks, "Nina, what's wrong?"

"Nothing," I say, fighting back tears. Up to this point, for well over a year, I have not mentioned my suspicions to anyone except his parents.

"Yes, there is. You are going to have a cup of coffee with me. You are not going anywhere being this upset. Something strange is going on, and we have to sit down and talk about it."

"What do you mean something strange is going on?" I asked. Her comment piques my curiosity.

"I've been getting a lot of strange phone calls from Bob," she whispers.

"You've been getting strange phone calls? Like what? What are you talking about?" I ask.

"He calls me all the time. He has never called me for anything before, let alone to just chat. Mostly he just talks about how depressed you are, how nervous you are, and how he thinks you are about to have a nervous breakdown. Nina, in all the years I have known you, you have never acted crazy, foolish, or irrational. I want an explanation of what's going on and I want it from you. Because I'm not getting it from Bob."

"Oh, Andrea, I could kiss you! I am so glad you are telling me this. I haven't been able to tell anyone for fear that they'd think I was out of my mind to think this great guy could do these things." I sit down and tell her of all the bizarre occurrences and his erratic behavior.

"You know you're right, Nina," she says.

"I can't be right, Andrea. You know what a great guy he is."

"I know the old Bob. I do not know this one and *you* do not know this one either. This is not the same man that I have known all these years. This is somebody new. This is a person who is definitely doing strange things. So let me ask, Why don't you prove it?"

"Well, how? You mean a detective?" I gasp.

"Why not?"

"First of all, it would cost money; second, it just can't be. It's probably just a little fling and it will end soon," I say.

"Have you mentioned it to him, accused him and has he denied it?" she asks.

"Yes, I've been accusing him."

"Well, you haven't gotten anywhere with that, have you?" she snorts back at me.

"Maybe you're right, Andrea," I say as I leave. "I'll consider it."

All the way to U of I, all I can think about is Bob. Andrea validated my suspicions and I could never thank her enough. I thank God for all that has just transpired. What courage it must have taken for our dearest friend to come forth and talk to me. Up until now, I have barely clung to my sanity. Now I know I am not crazy. He's trying to make me look crazy.

I pick up my son late in the afternoon and go home feeling a renewed sense of power. But I do not sleep well this night.

In the morning, I open the phone book to *detective* and call the first one. "Would you just listen to me before I decide whether I should hire you?" I ask, a little embarrassed to be calling.

He hears my story and asks, "Why did you wait so long to call me?"

"You're kidding. You really think there's something going on?" I say, excited.

"Of course there is. I'll probably prove it the first time I follow him," he says confidently.

"You're kidding," I repeat in disbelief.

"No. And let me tell you this; he has been getting away with this for so long now that he is feeling very secure. He is probably getting very careless. Also, he has been taking a lot of risks by working you into thinking you are insane. I would put money on it. I'll find him out the first attempt I make," he brags again.

The following day, we meet at The Abbey, and I give him cash from the cash box, a thousand dollars. It is an enormous amount of money, but Bob will never know. I do the bookkeeping. And I have to know, once and for all.

The detective asks me a lot of questions and takes notes. "I'll call you later with an update," he says assuredly.

A little later, the detective calls me as promised. He located Bob's car at the clinic and put a "trap," some kind of magnetic tracker, under the car. He explains he was able to follow up to a mile behind Bob via a radio signal. That afternoon, he followed Bob and Sue to Bradley Park, where they behaved quite playfully under a blanket. I feel joy. I should be upset, but I am so relieved that I am not going insane, as Bob has accused.

Later in the evening, the detective stands behind Bob in line, waiting for the phone at the bowling alley, where Bob has a conversation with someone about stopping over on the way home.

The detective then calls me and asks, "Did he just call you?"

"No," I reply. "Why?"

"Well, Bob just called someone making plans to stop over after bowling tonight. I wanted to make sure it wasn't you."

The detective tells me he will call me later. When he does, he confirms that Bob is at Sue's home. When he calls again, he tells me that Bob was on his way to our home when he got a flat tire. No stores are open, so he had to walk about a mile and a half to the nearest gas station. The detective alerts me that Bob will probably be calling me.

Sure enough. "Oh, hon. Sorry to wake you," Bob says softly into the payphone, "but I offered to drive one of the guys home and after I dropped him off, I got a flat tire. I had to walk to a gas station. Could you pick me up here and we'll send someone out to fix the tire tomorrow?"

"Oh, sure, honey! I'll be right there," I agree without letting on and he gives me directions.

As I hang up the phone, I feel the horrible tension that has been building for the past year dissipating, and I am at peace. Peace at last. I feel alive again to know that I can now be certain of what he is trying to hide. The person I trust most in the world is, in fact, doing these terrible things to me. He is, indeed, plotting to literally, drive me crazy. He wants me to believe that I already am crazy, in an effort to cover up his affair. But he is failing.

"I bet you are exhausted!" I tease him when I pick him up from the gas station. "It's quite a distance from where you left your car."

"Yep, it was. Let's get home," he says, and we say nothing more.

The following day, the detective meets with an attorney and a judge to obtain a court order for a "tap" to be put on our phones. We have to prove that not only is he having an affair, but he is also misusing the telephone, which is illegal. Every time I receive one of those calls, I am to record the time of day.

In the days that follow, I play it up like a soap star and beg whoever is calling to please stop, as it is driving me crazy. "Crazy" is the magic word. Sue and Bob are likely beginning to believe they have me right where they want me. If I am declared insane, he can put me away, keep his kennels, keep the children, keep the house and the properties, and look good in the eyes of his parents, who, regardless of their feelings about his affair, will undoubtedly take his side in the end. "How perfect his life will be," I think.

After a few weeks, with all the phone call times noted, the judge subpoenas the phone company's records. Lo and behold, all of those calls came in from the clinic or from Sue's home.

The very next day, I call Rodger Rooker, an attorney my detective suggested, and I file for divorce. We draw up the papers and plan to serve them to Bob at the clinic with all of his assistants and patients there to observe. I wish I could be a fly on the wall so I can see his face.

That afternoon, he is served. He calls me, furious and nearly uncontrollable. I knew that he might react violently, so I planned for the children and me to stay at Dr. McGinn's house for a couple days. He keeps calling me there but I will not talk to him. I want to wait until he calms down. I do not go to the kennel, so our receptionist fills in for me.

I let several days pass before I finally accept his call. "You know, Bob, it's difficult for me to process that you hate me so much that you tried to drive me crazy," I say to him.

"Honestly, Kitts, I wasn't trying to drive you crazy. I just wanted you off my back. I just wanted to escape and I am not sure from what. It all just got out of hand. I love you, Nina. This was just a fling. I do not love Sue and I never did. Please do not tear up our family. I will do whatever it takes to prove to you that the situation is over. Please, Kitten, please. Let's take some time." He even offers to go for counseling.

"I'll think about it," I say, and I hang up on him.

Now that he's admitted it, I call Chuck, Sue's husband, and tell him I filed for divorce.

"Yes," he says. "I know. Sue told me."

I proceed to tell him about the detective's findings and the phone calls. "Sue says you're just jealous and that none of that happened," he says to me.

"Chuck, I just gave you the recorded facts, the phone company's legal records, and the court's findings, and you still think I'm lying? I'm sorry for you Chuck," I say. "You can call my attorney. I've given him my permission to show you the facts!"

I slam the phone down, furious. "How can anyone be so stupid?" I think to myself. "Honestly, some people are too dumb to come in out of the rain. Chuck is one of them."

I question myself constantly about following through with the divorce. I want to believe that the affair really is over and that maybe I should give our marriage another try. His folks and the children are begging me to try again. I vacillate between following through and giving it another try dozens of times each day.

People make mistakes sometimes. Sometimes, they are big mistakes, but even I know that was not *just* a mistake. Nevertheless, I make the decision to cling to what is left of our marriage and begin the search for a marriage counselor. That soon becomes a problem too. Bob objects to paying the stiff fees. He argues that because the kennel is not on solid financial ground, money is at a premium.

In an attempt to compromise, I contact a priest, Father Dickinson. I am told that he is extremely well educated in the field, very friendly and easy to talk to. But the biggest plus of all is that he charges almost nothing. He asks only for a donation, and Bob cannot object anymore. I make an appointment to discuss our situation. He informs me he would like to set up one appointment for each of us, an hour for me and an hour for my husband. He will then contact me to make arrangements for counseling.

At my appointment, I tell him of all the circumstances that bring me to him. He says he will talk to my husband, who has an appointment the next day, and that he will contact us after that. I do not hear from him the next day, so I call him the day after.

"I'm sorry I didn't get back to you as I promised. I have put a great deal of thought into my decision. That decision is *not* to counsel you. I cannot counsel you," he says.

"You can't? Why not?" I ask, surprised.

"Nina, I truly believe this man's problems are extremely complex. I listened to his criticisms and complaints, and I think his problems are very deep and too intense for my accreditation. I can only suggest that you both see a psychiatrist. You will need to go together," he said. "However, having said that, my real recommendation to you is not to do it. Sometimes, people go to a psychiatrist for years, forever, and really never find out what is wrong. He definitely has a problem, I assure you, but you may never find out. I recommend a divorce."

I cannot believe what I have heard. A Catholic priest just recommended that I commit a sin in my faith and divorce my husband. "What could Bob have said?" I think to myself. "What could I have said that would make a priest think this great guy has such a serious problem? This family man who's just going through a mid-life crisis and having an affair?" I am dumbfounded, shocked, and completely confused.

Later that day, I call my husband and explain that Father Dickinson has chosen not to counsel us and instead suggests we see a psychiatrist. It will take someone with special training to work out our problems. I neglect to tell him that the priest says the problem is primarily his. However, I tell him the priest thinks divorce is also an option. Bob just laughs and says, "Well, what do you expect from a stupid priest? You know, you tell them you stole a candy bar from the grocery store and they're grasping at their hearts."

"Well, if you want to put this marriage back on track, you are going to go with me," I demand.

I make arrangements with a highly rated psychiatrist. I have an hour-long meeting with her and she says, "Of course, I cannot counsel a marriage problem unless both parties agree. Sometimes you will come together, and sometimes you will have to come at separate times." Needless to say, the visits will not be inexpensive. I decide if we can afford to go to the dog shows, we can afford to see a psychiatrist to help our marriage. I go, but Bob never does. He absolutely refuses and uses the cost as his excuse.

A few weeks later, I tell Andrea all about it. "God, Andrea, I don't know what he said or what I said that made Father think we need psychiatric help."

"I know someone who I think can help you, Nina," she says.

The next day, she calls with good news. "His name is Reverend Roberts and he's the pastor of our Presbyterian church. He used to be the pastor at San Quentin prison. There is nothing you or your husband could tell him that would shock him. He has heard it all. He offered to do this as a favor to me at no charge to you. If you wish to give a donation to the church, it would be welcome, but there would be no set fee."

Bob finally agrees and we begin our sessions. Reverend Roberts really is wonderful. He makes jokes and helps us relax. The work on our marital problems begins. It looks as if we are on the mend and maybe we will be able to put our life back together. The phone calls stop and life begins to return normal.

I feel like it is time to dream again. I hope that I am right.

CHAPTER FIFTEEN
DAY FIFTEEN
IN THE HOSPITAL

"Rodger, this is Nina. I'm ready to go ahead with the divorce," I tell my attorney.

"Are you sure?"

"Yes, now I'm sure. I was so confused about which direction to take, but something happened yesterday that made me realize my marriage is over. My dream is as dead as I was on that table two weeks ago. Everyone has tried to convince me that this is my only choice, but I just could not give up on it. Yesterday, Chuck, Sue's ex-husband, called and told me things he thought I should hear. He said he had not given me the information earlier because he did not want to believe what he had heard, and neither did I. But as badly as we do not want it to be real, it is. The conversation with Chuck convinced me of what I need to do."

"Well what was it you learned, Nina?" my attorney asks.

Exhausted going through it again, I tell him everything that Sue's ex-husband told me.

"Also, Rodger, I've consulted with one of Ann's best friends, Father Jacobs. He is a priest who also holds a master's degree in psychology and he is a counselor. He helped me put everything into perspective. He said to me, 'Nina, every time he comes home late, you will look at the clock and wonder. Leave it to God to forgive him, not you. Next time you may not be so lucky!' I am positive now. I want to file for divorce."

Rodger thinks for a second and says, "Okay. This is my suggestion. I have already spoken to Bob's attorney about this plan and he is willing to suggest it to Bob. You are holding all the cards. Make a deal with him. Explain that all the evidence we have against him will put him in prison. Tell him you want all the properties in lieu of alimony. You will also ask for the maximum child support, which is dependent upon his income, in exchange for his freedom. He will then retain his physical therapy license, which will enable him to work and pay you child support. On the other hand, if you choose to press charges, he will go to jail. You will have no child support and the children's father would be in jail. None of that would benefit you or the kids."

"I have to start thinking practically, but I still feel torn. His psychiatrist assured me that since this has all happened, he is no longer a danger to me. He assured me that Bob would be scared to even be near me at this point. On the other hand, I cannot help but think he might try again. After all, I will have taken everything from him and he will have nothing left to lose," I think out loud. "Okay, let's do it."

"Well, for your protection, I will place an injunction on him prohibiting him from ever setting foot on your property. I will prepare the quitclaim deeds and everything will be turned over to you upon divorce. Bye for now. I'll call you later," my attorney ends the call.

I hang up the phone and realize I have to call Bob and speak to him in person. I want to talk to him myself.

"Hello," he answers.

"Bob, it's me," I say.

"Hi, Kitts. It is so good to hear your voice. I miss you so much. I'm still hoping you will change your mind," he says with sadness. "You'll see; you'll see," he insists. "I'll get well. We will be back together again, Kitts. It will not be long. I will do anything you ask. I love you." He sobs into the phone.

"We'll see, Bob. I would like to believe that. Time will tell. But in the meantime, I am making sure that I secure everything I can. I cannot be sure of why you did this to me, but I do not feel safe with you. I do not know you anymore. You are not the man I married, and I do not even know if I can ever be in the same room with you again.

"I remember once many years ago, you slapped me on the face while we were arguing. You shocked both of us. And then you sat down and cried. And now *this*? You tried to *kill* me, Bob.

"I surely do not know what has happened to you, mentally or emotionally. I do know, however, that I cannot trust you. I'm filing for divorce and I'm taking all of our assets to secure our children's futures." And then I begin to cry with him. My heart is breaking. I loved this person so much, but regardless of the reason for this attempt on my life, we cannot continue. "Goodbye, Bob," I say as I hang up the phone, not even waiting for him to respond.

Hot tears stream down my face as I allow myself to experience this painful paradox; the gift of my life in physical form but the death of my life, as I knew it. Our beautiful dreams are shattered beyond repair and now it is time for me to face the truth. I cannot help but think about how unsettling it is that throughout the time I have spent in the hospital, he has begged for me to not divorce him but never once has he even attempted to apologize for any of this.

My decision is final as I think back to our fifteenth year of marriage.

YEAR FIFTEEN
OF OUR MARRIAGE

"Bob, are you okay?" I ask.

"Yes, I'm fine."

But he does not look well, and he seems emotionally distant. He is not here with me.

One day, while having my hair cut at the beauty shop, my stylist bends down and whispers into my ear, "So, what do you think about Sue and Chuck?"

Somehow, my hairstylist of over twenty years has also become Sue's stylist. I assume Bob must have told her about him.

"Sue and her husband, Chuck?" I ask. "I didn't realize you knew her husband."

"Well, I don't know him personally. I just know him through my conversations with Sue," he says.

"What about them?"

"You don't know?" he says as he steps back and throws up his arms. "She divorced him, and he didn't know it until he read it in the newspaper."

"How could he not know it?" I ask. "He had to sign the paper, didn't he?"

"She told me they'd been having marital problems for quite a while and that, over the past year, she would pick up divorce papers from the courthouse. They would sit down, fill them out, sign them, and then when the argument was over, she would tear them up and throw them away. That is, until last week. She actually took them into the courthouse and filed them, and voila, they were divorced. Then he read it in the paper. What an evil witch!" he exclaims. My stylist sees the look on my face and probably wishes he had not mentioned it. He just wanted to share the gossip to make conversation only to discover that I had not heard it yet. Neither of us knows what to say and the subject is dropped.

That evening, I say, "Bob, I understand that Sue and Chuck have gotten a divorce. Weren't you surprised?"

"Not really. Carl is such a stupid jerk. He deserves it. I guess she's dating every guy in town," he says, with a tinge of jealously.

I feel my heart fall to my feet. Lately, I had been feeling uneasy again and here is the reason. Something has changed in his demeanor, but I have not been able to pinpoint it. He is either still involved with her, or he is jealous of her dating other men. Whichever it is, I know our marriage is in trouble again.

The next day, I make a phone call. "Hi, Reverend Roberts. This is Nina. Remember me? I ask.

"A smile like yours, even your voice smiles. What can I do for you?"

I tell him of my suspicions about Bob's behavior and Sue's divorce.

"I hate to say this to you, Nina, but she is going after him. She got her divorce, and she is teasing and testing him by going out with other men. I have no doubt that your suspicions are correct. It does not make any sense to counsel the two of you again. In all my years of experience, when a woman says, 'I think my husband is having an affair,' she is always right. Women have a sixth sense that men just don't have. They can feel, hear, and see things – right through us – and they're always right.

"I have to tell you what you don't want to hear. It is only a matter of time. You will make the decision in due time, and you will make the correct decision, Nina. You are much stronger now than you were before. If you decide to get a divorce, you will do it confidently. You must fight for everything you can get, every penny for you and for your children. It is a man's world. You will need it to raise your family.

"By your silence, I realize this isn't what you want to hear. However, now that she has gotten her divorce, I can see the writing on the wall. I think you can, too. I will talk to you anytime, Nina, but I will not counsel your marriage. Do you hear what I'm saying?"

"Yes," I mutter, nearly speechless.

"Call me anytime," he reiterates as we end the call.

My hope has been sucked out of me once again. I did not expect that he would be so callous. I do not know what to do. I do not want to give up, but I have run out of people to talk to about it. I call Father Dickinson again. He said he was not equipped to counsel us, but maybe he will consent to help just me. I need the help to deal with this emotional roller coaster.

"Hello," the lady says as she answers my knock.

"Hi! My name is Nina. I'd like to speak to Father Dickinson."

"I'm Rosa, the housekeeper, and Father is in the hospital awaiting surgery tomorrow."

"I've talked to Father Dickinson before about my marriage problems," I tell her, "and I had hoped he could give me a few minutes. But if he is in the hospital, I'll make an appointment to see or talk to him another time." I turn to leave.

"Just a minute," Rosa says. "Let me call him. He is a nervous wreck. It might do him some good to turn his thoughts away from himself." She disappears into the next room, and when she returns, she says, "He'd like to see you. He remembers your situation and has wondered about you. I'll write down the room number for you."

As I leave, I cannot help but wonder why he remembers me. Surely, he has counseled so many people in my situation. It seems strange that I would stand out. I knock on the door and the familiar face of Father Dickinson opens it.

"Hello, Father. If you're not up to seeing me today, I'll make an appointment," I say, apologetically.

"No, no, come in. Rosa always knows what is best for me. Tell me what's going on, but first tell me what happened after we last saw each other."

I sit down on the chair he ushers me to and I fill him in on the past year. "I'm hoping that you will consider helping me weigh my options," I say. I then share with him the advice Reverend Roberts offered.

"He's a bright man and such a nice guy. We have met at several get-togethers. I'd like to be optimistic, but I can't," Father Dickinson begins. "I remember when you first came to see me. The reason I remembered you was because of my fear for you, and I did not feel that I was equipped with the knowledge I needed to help you. I still do not. Now, I will not try to help, because I do not have the tools to fix it. I will tell you what I thought, which may be what I should have told you at our first meeting."

After a long pause, almost as if he is trying to find the right words, he continues, "Nina, I believe you are in great danger. Your life is in danger. I want you to run. Run away from this marriage. It is not healthy. *He* is not healthy."

I sink into the back of my chair, and my jaw drops. "But, Father-," I begin.

"No, no. There is no 'but Father,'" he interjects. "Your life is in danger. He needs to be out of this marriage and he is desperately looking for a way out."

"He says he loves me," I protest.

"He does, Nina, but he also loves her. I am telling you, get a divorce before something evil happens. Yes, I said "evil" and I mean to use that word. I cannot put my finger on it, but I am sure that you are in her way and he does not know how to get rid of you gracefully. I hate to alarm you, but I don't want you to keep on trying to fix something that is broken beyond repair."

He stands up and walks to the door. "I couldn't tell you this before, but I will now. Run, Nina. Run! Let him go, child. You are in great danger."

I sit waiting for more but he offers nothing else. He opens the door. "And don't wait," he says. I realize that is the last word on the topic.

We say our goodbyes, and I leave the hospital. My heart is racing, pounding so hard against my shirt that I can hear every thump. I wonder if passersby can see the fear in my eyes.

"This damn parking deck is so dark," I complain to myself. I walk up to my car and try to put the key in the keyhole, but my hand is shaking so badly that I have to use my other hand to steady it. I finally make it into the car and I wonder why I feel safe, or rather, why I felt threatened. I am so confused, I do not even know what I am feeling or why. I cannot drive yet. My hands are shaking too badly. I just need to sit for a few minutes. I put my head on the steering wheel and try to calm myself.

Suddenly, there is a pounding on the door. I shriek. I look to the door, and a man jumps back. He screams in response. "Lady, lady, I didn't mean to scare you. I could see you were having trouble getting into the car and then when you put your head down, I thought maybe you were sick. I just wanted to help," he says, holding his hand to his heart, looking as terrified as I am. "I'm sorry; I'm sorry!" he says.

I open the window. Tears stream down my cheeks. "Thank you, sir. Thank you for being so kind as to care. I'm okay." I wave to him and pull out of the spot. Suddenly, I am home without remembering how I got here.

As I fix dinner, Father's voice resonates in my head: *"Run."* I wish I could see what he sees. I did not follow his advice and I waited. I waited to see if things would get better. I was not ready to give up on the dream.

The summer is coming to a close and I begin to feel more confident about our marriage again. The tension in the atmosphere of our home suddenly dissipates, as quickly as it had reappeared.

One evening, I question Bob how Sue is doing and he tells me she is seriously dating a cop.

"She's still at the clinic then?" I ask casually.

"Yes, but I don't see her often. My department is growing so fast, and I'm so busy that I'm lucky if I have time for lunch." And I believe him.

He seems happier over the next couple of months. He is more affectionate than he has ever been. We start going out to dinner and we are laughing more often, like we did in the early years of our marriage.

Then, in October, that familiar tension returns. We still occasionally go to a movie or out to dinner, but it isn't the same. Now the evening ends by going for a car ride out of town or a little off the beaten path. And sometimes, we go for long car rides on dark country roads late at night. I am uneasy about the tension between us.

One evening, I ask him what we are doing.

"Why go straight home? Let's just go for a little ride! It is the weekend. Lucy can sleep late tomorrow," he assures me as he pats my hand.

"Let's go for these rides in the daytime when we can see things. I have told my girlfriends about these late romantic rides. They agree that even if they are romantic, what the hell can we see?"

"Maybe we could park and look at the stars," he suggests. The rays from a streetlight flash into the car and just as Bob turns to look at me, he snaps. "You know, I can never please you," he says with pursed lips, his eyes narrowing. "You complain that I'm not romantic, so I do these things, and you still complain. You don't appreciate anything!"

"Of course I appreciate the loving things you do for me! I'm just not enjoying these senseless, late night drives," I reply. But really, I am frightened. Frightened enough to have told Bob that I mentioned these rides to my girlfriends, just to protect myself. "Why am I staying in this marriage?" I ask myself. I have no answer.

After that night, thankfully, the long, dark night rides end.

"Hi, Sy," I say into the phone days later. It is Sylvester, a friend of ours. Sy and Jen are social workers. We love them, and even though they are ten years younger than we are, they enjoy our company. Jen is Catholic and Sy is Jewish. He converted to Catholicism when they married. Whenever his parents visit them from New York, they put the crucifix away and bring out the menorah.

We do a lot of entertaining. Friends love my cooking and Bob's jokes. The time we spend with friends is always joyous.

"Hi, Nina. Jen and I want to invite you guys out to dinner tonight," he announces.

Before now, they have never invited us to go out with them, so I am eager to go. "That sounds great Sy. Bob and I have plans for tonight, but I do not see why they cannot be changed. We already have a babysitter. I'll call Bob and then I'll get back to you."

I dial the number for the clinic. "Physical therapy," he answers the phone.

"Hey, hon. It's me. Sy just called and invited us out for dinner tonight. I told him that would be great. We can always go fishing another day."

"No!" he yells. "No, not tonight! Tonight we are going fishing."

"Don't be ridiculous. We can go fishing whenever we want. Sy and Jen never invite us out. You know how frugal they are. Sy sounds so proud of his invitation. Come on, hon, let's go out with them." I beg. "Hey, I have an idea! How about they go fishing with us some other night? I just think we should take the offer while it's on the table."

"I said no! Make any excuse you want. Lie if you must, but the answer is *no*! We need to spend time by ourselves." He hangs up on me.

I am shocked. I have no idea what I will say to Sy. The whole situation is absolutely ridiculous. We have so many opportunities to go fishing at the Vanguards' lake that I cannot understand why Bob refuses to postpone the plans. We love to take our family fishing there and we visit them often. The plan is to have a romantic evening alone, but the idea of going out with the Goldmans is a rare opportunity, and we always have a great time with them.

The sky looks dark. We probably will not be able to fish, anyway. I do not understand what Bob is thinking and why he is so insistent, but this insistence is not normal for him. Then again, I have no idea what normal is for him anymore. Something is *very* wrong.

The Vanguard's home is deep into the rural countryside, about twenty five miles from our home. Sometimes it is difficult to drive out of the long driveway in the deep snow of winter. This year, like last year, they decided to rent a house in the city for the fall and winter, however, we are welcome on their property whenever we wish. All we have to do is call ahead and go fishing.

I finally come up with a lie and call Sy. "Sy, this is Nina. We are not going to be able to take you up your offer for dinner. Bob said that we have to visit one of his patients tonight to discuss some new therapy with him. He recently lost his leg, so he would not be comfortable with you and Jen around. He lives close to the Vanguards. After the therapy session, we will go straight to the lake. I hope that you'll give us a rain check?"

"Yeah, of course. We will get together another time. Bye for now." I can hear the questions in his intonation, but he does not ask anything further.

I close The Abbey for the night, walk to the house and enter through the front door. Bob comes in the back door with Lucy following behind him. I previously fixed a quick dinner for all of us, so we eat together. As I take the dishes off of the table and place them in the sink, I notice the wind outside. "Bob," I call to him, "I think it's too windy to go fishing."

He yells back to me, "We're going!"

"I'd better go to the bathroom before we leave then," I say begrudgingly. I can hardly pull my pants down because my hands are shaking so badly. I cannot even undo the button. "Oh, my God," I think. "What the hell am I doing?" I am terrified, but I feel I *have* to go with him. After all, I have no valid excuse not to go. I try to convince myself that he only wants to take me out for a romantic evening, but my gut will not allow my brain to believe it.

I leave the bathroom and head straight for the kitchen. I take a long, sharp knife out of the drawer and put it in my jacket pocket while no one is watching. A voice in my head tells me that something is wrong and that I need to be able to protect myself. "This is crazy," I think to myself. "Maybe I really *am* crazy. Or maybe Bob is."

Bob walks into the kitchen in his fishing clothes, ready for our outing, with all of his fishing gear. And I hear Father Dickinson's warning in my head: *You are in danger.*

I try to push the warning out of my mind but I say, without thinking about it first, "Lucy, if anything happens to me... Like, if I drown, you need to know it was *no* accident. This man sure is eager to be *alone* with me tonight. I even had to lie to a friend and get out of another commitment so we can be alone," I warn her, again trying to make it sound like a joke. She laughs, and we head out to the car.

As I step outside the back door, Bob grabs me by my arm and glares viciously into my eyes. "That wasn't funny!" he says in a low, threatening voice. He is holding me by the arm, quickly ushering me to the car.

Startled by his demeanor, I tell him I was just joking.

"You weren't joking," he says as he slams my car door, just about shutting it on my leg.

He remains silent all the way to the lake and I don't want to anger him further, so I remain silent as well. Throughout the drive, I can see Father Dickinson and hear his warning again and again. I hope that I have protected myself adequately with my statement to Lucy and with the knife in my pocket.

As we pulled up to the Vanguards', I notice the chain is strung, blocking the driveway. Another thing out of the ordinary. "Didn't you call will to tell him we were coming?"

"Of course I did. You know Will. He probably forgot," Bob, answers.

"Well, let's go home," I say. "So much for that. We'll go another time."

"No, we're not going to go home. We're going fishing," he insists. "We'll just walk up to the lake."

"The lake is almost a block away. We have all the fishing equipment to carry," I say, shocked that he still intends to fish. "Besides, don't you think the Vanguards would be upset if we didn't even call them and tell them we planned to come here? What if someone sees us? They always allow us onto their property, but I don't want to take advantage of them."

"I *told* you, I called Will. He just forgot. He forgets everything. I'll carry all the shit myself," he blurts out.

He walks toward the lake and then turns around to face the car. "Are you coming? Or do you think I'm going to murder you?"

"Don't be silly," I say. So I walk with him. As I do, I look at the house, hoping that maybe our friends are home. They gave permission for other friends and family to fish there too. So I hope maybe one of them might be here. But I see no one and no lights are on in the house.

"Let's go back, honey. It's really gotten cold," I beg. He does not answer and I continue to follow him to the lake, convincing myself that I am acting foolishly. I cannot, for the life of me, understand why I feel my life is at risk when I am alone with my beloved husband, but I cannot shake it, either.

He puts the fishing equipment into the boat. "Come on. Get in," he says.

"Why are you putting the stuff in the boat? We've never gone out in the boat." I say

"We never go out in the boat because the kids are with us." He says matter-of-factly.

"I don't want to go out in the boat. I just want to fish from the shore," I say. I look around. No one is here in this isolated place. I wish there were someone else out here.

I survey my surroundings as if I have never been here. The property is in the middle of many acres. The house and lake are in the center. On one side, there is a cornfield; on another side there is a row of giant evergreens which are probably hundreds of years old; and on the other side, behind the other cornfield, is an airstrip. They lease some acreage out to a farmer to plant corn. Joyce's father used to be in the oil business and flew his own plane, so the airstrip once served a purpose but it is no longer in use. It is usually beautiful out here, but tonight, it is dark and ominous.

"Are you afraid?" he asks.

"I'm getting in," I say.

Bob rows out to the middle of the lake. As he gets the poles ready, he asks, "Aren't you going to fish?"

"No. I am afraid to be out here. It is too windy and cold. Please, let's go back in."

He does not listen to my plea and he continues to fish. He says nothing to me. I sit silently, holding the knife in my pocket. As I look at him, he appears to be a stranger to me. I silently ask myself where my funny, easygoing husband has gone. A few minutes later, he puts the pole down and rows in without a word.

I am so relieved and I leap out of the boat so fast that I trip and fall to the ground. The knife slices through the pocket of my jacket and exposes itself. I quickly stand up and notice that Bob has not seen the knife. I also notice that the sharp knife cut my finger slightly and it was bleeding. I put pressure on my wound and hoped he wouldn't see the smear of blood on my slacks. I find myself running to the car, leaving Bob to pick up and pack up the equipment. When I reach the car, I jump inside. He puts the equipment into the trunk and climbs into the car, looking at me all the while with vacant, empty eyes.

"Your hands are shaking," I say to him.

"It's colder than I thought," he replies without emotion.

He drives home. We do not talk. I never take my hand off of the knife. "Thank You, God. I am not even sure why I am thanking You. This whole situation is crazy, or maybe I am crazy, but thank You, God. Please get me home safely," I pray silently.

"Well, you are home early," Lucy says as we enter. "Yeah, it was cold. But I did not drown her. See?" Bob says with a completely straight face.

Lucy ignores his response. She collects her belongings and leaves, and I run to the bedrooms to check on all the kids. The girls are still awake and I hug them tight. I feel so lucky to be home to take care of them, but I still cannot make sense of or tell anyone about my instinctual discomfort. I decide I will call Will the next day.

"Will, it's Nina. We were at the lake yesterday to go fishing. You forgot to take the chain off," I said.

"Why, was I supposed to?" he asks.

"Yes," I answer. "Bob called you a couple days ago and asked if we could go fishing. You were supposed to take the chain off on your way home from work. Remember?"

"Nina, I haven't talked to Bob in months. What the hell is going on? He didn't call me," Will says.

He calls to his wife to ask if she recalls talking to Bob. "No, I haven't heard from him. Is that Nina?" she asks. "Tell her I said hi!"

"What's going on, Nina?" Will asks.

I explain Bob told me he had talked to Will and suggest that maybe he forgot that Bob called him.

"Hell, he's full of shit," Will says.

"Thanks, Will. I love you,"

"Girl, you be careful," he says, sounding concerned.

After I hang up, I pick up the phone again and call Bob. "Bob, I called Will to scold him for not taking down the chain. He said that you never called."

"Well, he's nuts. Typical Will. He screws up and then lies about it. I'm busy, got to go." He hangs up on me. I am mistrusting him, and I am shaking at the thought he is once again forcing me to question my own sanity.

A few more months have passed and Bob does not look well again. His complexion is pasty, and he seems so unhappy. We do not really talk about our future anymore. In fact, we do not really talk at all.

Our four-year-old, Eric, on the other hand, is quite the talker now. One day, while I am putting on my make-up and looking into the mirror, he crawls up on the toilet seat and stares at me. He does this for a while until it appears that he has suddenly put together what he wants to say. He looks at me and says, "You know what, Mommy? You are beautiful. But you know what?"

"What?" I say.

"You're more beautiful with your makeup on than with it off!"

I laugh. Those kids always keep us on our toes.

And time marches forward. My brother is getting married today. He looks so handsome. I'm happy for him and pray that he never has a marriage like mine. My Dad is proud of him and yet also disappointed because Joe switched majors from Medicine to Pharmacy claiming that he wasn't cut out for it. The wedding ceremony and reception went off beautifully but my husband was aloof, disinterested, and not his jovial self.

Over the next couple of months, things seem to smooth out again. Bob and I are not back to our old selves, but the thick, ominous tension also seems to have melted away again.

I love spending time with my family and Christmas is one of the few times a year we are always able to celebrate together. By Christmas Eve, everything in the house is decorated festively. There are decorations on every doorknob, light and door. The dishes are Christmas. The toilet seat is Christmas. Everything is Christmas.

It is Christmas Eve. Bob and I are lying in bed awake in our Christmas PJs, waiting for Santa. We have such a wonderful little tradition every Christmas Eve to make the spirit of Santa Claus come alive for our children. Brook is now eleven years old but we think she still believes in Santa Claus. That may sound incredulous, but Santa is pretty believable at our house. There is a man we know who magically becomes Santa once a year. He is the father of a friend of ours, and he makes a very convincing Mr. Claus. He had a beard custom made out of genuine hair that looks just like Santa's beloved white beard. He had a Santa suit and boots made, too. When he is suited up, even a grown-up would believe he is the real deal.

On the twenty-third of December, we phone him and he gives us our special number from one to one hundred. Then on Christmas Eve when the children are asleep, we place a call to the phone in his car and tell him that our number is ready. When he is in the area, he pulls into the driveway with the car lights off and comes in the back door. He unscrews a few white bulbs on the Christmas tree so that the room is very dim, creating the perfect setting. He places himself under the tree with his back to the area of the room at which the children will enter. We give him one gift for each child, unwrapped. Each child can only ask Santa for *one* gift. They cannot be greedy. After all, Santa has to deliver toys to the whole world. Once Santa receives the children's gifts from us, we wake the children and tell them that Santa has arrived.

We walk them in their sleepy state to Santa under the tree. He pulls a gift out of his sack and we bring forward the child who will receive that gift. Then, the children are rushed back to bed before they are fully awake. When they wake up on Christmas morning, the gift Santa brought each of them is lying alongside them, and they have a faint memory of Santa giving it to them.

On this Christmas Eve, Brook is the last one to receive her gift. She hugs Santa and smiles at me, knowingly. I realize that, for her, the magic is over. But she would never ruin it for her sister and brothers.

On Christmas morning, I lie in bed remembering the magic of the night before and also the first time Santa visited our home. I can still hear the girls, who were five and three years old at the time, waking up that Christmas morning with the giant candy canes and Christmas gifts next to them in bed, arguing where the stuff came from. Sommer argued that they got their treasures in Candyland, while Brook was adamant that they saw Santa under the tree. What made that first Christmas Eve even more special was that, while Santa was under the tree, Bob was helping our female Doberman, Joy, deliver her puppies in the kitchen with a flashlight as his only light. I smile and I think about how simple everything was then.

I wonder about the boxes under the tree this year. Bob placed them there on Christmas Eve after Santa left. I am curious because he never buys me presents. He just tells me to buy whatever I want for myself. He sometimes goes with me and we shop together. Usually I choose something for the house. But this Christmas, presents are wrapped and under the tree. I look at the tags and they are for me.

"Mom, Mom, it's Christmas morning!" Eric announces as he marches into our bedroom carrying the game Santa gave him. He crawls over me and lays down between us. "Santa ate all the candies and he drank all the milk. See my present?"

We lay together in silence for a few minutes. "Come on! Let's go unwrap our presents," he begs us.

"It's barely light outside," Bob slurs, half awake.

"We have a special present for you, Mommy. Want a hint?"

"Sure." I answer.

"It's glass."

"Could it be a new set of dishes?"

He shakes his head, "No."

"Could it be a glass casserole? Could it be drinking glasses?" I ask.

"No. Do you want another clue? It's glass and it's bigger than me."

I look at Bob and we both laugh uncontrollably. Bob knows I have guessed it.

"Damn that kid," he mumbles to me.

I get out of bed and put the coffee pot on and the rolls in the oven.

"You get the first present, Mommy!" Eric and his Daddy bring my big, glass bottle into the living room from where it is hidden downstairs.

"Voila," I say as I pull the wrapping off of a box almost as big as me, "a wine making kit! Thank you, all! How did you all know this is what I wanted?"

The kids are as excited as I am. We open presents for hours. It takes us quite a while because we open only one gift at a time so we can all appreciate the gift and the giver. Bob gives me a fabulous cashmere coat with a large mink collar and a beautiful suit. He also took it upon himself to buy me a collection of beautiful bras, telling me that I never buy luxuries for myself. How true that is.

This Christmas is the most special I have ever experienced. We laugh a lot and play games all day. We went to Mass on Christmas Eve, so Christmas is *our* day. We cannot go home to Chicago and be with our families because The Abbey keeps us at home. Sometimes, our folks come to our home, but this year they spend it with other family members. I make a big beef roast for supper, and we sit around the dinner table, kids still in their pajamas and Bob and I in the casual clothes we wore to work the kennel that evening. We never ask our kennel helpers to work on Christmas Day.

All the kids laugh and tease that the presents they asked for we gave to the wrong child. Bob gives it his best shot, but he never fully engages our Christmas spirit. His complexion is sallow. He looks as though his very spirit has died.

CHAPTER SIXTEEN
DAY SIXTEEN
IN THE HOSPITAL
— IN THE MORNING

I look at myself in the mirror and cannot help but wonder if my kids will recognize me. I take a silk scarf, fold it diagonally, and tie it in a knot at the nape of my neck. I look sort of like a farm maid from the old days. I have no hair but this scarf covers my bald head beautifully. I will have to buy a wig or wear the one I borrowed from my friend, but I am not sure I will be able to tolerate it touching my ears. "I'd better retie this scarf and make it looser even though it already feels as though it will fall off my head. My ears still hurt so badly," I think to myself.

I pick up the hand mirror, turn around, and angle it so I can look into the mirror on the wall in order to see the back of my head. I stare intensely, trying to see every detail of my scalp. All the stitches have been removed, and it looks like the incisions are healing. They form an appearance of an oddly shaped patchwork quilt. I see a large area where a scab is forming which is turning dark brown. That is the area where a large patch of my scalp is missing and where the compression bandage once was. I wonder if hair will ever grow back there or if I will always have a bald spot, and tears begin to roll down my face.

I turn to the left and gently fold my right ear forward to see the back of it. I am not able to fold it flat as the scarring of the cartilage is very thick. My right ear was also cut in half about a third of the way up, so it has a thick scar on the front side, too. "Oh, my God, I shouldn't have done that," I think as I wince.

I turn my head again to check the backside of my left ear. It is not quite as bad as the right side. Bob is right-handed, so when he struck me from behind, he hit me more times on the right side of my head than on the left.

Even when I am not touching my ears, they feel as though they are on fire. As I stare into the mirror, I try to imagine how I would have looked without my ears. Only a small flap of skin held them onto my head, according to the doctors. "Oh, thank you God, for allowing me to keep my ears," I pray silently.

On my cheeks, there are long, deep scars running across both of them, and the flesh is puckered around the scars. It looks as though someone needs to cut the thread and smooth out the skin. I also have many scars developing above and through my eyebrows and along my forehead.

The plastic surgeon tells me that my skin is not going to smooth out by itself. It will take at least two surgeries, cutting under the puckers to separate the layers of skin and scaring, thus creating new scarring on the inside to soften the grip of the original scars. However, since the lacerations went all the way to the bone, some indentation and scaring will always remain.

The surgeon tells me that when my wounds heal, he will cut a section of my scalp loose, about three inches wide, starting at my forehead. He will pull the heavily scarred area of my forehead up and place an unscarred part of the scalp over most of the forehead. I can't imagine that I will ever look as I did before. I finish examining all the scars in the mirror and retie the scarf on my head as I sit on the bed and sigh. I am filled with self-pity.

My hospital bags are packed. There is nothing much in them -- just a little makeup, instructions on how to care for my wounds, a list of doctor appointments, and the hospital release forms. I am waiting for my friend to pick me up. I walk to the windows and notice that the sun is peeking out from behind the gray clouds, which is an especially welcome sight in February.

The phone rings. I walk back over to my bed and pick up the receiver. "Hi, Mama," Brook says to me. I can hear her tell Sommer, "I'm talking to her first because it's my birthday!"

"Happy Birthday, sweetie," I say and smile.

"Mrs. Seller is giving me a party today, Mommy! She let me invite some friends. And Mrs. Crawford is bringing Jon and Eric here!" she exclaims into the phone.

"You are going to have a ball! I hope you feel as special today as I did eleven years ago, the day you were born."

"I love you, Mama," Brook says.

She hands the phone to Sommer. "Hi, Mommy," my nine-year-old says.

"Did you have a good night, baby?"

"It was okay. Mrs. Crawford told me you are coming home real soon. I can hardly wait! I have to go now. I love you, Mommy!" She hangs up before I can even say goodbye.

I smirk because I know something they do not. I will be at the party too. "What a fabulous day this is going to be!" I think, attempting to feel more optimistic.

The boys did not call me this morning as they usually do. I guess Mrs. Crawford is too busy packing them up.

The Crawfords, Will and Joyce live right down the road from us. We met them when we knocked on their door. We needed their approval to re-zone the property that we were going to purchase. We wanted to change this property, house and land from agriculture to commercial, in order to build the kennel. We quickly became close friends. They felt the happiness our adopted child Brook brought to our lives. At their age of 40 and 42 they adopted a son and a daughter.

The boys don't know, but they are not only going to Brook's birthday party, but also going home to their own beds. I know the boys are more excited about being able to play with the Seller's boys than going to Brook's party. But that is alright because the important thing is we will all be together again.

I wonder how the kids are doing emotionally and how they are going to deal with the fact that Daddy is not going to be living with us anymore. I have no idea how to handle all of this. How do I tell them their entire world is about to change? The one thing I know is that I need to make them feel safe. The Sellers and Crawfords have told me that the kids are frightened of Bob. They know that he hurt their Mommy but that he still loves them – and me, too. That is the message I have made sure they have heard from all of us. "Once their arms are around me, everything will be okay," I say out loud to myself in a strong, confident tone of voice. Yet, I realize I can only hope this is true.

I quietly pray aloud: "Dear Heavenly Father, You gave me back my life. Now, you sure better help me live and take care of these children!"

It dawns on me I have been in the hospital for sixteen days and that Bob and I have been married for sixteen years. "How ironic," I think. I remember the events of our sixteenth year of marriage and the day that brought me here.

YEAR SIXTEEN OF OUR MARRIAGE

"Golly, Colleen, life is good!" I exclaim to our dog groomer. "1974 is shaping to be a much better year than the last one! And the last couple of weeks have really, really been nice," I say through a warm smile.

She smiles back and says, "Well, it's about time. You look more relaxed, and you smile more than you have in a long time."

I walk over to the grooming table and take hold of the dog being brushed out. "Here, let me help you steady this one," I say to her.

She is attempting to groom and trim an uncooperative poodle. I look at her and think to myself, "I'm so damn lucky that she walked into my life and begged me to train her to be a dog groomer. She is really, really good. Much better than her teacher."

"We're going out to dinner tonight with the Costellos. The Costellos are among the many friends we've acquired when we joined the local kennel club. They also have a boarding kennel and are breeders of dogs. Then we're going to play pinochle at their home afterwards. Just a nice evening with friends," I say to her.

"Nina, have you looked outside?" she asks and looks at me like I am nuts.

"Yes, I know it's snowing. Maybe it will lighten up as the day goes on. We'll just have to play it by ear," I reply.

"It sure is nice to see you happy again," she repeats, smiling.

"You know, Colleen, everything is *so* good. It is almost *too* good! I cannot quite put my finger on it. Everything is so right that it feels *wrong*. Maybe it's been bad for so long that now, normal is almost too good to be true," I reason. She does not respond and I chalk it up to her concentration on the poodle.

She finishes grooming her difficult client and I walk over to the window. "It's snowing heavier. I'd better give Bob a jingle," I say.

"Therapy," Bob answers.

"Honey, I think we better call off our evening with the Costellos. It's snowing hard and it seems to just be getting heavier," I tell him.

"No, we're not calling it off. We have already canceled twice. They'll be pissed if we do it again."

"Don't be ridiculous! They would cancel on us if the shoe was on the other foot," I assure him.

"No canceling. It'll probably stop snowing soon," he says.

"Okay. We'll just keep watch," I say to him.

As soon as I hang up, the phone rings. "The Abby" I answer.

"Nina, this is Fay. I think we had better call it off tonight. Phil and I think it is looking pretty rough out there," she says.

"I agree, but Bob is insisting we go. Let's see if it lets up. Plan on our meeting at the restaurant if you don't hear from me."

I look at Colleen and she shakes her head, letting me know that she thinks we should not go.

"I'm going to the house, Colleen. The kids will be home soon and I want to get their afternoon snack ready for them. I'll be back before you leave."

I trudge up the hill to the house. Several inches of snow have fallen.

"Leave your shoes in the hall!" I order the gang as they enter the house.

Sommer asks, "After we have our snacks, can we go out and play?"

"You bet! This is a terrific snow to build a snowman. Get out your snow pants and put on two pairs of gloves."

I head back to the kennel. Colleen says, "I'm leaving, Nina. I want to get home before the roads get too bad. And you'd better call off tonight! This storm is turning into a blizzard."

I call Bob again. Lucy answers, "Therapy."

"Hi, Lucy. Can I talk to Bob?" I ask. He picks up the phone and says hello. "Honey, I'm canceling our date for tonight," I inform him.

He abruptly cuts me off. "The hell you are! We are going!" he yells into the phone.

"Have you looked outside? There's a blizzard!" I yell back at him.

"I'm driving, so what the hell do you care? I am the one who drives, so I make the decision whether we go or not. I will be home soon. Lucy is riding home with me because she is afraid of driving in the snow. I'll drive her home when we get back from the Costellos' tonight." He hangs up before I have a chance to respond.

"Well, at least *she* has some sense," I think to myself as I hang up the phone. I lock up the kennel early so I can get ready for the evening. If a customer should arrive, he or she will ring the bell and I will run back to over here.

I trudge back to the house and dress for the evening. While I get ready, I mutter to myself, "Stupid. This is stupid. They live twenty miles from here. There is a blizzard out there and we will be right in the middle of it."

About an hour later, Bob appears with Lucy. "You people are crazy!" she laughs.

"Not me! It's him," I say, pointing to Bob. "He's driving and he's most likely going to be digging us out of a ditch, too."

"Wow, Nina, you look great!" Lucy says as she admires my new coat.

"It's my Christmas present from the big guy," I say as I run my hands over the long fur collar. "And see my new suit? He also bought this for me. And lingerie, too!" I brag.

Lucy steps back and looks at him curiously as she removes her own coat. "Well, Bob, you must have gotten a raise," she says wryly.

She sits down in front of the TV. It is easy to babysit our crew now. Thankfully, all the kids are pretty self-sufficient, as Lucy is too old to deal with babies. No more diapers and bottles, just popcorn, treats, and to bed by eight.

Bob finished changing his clothes and called the kids. "Come on, everyone, let's get kisses. Behave yourselves. Don't tie Lucy to the chair again," Bob teases. Everyone laughs as we leave the house.

I begin walking toward the car. "No, not the car. We're taking the van," Bob says more like an order that a statement.

I stop in my tracks. I am completely confused. "Why in the hell would we take the van? It has no traction and you know it slips and slides on the snow and ice! The car hugs the road. We're taking the car," I say more like an order than a statement, and continue walking toward the car.

"The car is low on gas," he says as he grabs my arm and walks me to the van.

"Well, I guess you're the one driving," I say as he opens my door.

"I'm always the one driving," he retorts. The snowfall is heavy, but the rush hour traffic moves along slowly but for the most part, smoothly.

As we enter the restaurant, Phil Costello greats us with, "You two are nuts!"

"We just miss you both so much, or at least Bob does, so we weathered the storm," I cheerfully say as I kiss them both on their cheeks.

Dinner is delicious and as usual, we share a lot of laughs. As we leave the restaurant, Phil says, "Be careful going home now. Looks like it's gotten a lot worse!"

Bob asks, surprised, "Aren't we playing cards? Your house is only minutes from here. Maybe the plows will be here by the time we leave your house."

Fay responds, "You've got to be kidding! We'll play some other time, Bob."

"Nope, nope. We will play tonight. I have a slight headache and don't want to drive home right now. Maybe it'll go away by the time we leave your house," Bob insists.

They look at each other and I can read in their facial expression that they are in disbelief. But they give in and we proceed to their home to play cards for a couple hours. I can't believe we played as long as we did. It's almost midnight," I say as we hug one another, readying to leave.

As we walked out toward the van, Bob says in a low but stern manner, "You drive."

I am stunned! "But I never drive, and I'm especially not driving the van in this weather! You made a big thing about you being the one to drive, so you will have to drive," I state. I continue to walk toward the passenger side door, but before I make it there, he literally pushes me aside and climbs in.

"I have a headache," he says to me before closing the door in my face. He leaves me standing in the snow, staring at him through the passenger door window. He is looking straight ahead, avoiding my stare. "Damn you!" I yell at him as I walk around to the driver's side.

I crawl into the driver's seat and tell Bob, "You'd better direct me. You've driven this road plenty of times, so you know it better than I do. This is crazy - I can't even see the road!"

I start the van and back up onto what I hope is the road. "Stop!" he screams at me. "You're already on the highway. Turn left and go!"

"How am I supposed to know I'm on the highway?" I ask. "There are no tire marks in the snow!"

Visibility is almost nonexistent. I grow terrified and increasingly frustrated. "I'm scared, Bob," I say as I drive at a snail's pace. "I've been driving for about eight minutes and I haven't seen one car. I'm following the light poles." My hands are aching because I am grabbing the steering wheel so tightly.

"I'm going to lie down in the backseat," Bob responds, completely ignoring my concern.

"What do you mean you're going to lie down? Oh, no you don't! You stay right where you are and direct me!" I scream at him.

He sits up straighter in the passenger seat and turns toward the middle of the van. "Where the hell are you going?" I yell.

He continues to move toward the bench seat behind us and he lies down. "Bob, you have to help me! I'm not sure I'm even on the road," I beg him.

"I have a headache," he mumbles again.

I have now driven about another five miles when Bob says, "Pull over. I have to vomit."

"You open the window and vomit! There is no way that I'm pulling off of a road that I'm not even sure I'm still on!"

"Pull over NOW!" he demands in a deep, dark, ugly tone of voice I have never before heard from him.

But that tone of voice made me angrier, and I responded, "I'm not pulling over! Get up here, open the window, and vomit!" As I look over my shoulder and in the rear-view mirror, I see that he is now sitting up on the back seat, not laying down anymore.

"Pull over there," he orders as he points to the entrance to the animal clinic where we take our dogs.

"Okay, okay," I reluctantly agree. I remember that the entrance to the clinic is wider than the driveway up to the parking lot. So, I only pull onto the apron of the driveway, afraid to take it any further, as I may miss the driveway. "Now open the door and vomit," I order him angrily.

"Put the van in park," he orders from the back seat.

"Put the van in park?" I question.

"Yes, *put the van in park!*" he yells back emphatically.

"Jesus Christ, Bob, why in the hell do we need the van in park? Just vomit!"

"We could slide," he insists.

"Slide? Where in God's name could we slide?"

"We could slide down into the ditch alongside the driveway," he says and points to a gully. "Now put the goddamned van in park!" he screams.

"Don't be ridiculous! Just open the door and vomit!" I insist, again.

"Not until you put the van in park!" he repeats.

Finally, I give in, too tired to argue anymore. "Okay, the van is in park."

"Are you sure?" he asks.

"Of course, I'm sure. See for yourself and then vomit so we can get out of here!" As I finish my sentence, I feel a blow to the back my head. My immediate thought is that we have been hit by another car.

I quickly turn around to see if we've been hit but what I see is that Bob is standing, hunched over due to the height of the van, and he is hovering over me. He has something in his hand. All I can process in this moment is that it is large and orange. And it is coming toward my face. I turn my face away and feel another heavy, violent blow to the back of my head. The force throws me into the steering wheel and while I feel pain, it seems to be a second thought to my mind racing, trying to understand what is happening. I manage to pull my head up and as I look over my shoulder, he strikes me again with the large, orange object - this time in my face.

I instinctively scream, "Bob! Bob! My God! What are you doing? My God! I love you! What are you doing?"

He hits me again and again, over and over. All the while, I plead and tell him I love him. He says nothing and continues to bludgeon me. Each blow sounds like a loud drum reverberating inside my skull. I hear bones breaking in my head and face. As he pummels at the side of my face, the orange object slips down my chest. I capture it under my right armpit and hold on to it tightly. He struggles to pull it loose. With my left hand, I reach for the car door and open it. I know I have to get out of this vehicle or he will kill me. But before I have a chance to get out, he crawls on top of me, between me and the steering wheel, facing me. He looks at me but his expression is devoid of any emotion. His eyes, usually a beautiful blue, are dark and empty, as if absolutely soulless.

He lifts his right hand, makes a tight fist and throws another blow to my face. I notice that he is wearing the new leather gloves that I gave him for Christmas and I fleetingly think, "What an odd thing to notice right now." He punches me in the face again and again and again, bloodying his beautiful gloves with each violent contact.

"Bob, I love you!" I scream over and over. But my pleas do not faze him.

He continues and continues and continues to bludgeon me. With the next blow, he hits a vein in my forehead and blood squirts, over his head, all across the windshield in a left-to-right pattern that draws the shape of a morbid rainbow. I watch the blood slowly slither down the windshield, melting the rainbow.

Then suddenly, words are placed in my head by someone else, I yell in desperation, "You can't murder me! Lucy knows! Lucy knows that you plan to murder me!" And after hearing those words he stops the beating and then there is complete silence.

"Lucy doesn't know anything," he says with very little emotion.

"Yes, she does! Yes, she does!" I try to convince him. "Bob, you are sick! You need help! Please, take me to the hospital. I think I'm dying."

"You are not dying," he responds, sounding disgusted, as if I am being over-dramatic in my statement.

"Please, please Bob! Take me to a hospital," I beg.

"I can't," he says, still perched on the steering wheel. "I can't! They'll put me in jail! He looks frantic and in his facial expression, I see panic.

"Move over to the passenger seat. I have a plan. I will drive the van into a light post on your side of the van. But before I do that, you will move to the backseat behind me. It will appear that we were in an accident and that will explain why you are hurt. I will jump out of the van just before we hit and take my chances. You'll be okay because you're in the backseat."

"No, no, honey, we could both be killed. Who would take care of our children? Please, honey, listen to me!" I beg. "I'll tell the police we slid off of the road and that you decided to walk to that farmhouse to get help and while you were gone, a car pulled up alongside us. Yes, a car pulled up and then a guy got out, demanded money, and then beat me up. I love you, honey. Please, you are sick. You need help. Get me to the hospital," I relentlessly implore him.

"Okay, okay, but make it that house there," he says as he points to another one. "It has a light on."

I cannot believe that he is listening to my plea, or that we are making these sick plans on the fly as we are. "Then again, maybe he's agreeing for the time being so he can rethink how best to kill me," I think to myself.

He moves off of the steering wheel and to the center of the van, between the front and back seats. He helps me move to the passenger seat. He then climbs into the driver's seat. I still have the orange object smashed between my body and my right arm. I look into his face and see nothing of my husband there; there is absolutely no emotion in his eyes. The tall driveway light at the animal clinic shines into the car and I notice how pallid his complexion is. His eyes are empty and his face is emotionless. He puts the van into drive, and off we go.

"Open the window and throw out the pipe wrench," he demands.

Pipe wrench. So, that is what the orange object is - and a huge, industrial-sized one at that. He must have picked it up from the clinic. I open the window, but instead of throwing it out, I lay it gently next to the seat. He does not notice that I pretend to dispose of it. I gingerly rest my right hand on the door handle. If he makes the slightest move toward me, I will jump and take my chances.

Bob commands, "Practice what you are going to say when we get to the hospital, telling them about the robbery."

So, I repeat our story through the pain that is now overtaking my senses.

"Repeat it again."

I try. "Bob, I can't say it anymore. My mouth is so sore. I can barely speak. My lips are numb," I tell him.

As we drive to the hospital, my mind is working overtime, trying to determine how he intended his plan to work. It occurs to me that what he proposed to hide the truth was very likely his plan all along. I think he intended to knock me unconscious and then drive the van into a light pole, making it look like an accident. He would jump before it hit, but I would have been killed. The plan failed because Bob did not have the leverage he needed to do the job. The van ceiling is not high enough to allow a large enough swing, or maybe he just did not hit me hard enough. Whatever the reason it failed, I am sure that that was his plan.

"Where did I get the idea that Lucy knew he planned to murder me I come from?" I wonder. Then like a warm, soft blanket, I feel the glow and spirit of my mother all around me I silently speak to her, "Mama, I know you are here. I can feel your presence. I can hear your voice. I still remember that one night, long ago, when Bob and I were dating and you put your hand on my shoulder and whispered to me, 'Be careful. I think he could be dangerous.' How did you know, Mama?"

I become aware that my clothes are wet and I feel sticky. The fur collar lying around my neck is saturated with my blood. I feel nauseated. As we near the hospital, I pray, "Dearest God, please keep me alive long enough to tell them what really happened. If I should die, he will raise the children.

He could hurt them, too. Mama, please stay with me. I am so scared, Mama. I don't want to die."

We pull up to the emergency door and I truly cannot believe that he actually brought me here. A police officer approaches the van. As he comes closer, I can tell he sees my face more clearly. He quickens his step and yells for a stretcher. The police officer opens my door and I calmly reach down and pick up the orange pipe wrench. I gently hand it to him and say "Here. He tried to murder me!"

Bob erupts and yells, "You promised! You promised!"

"You're dangerous, honey. You might hurt the children," I tell him.

I am sick to my stomach as I close my eyes. I feel hands guiding me and helping me onto a stretcher. Voices scream orders back and forth and I sense the urgency in their tones. The cart I am lying on starts to move and as I am wheeled away, Bob continues to scream, "But you promised! You promised!" My eyes are closed, and I can no longer see him. The doors to the emergency room slide closed with me inside and him outside. I am safe from him.

"Nina, do you have family here?" a voice asks me.

I recite the name of our babysitter and our home number and then the names and numbers of my Dad and my in-laws. I ask that they also call our best friends, the McGinns and the Sellers, our "Peoria family," as we call them.

I feel my chariot moving to another room and my clothing is being removed along the way. Someone takes my hand and does something with it. "What are you doing?" I ask.

"I'm taping your ring onto your finger so that no one steals it. It's very beautiful," a female voice answers.

"Please get me a priest. I am dying," I beg her.

"You are going to be fine," the voice reassures me. I know in my heart that I will never be fine again.

DAY SIXTEEN IN THE HOSPITAL — IN THE AFTERNOON AND EVENING

As I sit on my hospital bed, I remember back to that day, just sixteen days ago. I cannot help but wonder how this man, whom I love with all my heart, could have done this to me. How desperate and greedy he must be. I offered him a divorce and even filed for one once, but he declined and begged to stay married, telling me how much he loved me. I am convinced he loves what we had built - the kennels and the house. But he could not love me and have done this to me.

I walk to the door of my room and peek out into the hall, anxious for my friend to arrive and take me home. I sit back on the bed and notice a deck of cards on the dresser. I pick them up and look at them, and think to myself, "Life is like playing a game of poker. You pick up five cards, discard the ones you do not want, and hope the new ones give you a better hand. Sixteen years ago, I was dealt what I thought was a good hand, and worked hard to make it even better. Out of nowhere, a harsh wind has come along and has blown the cards out of my grip. Now I have been dealt a new hand, one I have not yet looked at. But I must say, dear Fate, I am a damn good poker player."

I open my right hand mindlessly, looking at the lines, and gasp. The heavy line that Mary, the fortune teller, pointed out to me so many years ago, the one that cut into my lifeline, has completely disappeared! I thought maybe the car accident a few years ago was the incident Mary said might occur, the one that would cut my life short, but that line remained intact until now. Today it seems unbelievable, even to me, but it is gone. I keep pressing my palm to try to make that line reappear but only a tiny stem remains. I now feel completely and utterly calm. I cannot explain it, but I am relieved and I know that I have survived that which tried to kill me.

I take one last look in the mirror and I cannot help but laugh out loud at the person looking back at me. I have a yellow print scarf on my head, a red jacket, brown slacks, and black fur-trimmed boots. My receptionist did the best she could putting my outfit together, but it is truly comical. I laugh out loud again at my reflection, and as I do, I remember a day in college when I was late to class. It was a typical freezing cold day in January and I took the cruel walk along Michigan Avenue to get there. By the time, I reached my school, my body was numb. I opened my classroom door and the entire class stopped working on their projects and looked at me, as I was late. But they didn't look away.

Don, my high school buddy who had become my college best friend, yelled out to me, "Stop!" He walked toward me and bowed, as if I was royalty. He snatched my books and laid them on a nearby table, took my left hand, pirouetted me in a full circle, and announced, "Blue knit hat, brown jacket, green plaid skirt, black boots, and wait! Wait! What do I see? I see a bit of white above those fashionable boots. I pull her skirt up an inch and what do we have here? Long underwear! Ladies and gentlemen, this is what a Polish debutante wears these days!" Everyone laughed and laughed, especially me. I smile at the memory now, as well.

"Well, world," I tell my reflection in the hospital mirror with my head held high, "I am once again a Polish debutante, and today is my coming out party!"

My friend, Ann, arrives and at the same time, a nurse pushing a wheel chair enters my room. "You are beaming," the nurse says as I sit in my buggy.

"Yep, today I get to feel the faces of my babies."

As we leave my hospital home, I take one last look at the cage that protected me, and it is unnerving. "WHAT IF?" my fear asks. I will be all alone now. A week ago, I called my aunts and asked them to come and stay with me for just a week, time enough for me to get my sea legs back. They each had an excuse why they could not come. I knew the real reason was because they were afraid of Bob and what he might do. I realize that I AM TOO!

We exit the hospital doors and I get into Ann's car. We are headed to the Sellers where Andrea is waiting for me.

When we arrive at the Sellers, Ann walks me to the door, gives me a hug, says she will call me tonight, and leaves. I watch her drive away, grateful she is in my life, and then I knock on the door.

"Come on in," Andrea says, happily. "I have some coffee ready. Come sit down and have a cup before all of our kids get here." We chat for about ten minutes about how it feels to come home. I confide that I am happy and afraid at the same time. Andrea nods, letting me know she understands. She tells me she has fixed a casserole that I can heat in the oven for dinner later in the evening. I am of grateful for her kind gesture.

Andrea looks at the clock and says, "It is almost time for your girls and my four to come home. Why don't you sit on this chair in the living room, so that as soon as they come into the house, they will see you? Since they aren't expecting you to be here, it'll be a glorious surprise!" She sounds like a kid on a Christmas morning.

We watch through the living room window and see them approaching. I sit in the chair and Andrea goes back into the kitchen. The kids enter, one at a time. My girls look at me, walk right past me, and begin talking to Mrs. Sellers.

I AM IN SHOCK! It is exactly what I had feared. They did not even recognize me! Hot tears slide down my cheeks and I cover my heart with my hands and press, trying to make it stop aching. I find it difficult to breathe. Andrea recognizes my pain, and she immediately brings the girls back into the living room and points to me. But she doesn't say a word as her eyes fill with tears as well.

Brook screams, "Mama!" Sommer asks softly, "Mommy?" They both rush over to me, fall to their knees and hug and kiss me. I stand up along with them and we all cry tears of joy as we hug and hug.

Only Moments later, Mrs. Crawford enters the house with my boys. The girls scream at them, in harmony, "Mom's home!"

The boys just stand there looking at me. Their eyes are open wide and I can tell they don't recognize me, but are trying to believe it's me. I walk over to them. They do not say anything so I look into each of their beautiful faces, and focus on making eye contact with them. Suddenly they break into tears and grab onto me. I can tell that no matter who explained how I was injured, it didn't prepare them for what they were now seeing. After all, they are only five and seven years old.

I sit down on the sofa, with all four of them cuddled around me, and I explain about the scars and how a doctor will take them away. I make light of the impending surgeries. I pull off my headscarf so they can see and touch my head. It feels bristly because of the new hair coming in and Brook tells me it smells like medicine.

"When are you coming home?" Eric asks.

"Tonight," I say and everyone yells, "Hooray!"

"I get to sleep with you first," Eric shouts out to the other children, just to make sure they are aware of my previous promise to him.

While this is happening, I notice the Seller family watching us from the other room. I see approval in their faces.

I caress each of my children's wet, crying faces and kiss their hands. "I'm home forever," I say. I feel as though a ribbon is wound around our bunch and God is pulling us closer than we ever have been. This happy crying goes on for long enough for them to calm down when from the kitchen, Andrea calls out, "Ok, girls, get in here. I need your help. You boys go to the rec room with my boys, this is a girls-only party."

My little supporters jump up and do as they are told. They all seem to be satisfied. <u>Mom is home.</u>

The partiers have arrived and the games begin. I remain seated on a chair, off to the side and really enjoy the party. Brook's friends occasionally look at me. I can tell they are having a hard time with how I look. But no one says an unkind word. Every now and then, Jon or Eric come over to me and give me a hug and then return to the rec room. No words are spoken, they just need to know that I'm still here. I understand that my main job is to make them feel secure, even though I certainly do not.

The past sixteen days, I have had to concentrate on fighting for my life and now I have to concentrate on giving the children the security they've lost in their lives. Now, more than all the uncertainties I face, the most important challenge I have is making these four gifts that God blessed me with feel safe, protected and happy.

The party has ended and Andrea has my children packing up their clothes. She'll be driving us to our home soon and I am pensive about what that will be like. I walk to the window and notice that it's already dark outside. I look up to the heavens and hold out my right hand, palm side up and whisper, "Alright, Lord. You've given me a new lifeline. Where is it taking me now?"

The ride home is quiet. I sense that the children may also wonder what lies ahead for us. The children exit the car and just stand there looking at the house they haven't seen for many days. Then they run to the door, pushing and shoving to be the first one in to what they think will be their previous "normal life."

Andrea helps us with the luggage, sleeping bags and pillows that the kids used while staying at our friends' homes. I hug her as she leaves us and notice that she is crying. In all the years, I have known her, I've never seen Andrea cry. "I'll call you tomorrow," she yells as she gets into her car and drives away.

"Okay, kids, get your homework done," I say as I put Andrea's casserole in the oven. "Mommy, where is Daddy?" Eric asks.

"He isn't going to be here anymore, Eric. He's eating with his friends," I say. And that satisfies my five-year-old's question for the time being.

After everyone finishes their homework, we sit down for dinner. We talk about the party and events at school that day. I wash the dishes while everyone prepares for bed.

Eric jumps into bed with me. It's nine o'clock, later than they usually go to sleep. Tears drip down from my eyes and fall onto Eric's head. He must feel secure in my arms as he falls asleep as soon as I cuddle him into my arms. I wonder though if I will ever feel secure again.

I feel my eyes getting heavy and I look forward to the end of this very long day. Suddenly I sit straight up as though I had been shot out of a cannon and find myself screaming. I startle my baby boy and he starts bawling. The other children come running into my bedroom and Brook flips on the light. "Mama, are you alright?" she asks.

I notice that I am holding my hand over my ear. It feels as though it is on fire. Eric must have inadvertently moved his arm and touched my ear while I was asleep. The pain is excruciating and I am crying even though I am trying not to so as not to upset the children.

All of the kids walk over to my bed and sit on the edge. "I'm sorry to frighten you," I tell them. "Eric must have bumped my sore ear."

Brook comes to my panicky rescue. "Mama, maybe we better not sleep with you until your ear heals." I agree that may be best and then see confusion and fear on the younger ones' faces. Jon begins to cry along with Eric.

I do my best to comfort them. "No! No, don't cry. Mommy is going to be fine. You know how it feels when you scrape your knee. It hurts a lot for the first day or two. Then it gets better. Well my ears are better but they still need more time to heal."

I reach and grab a tissue and wipe the boys' noses. The girls give them mothering too, as only older sisters can do.

I carry Eric back to his bed and Jon follows. I hug their tears away. I lay each of them down on their pillows. They are overtired from the evening at the Sellers home and from Brook's birthday party. Eventually, they roll over and fall asleep.

I look into the girls' room. They are huddled together and now they are crying too. "Mommy, the kids at school told us that Daddy beat you up, but Grandma told us you and Daddy were in a car accident," Sommer says.

"Your Dad did hurt me but the doctor says it was because he was sick. Now he is taking medicine and he'll never hurt me again," I say, knowing that I may be lying to them.

"Will he beat us up?" Sommer asks.

"No, he would never be that sick. He loves all of you too much."

"When we are with him we are afraid!" Brook blurts out. "We do everything he tells us to do because we don't want him to hurt us too. He doesn't seem like our Daddy anymore," and she begins to cry. "He never laughs anymore and he always looks sad."

"Just give him time; he'll be his silly self again in no time. Now you two get to sleep. You have school in the morning." They stand up, hug me tight and continue to cry. I cry too. I am not fooling them or myself.

I return to my bed and lay down. It is difficult for me to get comfortable because I have to lay flat on my back because of my ears. When I touch the back of them, they feel like raw meat. I have to turn the pillow over to the other side because it is wet from my tears. Exhaustion seems to be the answer, as I give way to sleepiness.

CHAPTER SEVENTEEN
BACK AT HOME

As I walk to the kitchen, I notice that it is just getting light outside. I put the coffee pot on and as I wait for it to brew, I close my eyes and notice the welcomed aroma. I have missed the smell of fresh brewed coffee. Before today, I could see a few of our dogs in their kennels from this kitchen window. Because of their great sense of smell, they would wake up and the barking would begin at the smell of the coffee brewing. Today there are no dogs and no barking to greet me. Some of the dogs are boarded at other kennels and some are at the Abby until I am strong enough to handle them. A simple friendly bump from one of our large Saint Bernards could topple me and cause more injuries.

I walk into the boys' room and choose the clothes that they will wear today. After all, they are only five and seven years old. The girls, however, insist on choosing their own. They have already begun to develop their own styles.

"Wake up sleepy heads. Wash your faces and brush your teeth." As I say this, I remember my Mom saying the same thing to me.

"Yeah, Mom, we know the routine," Jon responds.

"It's Pop Tarts or cereal. Your choice," I say. Today my crew is especially quiet. They are still tired from the happenings of yesterday. Nevertheless, the children scarf up breakfast. They dress in their heavy winter gear, as it is freezing outside.

The hugs and kisses are not as casual as usual. "You will be home when we get back won't you?" Jon asks.

"Of course, where else would I be?"

The kids walk out the door and down the long driveway to catch their school busses. The girls attend one school and the boys another. Our district has gotten so large that it is separated by grades.

I take time to bathe, get dressed and walk over to the Abby. I am neither excited nor dreading this reintroduction. It is simply what needs to be done.

As I unlock the front door, something catches my eye. It is our van at the far side of the parking lot. It is usually in our home driveway. I feel numb and trepid as I walk towards it, the chariot of my death. From the outside, it looks as it always did, two-toned gray with a little Polish flag pasted above the outside key opening.

I look at the keys in my hand, the key I used to open the Abby, and I confirm the key to the van is on this same set of keys. I try to insert the key to open the door but I am shaking so badly, I give up. "Come on, Nina," I encourage myself. "You must find the courage to do this. After all, this is the van you have to drive every day."

I try again but this time I use my left hand to steady my right hand, which holds the key. I turn the key and open the door. The smell of old, dried blood is overwhelming and I feel that I might vomit or even faint. I notice that the fabric covering the seats still has traces of my blood on it. But the blood is much more evident in the seams. The gray carpeting that extends from the driver door, over the hump between the seats and to the passenger side has heavy bloodstains on it. "There is so much blood," I think to myself.

"I have to do this", I encourage myself again as I climb into the driver's seat. I am sitting in the driver's seat, as I did that fateful night. As I close my eyes, I can literally feel the blows to my head. I feel my head and neck being jerked this way and that with each blow. I see the blood shooting from my forehead and splattering the windshield as if it came from a squirt gun. From left to right, my blood makes the shape of a rainbow. I watch it dripping down, like a melting rainbow. I force my eyes open and I notice that my entire body is shaking life a leaf. I wonder if I will ever be able to erase these images.

My mind starts ticking off the options. I cannot sell this van, who would want it? I cannot afford to buy another one this large. And I need this 12-passenger van to transport the dogs to and from the shows and veterinary appointments. I resign myself to the fact that this will be my means of transportation.

Bob is keeping the small economy car and the converted school bus, which we sometimes used to take our dogs and the kids to shows. He gets those items and a chance for a new life. However, most important, he will retain his medical license as a Registered Physical Therapist and probably his girlfriend, Sue, too. I am giving him a chance at a new life. It is better than the one he has given me.

As these thoughts go through my mind, I look again at the seats of the van and the blood crusted on the fabric and in the stitches. I buy large beach towels to cover the seats and rubber floor mats to cover the blood on the carpet. I now feel nauseous again and I run as quickly as I can to the bathroom at the Abby. I open the bathroom door and proceed to vomit.

I try to steady myself and make my way to my desk. I lay my forehead into my cupped hands and cry as I think back on last night's events, my first night back in my own home, and now this morning's visit to the van. Colleen, our groomer, walks in and interrupts the memories.

I stand up to greet her through my tears, "Dear Colleen, what would I have done without you?"

She holds onto me and we sob, both for the sadness and loss, and for the present joy of having lived. I love her so much. She is the kindest, most giving person I know.

Colleen tells me she has a few dogs coming in for grooming and that she will feed the boarders. As she walks to the other room, Andrea comes in the front door.

"Well, are you ready to go grocery shopping?" she asks. I am sure that she can tell I've been crying but she does not acknowledge it.

"Am I back to the real world already? I ask her. "You mean no one will fix me breakfast, lunch and dinner?" I joke as I grab a tissue and blow my nose.

"Get in! You have rested enough!" Andrea orders me, pointing to her car waiting outside.

At the grocery store, I need to steady myself by holding onto the grocery cart. When done, Andrea returns me to my home and-helps me put away the groceries. "What would I do without these friends?" I wonder. I can't even imagine doing this all alone.

Again, I walk to the Abby. As I arrive, so does Nora, our receptionist. She has brought lunch for Colleen, herself and me. We eat and they share what has happened at the Abby over the past sixteen days.

"I am ever so grateful to both of you for helping all these days. Go home ladies, you have served your purpose. You have been here way too much. I will lock up and put the sign by the bell instructing anyone who arrives to ring the bell. I can check out the dogs that have been groomed today. Since business is so slow now in the dead of winter and we have only a few boarders. I can handle closing up for the night.

They leave for the day. However, before I leave, I visit those of our own dogs who are boarding here. I reach into their pens and scratch their ears. They are so happy to see their Mommy that their bodies jump up and down. The Dobermans do not have a heavy enough coat to keep them warm and they are enjoying the heated floors here. They rub up against the chain link gates as I run my fingers over their fur. As they stand on their hind legs, I enjoy them licking my face. I cry again and wail aloud, "How could this have happened?" My wails reverberate off the tiled walls of the kennel.

As I trudge back to the house, a thought comes to mind. I cannot even imagine how much Bob must be missing all of this. After all, this was his dream too. Then I chide myself for feeling sorry for him and just as quickly feel sorry for myself again.

I get to the house just as the kids are getting off their busses. It is too cold for them to play outside this February day. They come in and just quietly do their homework, without having to be asked. I do not ever remember this rowdy bunch being this quiet and I realize they are not completely comfortable yet.

"Let's play Monopoly!" I shout.

"Hooray!" they reply in unison. As we play, the sound of their voices, laughter and teasing is filling our home once more and I am relieved and hopeful that they will adjust to what will have to be our "new normal."

"Ok, guys, time is up. I am fixing goulash for dinner. Go finish your homework now."

After dinner, everyone does his or her own thing. I answer the phone many times, as friends call to see if I need anything. I call our receptionist, Nora, and tell her she does not need to come in early but at 11 AM instead. I have doctors' and attorneys' appointments tomorrow and the next day. She agrees. The evening passes quietly and quickly.

In the morning, I get the kids off to school, clean the kennel and feed the boarders. I notice how tired I am and then remember that all I have done for 16 days is eat and sleep. When Nora arrives for work, I return home, bathe, dress and emotionally prepare for an appointment with my attorney. I am dreading this appointemtn. I have to terminate my marriage. I ask myself repeatedly, "How, why, and what could I have done better?" I blame myself and feel like a failure.

"Hi, Rodger," I say as I enter his office.

"You look a lot better than when I first saw you," he responds. We discuss my inevitable divorce and the general terms under which I will face the future. I notice that Bob looks so spiffy. I think to myself how classy I tried to look before all of this. Now I feel disheveled inside and out.

"Alright, Rodger, let's get this going." I say to him.

"Are you sure you are up to it?" he questions.

I nod yes.

"Okay. I have all the papers and quit claim deeds ready for you to sign. Your husband has already signed them," he says. He then goes over what Bob will get in detail. He gets the economy car, the school bus and his freedom. I will have complete possession and ownership of the Abby, our home, a college boarding house, and the blood-laden van. "Yes, all heavily mortgaged. We weren't making it before, how on earth will I make it now?"

I think to myself. I definitely do not want the school bus, as it broke down every other time we used it. I let him have it and hope that it, or his girlfriend, will do him in.

Rodger explains, "You'll have to face the grand jury in a few weeks. These are some of the questions that the grand jury may ask: Has he ever done anything like this before? You will answer truthfully, 'No.' They will ask about the psychiatrist's findings. You can tell them you believe his new medical diagnosis of hypoglycemia is the cause of this irrational act. In addition, you can explain that you are still getting a divorce because you do not feel safe with him anymore. However, do not volunteer the phone call episode that happened last year. That could give them evidence to indict him. But if you are asked about it, you tell the truth. Understand?" He goes on to explain that if Bob is indicted, he will very likely be convicted and I will be without any financial support for the children.

My attorney goes on to suggest other questions that I may be asked and we discuss my responses. Our session ends and I return home.

It's the third day of my being home and I have an appointment with the plastic surgeon that I met in the hospital. I'm sure that he'll be happy to see me. Especially after I woke him up at three in the morning when I had run out of pain medication.

The plastic surgeon enters the examining room and says "Hello." He thoroughly looks over my face, ears and head. Thankfully, he says nothing of my late-night call.

"Let me see you again in a few months, after your wounds have healed a bit more. I will reevaluate you and schedule a time for plastic surgery then." As I prepare to leave, he turns to me and says, "Maybe by that time, you and your husband will be back together."

I feel an instant swell of anger. "Are you out of your mind? Look at me!" I yell at him as I leave the office. I am definitely not returning to that son of a bitch, no matter how good he is!

My fourth day home is almost normal and like it used to be. The exception is at the dinner table. Bob is not here with us and there is little laughter.

It is now my fifth day since leaving the hospital and I am at Dr. Turner's office. He is my dentist. He takes many x-rays of my teeth and jaw. As I wait for the results, I find a mirror in my purse and look at my beautiful teeth. I have had only one cavity in my entire life, I think to myself.

"I have bad news," Dr. Turner says, as he sits on a chair beside me. "The blows to your face were so powerful that they cracked the roots of your front teeth. I will have to remove those teeth. I will fit your mouth with a temporary bridge, which will be completed that same day and placed in your mouth. Therefore, you will never be without teeth. A permanent bridge will follow in about a month."

"I don't understand," I say in disbelief. "The pain isn't nearly as bad as before."

"I understand," he explains, "but anything you bite into could be the final blow to those roots and that would be extremely painful. No one will ever know the fake teeth are not real. They will be as beautiful as the originals. I will make your appointment."

I stand up to leave but feel weak and fall back into my chair in shock. My dentist quickly helps me up and offers to walk me to my car. I feel like a puppet. Someone is pulling the strings and I do as I am asked.

"I'm alright, I say to him as I grab onto the arm of the chair to steady myself. He insists and walks with me. It is difficult to see where I am walking with my eyes so full of tears. "All that I have already gone through and now this. Why couldn't I just die?" I ask aloud. He puts his arm around me and gives me a hug. He has been our family dentist for years.

I drive away feeling that Bob is still torturing me.

I decide that I will not tell the children about this. I hope that they do not notice the difference because it would freak them out. I will call my close friends and family as soon as I get home, to tell them what has transpired and what will transpire.

As I walk into the house, the buzzer from the kennel is ringing and alerts me that someone is there. I guess that Nora has already left for the day. I scoot to the Abby and see that our long-time boarding customers, the Winters are waiting outside. They have come a day early to pick up their dog, Cookie.

I unlock the outside door and as Mrs. Winters walks into the reception room, she stops, walks over to me, cradles my face in her hands, and says, "Oh, Nina, you used to be so beautiful. I am sure that a little surgery will remedy that."

I stand here in utter shock: I cannot believe she just said that. Those words play repeatedly in my head as I go to retrieve Cookie.

I feel nothing as I return Mrs. Winter's dog to her. I am just numb. She pays me the boarding fee and leaves. I sit down at my desk and I am shattered beyond all belief. How could a person say such a cruel thing to a bird so badly broken? I cry so hard that my chest feels as though my ribs will break. I call Andrea and Ann and tell them what had just happened. I need their sympathy. I am overwhelmed with self-pity and grief.

I return to our house and soon my brood comes home from school. They are very attentive to me. They do little chores and tasks and I do not even have to ask. I say nothing about my day at the dentist. As I place dinner on the table, the phone rings and its Ann.

"Nina, you and I are going to the Westminster Dog Show!" I just smile at this crazy statement. Ann continues, "I talked to Dr. Melborne, your surgeon, and he says that if you think you are up to it, there is no reason that you cannot go."

"Are you out of your mind, Ann? I am barely walking and you are telling me I can fly and even show our champion dog, Boris? I do not know if I am even capable of showing him! What about flying in my condition and besides, I am terrified of flying. Think of the children. I cannot leave them again. I have just returned home. Who will care for them? We will be gone four entire days in New York City. Ann, I think you have had too many martinis. I'm saying goodbye, Crazy Lady," and I hang up the phone.

The kids overheard my conversation and after I hang up Brook says, "Mama, why don't you go? This is your big dream."

"I am not going, because it's a ridiculous idea." I answer.

"I remember-when you sent in the entry and you were all excited," she answers.

"That was then. This is now and I have more important things to do and that's that!" I cut off the conversation.

It is eight o'clock, everyone has taken their baths and they are ready for bed. It is still amazing to me how obedient they all are. There is no argument about who has the tub first, etc. I need to enjoy this calm, as I am sure that it will return to the normal sibling bickering soon.

Everyone is in bed and I sit down to watch a little TV but I cannot concentrate. I find my mind wandering back to a couple years ago. Bob had just come in from work, kissed me and grabbed the newly delivered 'Dog World Magazine.' Off he went to his library (in our house, the bathroom) to read. A short time later, he came out, walks over to me and points to an ad reading, "For Sale - Champion Borzoi Pup."

"My God," I said aloud, after reading the ad. "I've never seen a giant breed win its championship at ten months of age. It usually takes about a year and a half. Look at this, he won it in three major shows in a row. Wow!"

"You mentioned not long ago that you love the look and gentleness of that breed. What do you think?" Bob asked.

"First, and second and third for that matter, we can't afford $1,000," I respond.

"Can you think of anyone who can?" he smirks.

"You mean Ann?"

"No harm in asking. Do a co-ownership. Offer her a deal."

Without thinking twice, I pick up the phone and call her.

"Hello," she answered in her normal happy sing-song voice.

"Ann, this is Nina. How would you like to co-own a champion Borzoi?"

"I'd love to!" she says with glee.

"Really?" I asked, stunned at her quick response.

"Since I was a child and living in New York, my daddy took me every year to the Westminster Dog Show. I always told him that someday I was going to own a Borzoi and show it at Westminster."

"Are you serious?" I am giddy with excitement.

"Of course, I am serious. When Jack and I got our first dog he wouldn't let me have a Borzoi, because he did not want the long dog hair in the house. Therefore, we got a Doberman. However, I have always wanted a Borzoi. So, tell me more about this dog."

It is eight o'clock, everyone has taken their baths and they are ready for bed. It is still amazing to me how obedient they all are. There is no argument about who has the tub first, etc. I need to enjoy this calm, as I am sure that it will return to the normal sibling bickering soon.

Everyone is in bed and I sit down to watch a little TV but I cannot concentrate. I find my mind wandering back to a couple years ago. Bob had just come in from work, kissed me and grabbed the newly delivered 'Dog World Magazine.' Off he went to his library (in our house, the bathroom) to read. A short time later, he came out, walks over to me and points to an ad reading, "For Sale - Champion Borzoi Pup."

"My God," I said aloud, after reading the ad. "I've never seen a giant breed win its championship at ten months of age. It usually takes about a year and a half. Look at this, he won it in three major shows in a row. Wow!"

"You mentioned not long ago that you love the look and gentleness of that breed. What do you think?" Bob asked.

"First, and second and third for that matter, we can't afford $1,000," I respond.

"Can you think of anyone who can?" he smirks.

"You mean Ann?"

"No harm in asking. Do a co-ownership. Offer her a deal."

Without thinking twice, I pick up the phone and call her.

"Hello," she answered in her normal happy sing-song voice.

"Ann, this is Nina. How would you like to co-own a champion Borzoi?"

"I'd love to!" she says with glee.

"Really?" I asked, stunned at her quick response.

"Since I was a child and living in New York, my daddy took me every year to the Westminster Dog Show. I always told him that someday I was going to own a Borzoi and show it at Westminster."

"Are you serious?" I am giddy with excitement.

"Of course, I am serious. When Jack and I got our first dog he wouldn't let me have a Borzoi, because he did not want the long dog hair in the house. Therefore, we got a Doberman. However, I have always wanted a Borzoi. So, tell me more about this dog."

I unlock the outside door and as Mrs. Winters walks into the reception room, she stops, walks over to me, cradles my face in her hands, and says, "Oh, Nina, you used to be so beautiful. I am sure that a little surgery will remedy that."

I stand here in utter shock: I cannot believe she just said that. Those words play repeatedly in my head as I go to retrieve Cookie.

I feel nothing as I return Mrs. Winter's dog to her. I am just numb. She pays me the boarding fee and leaves. I sit down at my desk and I am shattered beyond all belief. How could a person say such a cruel thing to a bird so badly broken? I cry so hard that my chest feels as though my ribs will break. I call Andrea and Ann and tell them what had just happened. I need their sympathy. I am overwhelmed with self-pity and grief.

I return to our house and soon my brood comes home from school. They are very attentive to me. They do little chores and tasks and I do not even have to ask. I say nothing about my day at the dentist. As I place dinner on the table, the phone rings and its Ann.

"Nina, you and I are going to the Westminster Dog Show!" I just smile at this crazy statement. Ann continues, "I talked to Dr. Melborne, your surgeon, and he says that if you think you are up to it, there is no reason that you cannot go."

"Are you out of your mind, Ann? I am barely walking and you are telling me I can fly and even show our champion dog, Boris? I do not know if I am even capable of showing him! What about flying in my condition and besides, I am terrified of flying. Think of the children. I cannot leave them again. I have just returned home. Who will care for them? We will be gone four entire days in New York City. Ann, I think you have had too many martinis. I'm saying goodbye, Crazy Lady," and I hang up the phone.

The kids overheard my conversation and after I hang up Brook says, "Mama, why don't you go? This is your big dream."

"I am not going, because it's a ridiculous idea." I answer.

"I remember-when you sent in the entry and you were all excited," she answers.

"That was then. This is now and I have more important things to do and that's that!" I cut off the conversation.

I proceeded to read the advertisement. Then I explained, "Bob says that we can't afford it right now. But he has an idea. You pay the $1,000.00, all the vet bills and show entry fees. We will house him here, feed him and show him. What do you think?"

"Done!" she happily accepted.

The very next day we drove to Ohio and brought home Boris, our new champion puppy. My God, he was so beautiful!

"How weird that was," I think to myself. The memory from years ago brings a smile to my face. "It was Kismet; meant to be," I think as I relax into my bed alone for the fifth night.

It's my sixth day back at home. Colleen and Nora are not coming in at all. Business is slow and I feel I am strong enough to resume my normal kennel responsibilities. I've just finished the cleaning and feeding and walk back to our house. Even the cold air seems empty. I feel emptiness and dead inside my soul. The day passes with many phone calls from well-wishers again. I have just fixed dinner and everyone is seated at the table when the phone rings.

"Hi, Ann," I say and then just listen. Then I hang up the phone.

Brook has noticed that I have not said a word.

"What's up, Mom?" she asks.

"Ann called to tell me we are going to Westminster in New York. She booked the flight, hotel, and even Lucy, your babysitter. She said that I need some fun and she wants her dream and then she hung up on me."

"Hooray!" all the kids yell out, again in unison.

"But I can't leave you. I just got back home," I say to them.

"Go, Mama!" Brook says.

"You need to have some fun," Sommer adds.

"Oh, my God," I say aloud. "I'm going to Westminster next week!" Then I think to myself but do not say aloud, "And just a few days ago, I was fighting for my very life."

I find it difficult to sleep tonight. It is just all too much.

Day seven at home and Bob is supposed to pick the kids up for the weekend. They say that they do not want to go. "Your Daddy loves you and

God knows how very much he misses you," I tell them, hoping in my heart that it is true.

"We are afraid of him, Mommy," Sommer chimes in. "He beat you up and maybe he'll beat us up too."

"He never spanked you before, why would he spank you now?" I ask. "I'm sure that he has plans that you'll enjoy. I will be here waiting for you on Sunday. Just pick up the phone and call me if you are frightened or want to talk to me. I will be here except for Saturday night. I will be playing poker at Mimi's house and you can call me there."

At that moment, Bob's car pulls up and the kids place their overnight cases in the trunk and climb into the car. Complying with the injunction, he does not get out of the car. He is not to set foot on my property. "MY property," I think again, so angry at what he did to me and our dreams. I watch the car until it is out of sight. I fear for them and I fear for myself. It is the first time that I have been completely alone. I am honestly terribly worried about the safety of our children. I do not know this man anymore. Should I trust him? What would prevent him from taking their lives too? I cannot help but wonder if Bob is happy and feels lucky that he is not going to jail. I am sure that he is resentful that I have taken all of his dreams away. Then I ask myself, "What does he have to lose if he kills me now? I have taken about every monetary item from him." I feel a chill running down my back.

The internal dialogue continues, "But what have I really taken? Everything is heavily in debt. We could not make it before when we used all of his salary, now I only get 40% of his take home pay for child support. I have already missed the January and February payments because Bob used the money from the Abby's huge Christmas holiday income to bail himself out of jail. The bank assures me not to worry, I can make it up. One thing I know, is that I have to sell or give away some of our show dogs. I cannot afford to feed them."

The weekend is almost over and I watch as the kids get out of Bob's car. They are safe. The house has been so quiet. Now my noisy bunch has returned.

Brook tells me she found a pair of bikini lady's panties behind her Dad's bedroom door. Funny, I think to myself, "Instead of being sad or angry, I am comforted and I feel safer. He is with Sue."

It's Monday and the kids have left for school. I'm done with the kennel work. I make a fresh pot of coffee. As I sip a cup, I find myself laughing aloud. I must be crazy. I am going to show a dog at the most prestigious show in the country. I close my eyes and imagine myself at the show with all the other dog handlers and dogs running around the ring when my wig falls off. All the dogs run into it and tear it to bits. I laugh aloud at my imagination.

I spend the next few days packing for this journey of a lifetime. I smile at thinking it will be taken by a bald woman, her crazy friend, and their champion, Boris.

The day is here. Dr. McGinn and Ann pick Boris and me up and we are off to the airport. Boris and I sit in the back seat together. The animal crate is in the trunk of the van. Ann sits in the front passenger seat and she is wearing the white mink coat that Doc gave her for Christmas.

When we arrive at the airport, Boris is led away to be put into his crate to fly-in the luggage compartment which is pressurized. I have peed 20 times and we have not yet boarded the plane. I am scared to death of flying.

As it turns out, the flight is very smooth with little to no turbulence. Then suddenly the plane banks hard and it feels as if I will fall out the window. I see the ground and I scream, "Ann, we're going to crash!"

Ann is shushing me and explains that when flying into New York the plane has to do this to observe sound restrictions or something of that nature. I look around at the other passengers and notice their dirty looks. I guess that I have scared the BAGEEBIES out of them.

We get off the plane and retrieve Boris. We then find the location that the airport has assigned–for dogs to go potty. Because of this large Westminster show, there are plenty of areas for dogs to exercise.

We hop in a cab, dog and all, and check into our hotel. We walk Boris many times and carry a pooper-scooper with us. We dine at a fine restaurant, thanks to Ann, and I sleep very well.

After breakfast, we head off to Madison Square Gardens and the show. It is snowing but that is fine, as Boris loves the snow.

We settle Boris into his designated area. At this particular show, we "bench" the dogs. That means that each dog has his own spot and is tied with a short leash to a large screw. They can only leave their spots to go potty, urinate or eat. One of the owners or handlers is supposed to stay with the animal at all times. This is done so that the public can view all the dogs at any time, during the next three days. At most shows, you show your dog at a specific time and can then leave, once they have been shown. They can go home, or stay to be seen or judged again later in the group judging.

I hook Boris's short chain to the fastener. He lays down to rest. He is so beautiful. His coloring is mainly white with a splash of cream. His original breeder and owner sold him because she already owned his sire, or father and honestly felt that the sire was better. Wrong! She admitted to that a year after we bought him. She took a gamble and we won.

The judge scheduled to judge the Borzois has judged Boris three times before this and he always won Best of Breed. We therefore feel-that we have a great chance of winning. Not so quick, I find out. After checking with the other nine owners, we sadly discover that their dogs had never lost under this judge, in different parts of our country. We all had a sad laugh at the irony. We were all in the same boat!

We asked the people on either side of us if they would keep an eye on Boris, as we had to leave the show site for a few minutes. We have a mission to buy film for the new camera that Ann gave Doc for Christmas. It is turning out to be quite a big challenge because the camera is so new; no one has film for it yet. We trod without boots in snow above our ankles. At last, we find the film, return to our dog, and give the people next to us a break.

This is definitely the longest day of my life. Professional handlers come up to me and offer to show Boris if I do not feel able when the time comes. I guess that even through all of my scars, people still recognize me. I am happy for that.

The first day of showing is over. We are scheduled to show tomorrow. We return to our hotel and exercise and feed Boris. Then we head out to the restaurant that Ann's Daddy always took her to after the show. Its name is Paddy's Pub. We enter what looks like the old taverns in Chicago where I grew up. The floor is wooden. The waiters are dressed as though they lived in the twenties. They are wearing black slacks, a white shirt and a long apron tied above the waist that goes down to their ankles. I feel that this is an adventure all in itself and I am truly, truly happy for the first time in a long time.

We order our martinis and toast Ann's Dad. Dinner is wonderful. We return to our hotel and sleep, but not well tonight. Anticipation for the next day and our turn to be in the show ring is very unnerving.

Morning is here and after breakfast we head on over to the show. We exercise Boris and ready ourselves for the most important show of our lives.

Eleven o'clock is here. I am planning to show Boris myself. Since I walked the streets of New York yesterday, I'm confident that I'm strong enough to get through the judging. As we walk to the show ring several handlers stop me to tell me they will be standing ringside in case I need help. I am grateful that I have that backup.

I approach the show ring. I make sure that my armband with Boris' number is on and I enter the show ring. The judge begins examining the dogs one at a time. She checks their shoulder lay back, their teeth, their gait and more. She completes her check of the two dogs in front of me and now it is my turn. She finishes her checkup of Boris and puts us in front of the other two dogs. Now I am shaking with excitement because she is always very consistent in her procedure. She places her favorite in the first place. I am thinking, "Oh my God, is this possible? We may win!"

The judge finishes her judging of the other dogs and she places them all behind us in the line. She then instructs all of us to run as a group in a large circle, for the last time. We are in first place and I am so excited. Then as she usually does, the judge waves her hand with a dramatic flourish. Instead of pointing to the lead dog in line as usual, she points to the third dog in line.

I am dumbfounded and stunned! If she had put all of us back in our original order and then pointed to another dog in line, I could have taken the blow better. However, to think I really was going to win the biggest show of my life and did not, I am just devastated.

As I leave the show ring, thoroughly disheartened, I see Ann waiting outside the gate for me. But as I pass by the judge, she says to me with pride in her voice and demeanor, "I chose a beautiful dog, didn't I?" Why would any judge say that to the handler losing at the most prestigious show in the country? Now I am angry.

I exit the ring. Ann and I hug and cry a bit. Then I sadly say, "Oh well, Ann, at least we have the pictures to remember this day by."

Ann responds, "Oh my God, I got so nervous, I forgot I have a camera!" I stop crying because I want to kill her and then the judge. After a few tense moments, we make eye contact and both start laughing until tears roll down our faces again.

We stay to watch the Borzoi from Canada who won, as he is now competing against other dogs in the hound group. He does not even get a consideration. We delight in that.

We leave the building after the "Best in Show" dog has been chosen. We gladly return to Paddy's Pub for dinner and we turn in for the night, exhausted by the happenings of the day.

Morning is here and I open the window shade. I cannot see the building across the street. We are in the middle of a full-blown blizzard! Ann says, "I'll call Ozark Airlines and see what they say about our flight." She hangs up the phone and tells me the flight is scheduled to take off as planned.

I put the TV on and the local news station is predicting that it may be the largest snowfall New York has ever had. "There is no way in hell that Ozark will be able to fly," I say to her.

Ann retorts, "If they say they can fly, then they can fly!" Ann is such a "Pollyanna" at times.

I call the children and talk to each of them as I have at least two times a day since I have been here. I prepare them and Lucy that we may not make it home today because of the snow.

We pack up, hail a cab and we are off to the airport and home. I miss the kids terribly although each time I call them, they are happy that I am happy. The cab drops us off at the Ozark terminal. Our cab is one of only a couple dozen cars on this, I am sure, usually very busy highway.

We look at the board that lists the departures and almost all flights have been canceled except Ozark's. We check in. Amazingly, our flight is still scheduled to leave, but it is delayed. The airline offers to keep our dog in the office area and give us drink tickets. We go to the lounge and have a Bloody Mary cocktail. Shortly thereafter, our flight is canceled. Ozark sends us to American Airlines to see if we can be booked on a flight to Chicago with a connection to Peoria. An hour passes when we hear that this flight has been canceled as well.

I survey the physical situation at the airport. There is no way to explain to the average person who has not experienced it, the chaos I am observing. People are sleeping on their fur coats on the floor. Dogs are everywhere. Before, I could see the planes outside through the window, but now I see only snow. The planes are still there but I cannot see them.

Ann is now very worked up. Her bronchitis is flaring up, and she is beginning to have a panic attack. She gets up and tells me she is going to Ozark to complain. I wonder to myself if she believes Ozark can make the blizzard go away. She has now been gone for about thirty minutes when an Ozark representative appears and asks me if my name is Nina. I answer, "Yes. Is my friend, Ann, alright?" She does not answer but takes me to where Ann is seated.

Ann's white mink coat is off. An attendant is fanning her and indeed, she is having a panic attack. Unexpectedly, Ann screams out, "Do you know who my husband is?" Now she really has my attention. I know he is a pathologist. For all I know, he is on the board of Ozark Airlines. No one answers.

They continue to fan her and assure her they will get her to a hotel. A wheelchair is delivered for Ann and I am told that a limousine is waiting for us and will take us to a nice hotel. An attendant puts what she calls vouchers into my hand. "Dinner and breakfast are on us," she explains. "You will fly out tomorrow morning and we will send a limo for you. You will be on the first flight out tomorrow."

Another attendant brings Boris to us and tells us he had diarrhea all over their office. Between Boris and Ann, I understand why they are so glad to get rid of us.

We are only one of three cars that I can see on this gigantic highway. Our limo crawls at what seems like five miles per hour and for what seems like an eternity.

Finally, we check into the hotel. We walk and feed Boris. He seems to have calmed down since we were at the airport. We dine on steak and have our martinis. I start laughing.

"What is so funny?" Ann asks.

"You are not coughing or breathing hard anymore. From now on, I am flying with you. Ozark provided all these amenities just to get rid of us." She does not seem to be amused. "We will be telling of this adventure for the rest of our lives, Ann!"

Although we had not noticed when we first checked in, after dinner we noticed that our room was marked as the Bridal Suite. The room has only one bed so we sleep together. We get in our pajamas and slither into bed when I start laughing again.

"Now what is so funny?" Ann asks.

I answer with glee, "Ann look up at the ceiling. It is mirrored!" She hits me with her extra pillow. We laugh and giggle until we fall asleep.

"I am home, I am home!" I yell. My brood comes running to me. We hug and I go over the details I could not tell them over the phone because Ann could hear. I told them about the camera episode and the panic attack.

In the morning, I called Ann and I told her, "I cannot thank you enough. You gave me one of the greatest gifts of my lifetime. To think we made it to your dream, one I never dreamed, but will relive forever. I love you, dearest friend."

Weeks pass. The kids are adjusting well. Life and its routines here at the house are becoming normal. The boys miss their Dad more than the girls do. The girls are older and remember the many arguments they witnessed about Sue. The boys would run off to their bedroom and close the door during those times.

The kids tell me they are apprehensive when they spend time alone with their Dad. Sometimes when he has them for his every-other-weekend visitation, he takes them to Chicago to be with his parents, their grandparents, and they like that because they feel safe.

Bob was 'let go' from the clinic he worked at but his psychiatrist found him a job at a different one. Bob's psychiatrist never knew the full story about the phone calls Bob and Sue made to me, breathing into the phone and hanging up to make me feel I was going insane. Nor did he know how they substituted the powder in my antibiotic capsules with sleeping pill powder. No, I never told him because Bob would lose his medical license. I want to make sure he continues to work and support our children. I pray to God that I have made the right decision.

It is March 1974 and today I have to face the Grand Jury. As I enter the courthouse, I am terrified and do not know what to expect. I have to be so careful to tell the truth but not to offer the whole truth. I hope I can do it.

I look around the room and it is all brown wood. The people that make up the Grand Jury enter the room and then the Judge enters. I am so nervous, I feel as though I am going to wet my pants.

One juror asks me if Bob had ever done anything like what he did to me the night of my murder and I answered, "No." Another asks me if I feel safe and I answer, "I hope so." Another asks if Bob is working and I answer that he is. They ask me a few other questions, the last of which is whether I will stay married to Bob. I answer, "No, I do not trust him anymore." I look at them and I sense that they do not believe me. However, they do not ask any more questions and I am dismissed from the witness stand.

Shortly after I return home, my attorney calls to tell me that the Grand Jury decided not to prosecute Bob. He also told me that my divorce would be final tomorrow.

"How can our marriage be over? It was just yesterday that I was designing my wedding dress." I say aloud. I can still hear Bob and me vowing to love each other forever. Never in my wildest dreams did I think "forever" was to be only 16 years. I sit down at the dining room table, outstretch my arms across it, lay my head onto my arms and sob. As the tears flow onto my arms, I feel a raw emptiness in my soul.

A week passes and Ann drives me to the dentist because I would not be wise to drive myself home. The nurse calls my name and I leave my chair in the reception room to go to what I feel is the equivalent of the electric chair.

My dentist puts his hand over mine, which is tightly gripping the chair. "You will be fine, Nina," he reassures me. "I am sorry that I have to do this but if you do not tell anyone that that the new teeth are not real, they will never know." He then explains that he is injecting Novocain to numb the area. He leaves the room after telling me he will be back in a few minutes.

When he reenters the room, I ask, "Are you sure that this has to be done? Do I have to lose my teeth?" I ask one last time and I am crying uncontrollably.

"You know the answer."

He pulls my teeth. I do not feel any pain but I hear the horrible sound of cracking. He then inserts the temporary teeth and hands me a mirror. The teeth are shaped like my teeth but they look chalky and not at all shiny like mine were.

"Next month, when you come in, you will get the permanent ones and they will be even prettier than your original ones," the dentist promises. I do not believe him and I feel empty inside.

Ann takes me home. I kiss her and thank her for everything she has done for me. I feel numb, not just my mouth but my entire body and my heart as well. I cry a deep, mournful, soul-bending, sorrowful cry. I cannot help but feel that Bob continues to murder me, a little at a time.

It is late March and all the dogs who were boarded at a variety of kennels, homes and the Abby, have all been returned to our home and our kennel in the back yard. I put an ad in the newspaper that I have adult Saint Bernards and Doberman Pinschers for sale, gentle and good with children. I am faced with having to make gut-wrenching decisions about which ones I let go. I love them all. A few female Saint Bernards are five years old. They have had two litters each. I do not plan to breed them again. I insist that they are to be house pets. I want a better life for them.

I put a price on each of the dogs that must go. I cannot afford to feed all of these dogs or to take care of their medical check-ups. I give the prospective people a price and if I feel they accept that and feel that they will give the dog a good home, I just give them away free of charge. I want them to spend the next half of their life, hopefully, at the foot of someone's bed. I will not give them the AKC registration papers and hope that they will never breed them. I do not want my kennel's namesake animals to be used irresponsibly to make money.

Ann has convinced Doc to adopt one of the Borzois, a female named Image. I still have a lovely male named Echo, yet to be sold.

In just one week, I place all except Echo. I decide I can keep him because he is still a possible show dog. I have just put the phone down, canceling my newspaper ad, when a man walks into the Abby holding the newspaper ad. He says he would like to see the male Borzoi pup. He tells me that since he got divorced a year ago, and he is on the road a lot, his daughter could use a friend.

I have just finished cleaning the Abby. I am in my jeans and my yellow turbine; my old set of working clothes. I am embarrassed because when I am at the Abby I am always well dressed. I apologize for my outfit because it does not represent the elegance of the Abby.

He poo-poos my embarrassment and says he looks like that when he is working around the oilrigs.

"Echo is out at our show dog kennel in the back of the house. I will go there and bring him over here."

"Heavens no," he answers. "I will go there with you."

I look at him and notice that he is all dressed up in a suit and loafer shoes. "There is still snow on the ground and you will get muddy," I say.

"No, I insist. I will go with you."

I cannot stop looking at him. He is so handsome and has beautiful dimples in his cheeks.

We walk to the dog pens and Echo runs over to greet us. All the dogs that remain are barking their hellos. The man walks up to each kennel and greets all the barkers. He returns to Echo and looks deeply into Echo's eyes.

I explain that I am selling Echo as a pet because I am not sure that he has the bone structure to be a show dog. I want him to live in a home and not a kennel.

"I need to call my wife, ex-wife, to get her approval since the dog will live with her. I will get back to you later. Do not sell him until I call you. It will be later." He hands me his business card that reads Ken Bartley Oil Exploration.

It is the next day and I am again at the Abby cleaning when the phone rings and it is Mr. Bartley. "My daughter's mother gives her permission for me to get the dog. Do you think you can have him cleaned up by late afternoon? Today is my daughter's birthday."

"Of course I can," I answer.

I run out to the kennel and bring Echo over to the Abby. As I bring him from his run, I look at our kennel and there are still eight dogs left. Some are too old to sell or give away. They stay inside our house quite often. It would be too much of a transition for them and for us for them to leave.

I take Echo to the Abby and bathe him. He just loves his bath. "Dear God," I say. "Please watch over him and give him a good life." I asked the same thing for the other dogs that left in the past two weeks.

Just as I finish grooming Echo, the door to the Abby opens and in walks Echo's handsome new owner. Ken holds a new collar and leash in his hands. He puts them on Echo and they walk out of the Abby. Echo walks out of my life, jumps into a fancy sports car and off they go. "My heart has added yet another little crack. How many it can handle before it shatters," I wonder aloud.

A week has passed and I am at the desk at the Abby. I look up from my appointment book and see Ken with Echo, who is not on a leash. Echo runs around the reception room and rolls over at my feet to have his tummy rubbed as though he is saying "Hi, Mommy."

"You do not have him on a leash?" I am shocked. "Do you know that if he wanted to, he would run like the wind and be gone in seconds?"

"Nope, I have not used it since the first day. I take him to the park every day and let him run. He comes to me as soon as I call him. I housebroke him at my apartment so that my daughter did not have to deal with that. It took me two days and he has not had an accident since. I had to be here in Peoria on business today so I thought maybe you would like to see him and what we have accomplished."

"Are you going to be here in town long enough for me to bathe him?"

"I would be happy to pay you," he offers.

"No way. It will be my pleasure. I am in shock," I say. "I have never seen any dog trained so quickly, not so much the house broken part, but to walk alongside this `almost stranger` without a leash. You seem to have an unbelievable bond."

Ken continues to come to Peoria every few days, "on business," he tells me. Each time he brings Echo. I keep Echo in the kennel while Ken takes care of his business and then he helps me groom Echo. During these times, I tell him the story of the last few years of my life.

Today he tells me his. When he finishes sharing his story, Ken asks me if he can take me to dinner. My heart is beating so hard, I think it might be seen through my blouse. I am in shock that this handsome man wants to be in public with scar-faced me.

"It would be my pleasure, sir." I laughingly accept.

When Ken leaves, I call Lucy to see if she can babysit tonight.

"Of course," she answers. "I miss the kids." Lucy, Bob's former nurse, has just retired so she has some extra time. She previously told me that when the clinic let Bob go, it just was not the same without him. I know how much she loves him. He loved her enough to take her with him a few years earlier when he accepted the position at this new clinic.

I look into the mirror as I prepare for my dinner date. It is almost time for Ken to pick me up. I am dressed in a long, fashionable cotton dress that hangs to the ground and I am wearing a wig similar to my normal short, curly hairstyle.

The doorbell rings and Johnny answers the door. Ken walks into the living room and sees my brood for the first time. They all look both confused and fascinated to know that someone other than their father will be at my side. Their eyes are open wide as they scrutinize this man.

Then Ken announces, in his deep baritone voice, "Children, look at this woman. She is beautiful!"

The kids do not just look at me. They really study me. They have never thought of me as "beautiful." They have only thought of me as "Mom."

Recognizing that my children are looking at me for the first time as someone other than just Mom and knowing that this handsome stranger thinks of me as beautiful fills me with such sweet, joyful emotion. Tears well up in my eyes. For the first time since the fateful night of my murder, these are tears of happiness.

"Maybe this is the beginning of the new lifeline that God has given me," I think to myself as I take Ken's arm and head out for a wonderful evening.

NOTE FROM THE AUTHOR

Word-of-mouth is crucial for any author to succeed. If you enjoyed the book, please leave a review online—anywhere you are able. Even if it's just a sentence or two. It would make all the difference and would be very much appreciated.

    Thanks!
    Nancy

ABOUT THE AUTHOR

Nancy Lee lives in the Midwest of the United States. She is a fashion designer, breeder of champion dogs, entrepreneur, mother, and now she is following the advice of her teachers and professors in authoring her first novel, *Maybe You Die*.

Thank you so much for reading one of our **True Crime** novels.
If you enjoyed the experience, please check out our
recommendation for your next great read!

The Poisoned Glass by Kimberly Tilley

"A great read and a fascinating retelling of a long-forgotten murder,
that still resonates to this very day...
for anybody interested in the history of the Silk City!"
—Mark S. Auerbach, City Historian, Passaic, New Jersey

View other Black Rose Writing titles at
www.blackrosewriting.com/books and use promo code
PRINT to receive a **20% discount** when purchasing.